Political Theory and Ecological Values

Political Theory
and
Ecological Values

Tim Hayward

Polity Press

First published in 1998 by Polity Press
in association with Blackwell Publishers Ltd.

Editorial office:
Polity Press
65 Bridge Street
Cambridge CB2 1UR, UK

Marketing and production:
Blackwell Publishers Ltd
108 Cowley Road
Oxford OX4 1JF, UK

ISBN 0-7456-1808-1
ISBN 0-7456-1809-X (pbk)

A catalogue record for this book is available from the British Library.

Typeset in 10 on 12 pt Palatino
by Best-set Typesetter Ltd, Hong Kong
Printed in Great Britain by MPG Books, Bodmin, Cornwall

This book is printed on acid-free paper.

Contents

Acknowledgements

I would like to extend the warmest thanks to those who have given advice and support in the writing of this book. Russell Keat's probing and constructive criticisms at an early stage set the project on its way; Cecile Fabre's acute observations helped considerably to improve the final version; Avner de-Shalit and Graham Smith very kindly read the entire draft and made valuable suggestions for its improvement; Robin Attfield, Frederick Ferré and Soran Reader provided helpful comments on individual chapters. I am also particularly grateful for the insights, critical interrogation and personal support of Ted Benton, Andy Dobson, Angelika Krebs, Antonia Layard, John O'Neill, Anna Pärnänen, Stephen Priest and Susan Stephenson. Others with whom I have had pleasurable and instructive discussions include John Barry, Jane Harris, Alan Holland, Kimberly Hutchings, Michael Jacobs, Kevin Magill, Mary Mellor, Kate Soper and the members of the *Capitalism, Nature, Socialism* editorial collective. I would also like to thank the editors and readers at Polity Press, who have been friendly and efficient as ever.

Some of the material in this book was first presented at conferences and seminars between 1994 and 1997; I should like to make a general acknowledgement of the contribution of participants at: the Conference of the Society for Social Studies of Science, University of Bielefeld; the Political Studies Association Conferences at the universities of Glasgow and York; the Conference of Association for Legal and Social Philosophy, Durham University; the Workshop of the British/Swiss Joint Research Programme, Lancaster University; the Centre for Law and Society Seminar, and the Social and Political Theory Seminar at the

University of Edinburgh; the Philosophy Section seminar at University of Wales, Cardiff; and the Conference of Interdisciplinary Research Network for Environment and Society, Keele University.

A visiting fellowship at the Oxford Centre for the Environment, Ethics and Society (OCEES) in the Hilary Term of 1998 provided me with the opportunity to meet a number of people whose comments on parts of the manuscript were accommodated in some last minute revisions. I would like to thank the staff at the Centre for providing such a congenial working environment, and the Principal and Fellows of Mansfield College for their hospitality. I learned a good deal from the participants' comments on papers presented at OCEES, at the Graduate Seminar in Moral Philosophy, and the Political Theory Seminar hosted by David Miller at Nuffield College.

The book was written, though, at Edinburgh, and I count myself fortunate indeed to be part of such a friendly and stimulating intellectual community: this includes not only colleagues in the Department of Politics, but also a wider network of political, legal and social theorists in this university – among whom I'd like particularly to mention Zenon Bankowski, John Holmwood, Ruth Jonathan and Neil MacCormick. Thanks are also due to my students, especially those of the Green Political Thought course, from whom I have continued to learn.

This note of appreciation would not be complete without an expression of gratitude to Jez Collinson and the other members of our Tai Chi Chi Kung group at the Salisbury Centre in Edinburgh. Finally, the greatest delight is to write the name of one individual who is now able to read it, and so I dedicate this book to my son David Hayward.

Chapter 3 is a revised and slightly expanded version of the article 'Anthropocentrism: A Misunderstood Problem', which first appeared in *Environmental Values*, vol. 6 no. 1 (1997): the material is reproduced with kind permission of the publisher, the White Horse Press.

1

Introduction: Ecological Values and Human Interests

This book aims to show why political theorists must take account of ecological concerns as part of their core enterprise, and how they can do so. Ecological issues affect practically all spheres of social existence, and accordingly bear on political institutions, processes and policies at all levels. Yet this is not adequately taken into account in traditional political theory, which, indeed, even works with some assumptions that are ecologically counterfactual. The reasons *why* ecological concerns are as centrally important to politics as other of its more traditional social and economic concerns, I shall argue, derive from the fact – and this is my first premise – that humans are a part of nature; we are, to recall Aristotle's words, political *animals*. For the same reason, I shall argue, it is actually in humans' *interest* to integrate ecological concerns fully into their political institutions and policies; and with this reference to interests lies the key to theorizing *how* they can do so: for by seeing ecological concerns in terms of human interests they can be set in relation to other interests when devising institutions and policies.

Unfortunately, though, this neat theoretical proposal runs up against the practical problem that people often do *not* perceive it to be in their interest to take ecological concerns as seriously as other social and economic concerns. Indeed, on a view which is shared by both advocates of ecological politics and defenders of a more traditional conception of politics, there is a basic and irreconcilable conflict between the values appealed to by the former and the interests upheld by the latter.

However, I intend to challenge that view, to show, on the one hand, against mainstream non-ecological political theorists who may be sceptical about the possibility or desirability of distinctively ecological norms at all, that human interests do have ecological implications; and, on the other, against mainstream ecological theorists that the kinds of value and imperative they advocate can in fact be supported by human interests. Thus I shall seek to show how ecological values can be presented in terms that require a reasoned response from political theorists. This is not to say they must take on a specific set of normative commitments, for all sorts of legitimate disagreement is possible – indeed unavoidable – as it is in any other area, like social justice for instance; but it is to say that just as no one would today consider questions of social justice as extraneous to political theory, whatever specific view they hold on such questions, so ecological concerns are not an optional extra for political theory, the specialist preserve of 'green' political theorists.

In this chapter I shall set out the premises of the position to be developed in this book, and outline the argument to be developed from them. To begin with, though, I shall indicate how the practical problem is more complicated and less clear cut than appears from an initial statement of it; including comments on how it arises.

1   The problem

When we speak of either human interests or ecological values we are referring to complex concepts, but there is a quite straightforward sense of each in which they do appear to conflict. Humans have interests – associated with production, transport, housing, recreation and so on – whose satisfaction involves the utilization of land, resources and waste absorption capacities in ways that can result in ecological disruption. It is no less evident, though, that people have an interest in a healthy and life-supporting environment, and so, in this respect, the problem is not so much a straightforward conflict between human interests and ecological values, as, rather, a conflict between different human interests. In recent years there has been a growing recognition of environmental interests. Regarding pollution, for instance, there has been a move from initial relative inaction, through the increasing adoption of 'end-of-pipe' clean-up measures (such as filtering carbon dioxide emissions) to the growth of what Weale (1993) has called the 'new politics of pollution', which involves assessing the environmental impact of products throughout their life-cycle (from resource extraction through use to eventual disposal) and 'ecological modernization' of the processes involved. At the same time there has been a growing acceptance (as by the EC and OECD, for instance) of a general interest in adopting the 'precautionary principle' (cf. O'Riordan and Cameron, 1994) when dealing with uncertain environmental hazards. Moreover, some environmental interests, such as the need for energy efficiency, coincide with economic interests. It should also be mentioned that environmental clean-up is itself now a very substantial business interest.

Nevertheless, taking the range of environmental problems as a whole, it remains the case that governments and businesses tend to be slow to reach agreement about the existence of problems, set modest targets when problems are recognized, and make even more modest efforts towards their implementation: in short, at each stage other – especially economic – interests take priority over environmental interests. Yet this is not straightforwardly a case of one general human interest taking precedence over another. In fact, it is notable that often, perhaps even typically, those whose activities are the root cause of greatest ecological disruption and who reap its economic benefits are not the same people who bear the brunt of its environmental consequences. This is especially the case when interests are compared and contrasted on a global scale. So it is not necessarily, or even typically, humans in general whose interests are served by ecological disruption.

Here the environmentalist critique converges on recognizable positions in political theory on the issue of social justice. If today it is the rich who tend to benefit and the poor who tend to suffer from human environmental impacts, this is not a novel situation – even if it now has to be viewed on a global scale. In the earlier days of industrialization, it was the poor who suffered poor living conditions and often intolerable working conditions in mines and factories, not the rich owners. If this feature of ecological problems – their inequitable social distribution – has remained constant, so too has the justification for such states of affairs: namely, that while the initial benefits may be inequitably distributed, this inequity is merely an unavoidable price to pay for development, modernization – or, in short, for progress. Ultimately, though, all will benefit from this progress, because the greater general wealth will 'trickle down' to make the poor better off.

This in fact worked well enough during the twentieth century – within most liberal and social democratic states, that is – for the justification to go substantially unchallenged. It was only in the 1960s and 1970s that a distinctively 'green' protest began to be mounted. Conceptually focused around the idea of 'limits to growth' (Meadows et al., 1972), the challenge was to the very premise of the 'trickle-down' theory: given that the earth is finite and has a limited 'carrying capacity', there are ecological constraints to the possible extent of economic development, and so there are limits to how much the worst off can expect to benefit from it. Now the liberal/social democratic response to this challenge is, in essence, summed up in the findings of the Brundtland Report (WCED, 1987): agreed that indefinite economic growth is not possible, it is nevertheless desirable to develop within the limits possible; and if the poor do not benefit, then there must also be some redistribution. In the idea of sustainable development, Brundtland conjoined a recognition of environmental constraints with a recognition of the need for equity in distribution – these being two of the report's three desiderata. The third concerns future generations: this helps give a definition to sustainability – as 'development that meets the needs of people presently living without compromising the ability of future people to meet their needs'. The normative basis for this is effectively equity applied across generations as well as within generations to yield environmental criteria.[1]

This normative principle is now well established *as* a principle, recognized by governments throughout the world. But part of the reason it is so well established is that it is amenable to different – and conflicting – interpretations in relation to practical commitments (see Thomas, 1994). Still, if political theorists were systematically to examine the various meanings of the principle in relation to social justice and other core political concerns, I believe valuable insights could be generated for political theory.[2]

Nevertheless, the principle of sustainable development stops significantly short of what more radical ecologists demand. Up to this point, the whole discussion has been couched in terms of human interests, and no meaning of ecological values has been appealed to other than the value of ecology in maintaining the environmental conditions for human life and flourishing. But the more radical ecological critique challenges the view that the nonhuman world can or should be viewed merely as a resource for humans' benefit. At this point ecological values and a political theory based in interests do indeed seem to part company.

A more radical challenge for political theory is to accommodate the requirements not only of environmentalism, but of what can be called, by contrast, *ecologism* (Dobson, 1995). Although I have certain reservations about the ways 'ecologism' has to date been characterized (Hayward, 1996b), I think the term does serve to focus a central issue: the term 'ecology' refers to relations between organisms and their environment; because the environment of any organism itself includes other organisms, it therefore includes relations *between* organisms. So whereas environmentalism considers only the environment of – usually – the one sort of organism that we humans are, ecologism – to live up to its name – aspires to take account also of relations among other organisms and their environments. Hence it is often claimed to be more complete and holistic, accommodating the complex totality of all the interrelated organism–environment relations, rather than being restricted to a view of nonhuman nature as merely humans' environment. It also claims to consider the good of nonhuman nature 'for its own sake'. But we might reflect on what this means.

Consider the options for a particular feature of the nonhuman natural world, such as a forest for instance. Various human interests might be served by cutting it down: to make way for a road, to yield agricultural or grazing land, to plant different trees for timber, or for housing, and so on. However, various human interests would also support a policy of preserving it intact. For instance, the forest might be home to an indigenous people who depend on its flora and fauna for their survival; and who perhaps also hold it sacred as the abode of their ancestors. Then again, the forest might be valued by non-indigenous people simply because it plays a contributing role in releasing the oxygen humans need for their survival; or because it is aesthetically pleasing, or provides opportunities for recreation, or because they find it spiritually uplifting, or just because they like the idea of 'unspoilt nature'. Alternatively, the ecology of the forest might be valued for its biodiversity, particularly if it includes any endangered species; and the reasons for valuing its biodiversity are in turn varied: the preservation and discovery of different species of plants can be useful for pharmaceutical companies; it can also be valuable for pure scientific research, and there can be a presumption that all species might one day be of use to humans; or one might just take the view that it is inherently wrong to bring about the extinction of any species. Another reason which would apply, regardless of any potential human benefits or of whether any species is endangered, is that it is also the habitat of various animals and birds, as well as plant-life, and for these creatures the forest is an environment that it would be good to preserve.[3]

Among the points illustrated by this range of options is that the same policy can be adopted for very different reasons. Thus while it is true that some ecological values conflict with some humans' interests, it is not true that all ecological values conflict with all humans' interests. The significance of this for politics is that it would be a mistake to divide up types of ecological/environmental movements into those dedicated to the pursuit of human interests and those dedicated to the pursuit of ecological values. I have already argued in my previous book (Hayward, 1995) that this sort of dichotomizing constitutes an unnecessary obstacle to constructive dialogue between proponents of ecologism and environmentalism, and that quite 'radical' ecological aims can be achieved by 'reformist' means. But whereas in that book I largely accepted the terms of opposition as conventionally presented, seeking ways of reconciling them, in the present book I deepen the analysis to question the very basis of such oppositions.

Thus a further point to recognize is that some ecological values conflict with other ecological values, since what is good for an ecosystem as a whole, for instance, does not coincide with the good of each of its constituents (cf., e.g. Callicott, 1980). It is therefore to be noted that sometimes the same policy can be supported by different value commitments; and sometimes one value commitment can have contradictory implications. For this reason, the radical critique of reformist values and motivations can be misguided not only politically, but also at a conceptual level, since the standpoint of the critique is itself not without its own internal contradictions. This means there is room for legitimate differences not only about policies, but also about the underlying reasons for them – so that critics should be cautious when tempted to say that a policy-maker has done the 'right' thing for the 'wrong' reasons. Recalling the illustration given, I would suggest it is not clear that any of the reasons for preserving the forest is inherently wrong; nor, in a broader context, is it obvious why preserving the forest is necessarily the 'right' option. At any rate, clear and unequivocal value guidance is needed first.

So what are ecological values? If we assume that ecological values refer in some sense to 'good relations' among organisms and environments, between different local environments (such as biotic communities and ecosystems), two sorts of question arise: what counts as a 'good' relation; and how does this translate into human values? Given the immense complexity of ecological relations, they can be brought under an indefinitely large number of descriptions; and a similar point applies regarding values. Moreover, the aspects under which ecological processes could be valued are not only innumerable, but also, from the perspective of humans – who are, after all, just one set of constituents – imponderable. In short, if there might be as many ecological values as there are relations between organisms and environments, and if some guide to action is to be provided, then some more general evaluative principles would appear to be required.

To be sure, various attempts have been made to distil certain more general value guiding principles from ecology,[4] but as already mentioned, these can conflict: because all organisms 'use' other organisms as environmental resources, any general principle of ecological value would have to strike a balance between competing 'claims' of different organisms, and so be faced again with imponderable complexity that could only be cut through by arbitrary favouring of some ecosystemic constituents over others. Another possibility, of course, is to take the integrity of the whole ecosystem as a principle of value, but the only principle this could generate for guiding human action, without reviving the problem just mentioned, is one of complete non-intervention. This principle has some intuitive appeal, and it seems fair to say that ecological thought has a presumption in favour of intervening as little as possible in the relations of nonhuman nature. Nevertheless, given that humans do, as a matter of ecological fact, interact with nonhuman nature, they have to make decisions about which interactions to promote and which to avoid, and so the principle of non-interference yields little guidance for practice: ecological relations being as they are, apparently small interventions can have dramatic consequences. The problem of imponderable complexity returns.

So if we are not to give up on the idea of ecological values, I propose a different approach. Instead of asking after values in ecology, trying directly to find values in ecological relations, I propose the principle of examining our existing values to see how consistently they can be maintained in the face of ecological realities. Of course, to try to work out how such a principle could be applied in real investigations would be a mammoth task in itself. However, I propose a further complexity-reducing move: since what we are concerned with here is the sort of value that political theorists are or should be committed to dealing with, what can appropriately and more realistically be investigated is whether a theory includes amongst its basic assumptions any such that belief in them would entail further beliefs that were ecologically counterfactual. If it does, then it is unecological.[5]

Clearly, many of the assumptions a political theorist might make have no determinate ecological implications. However, one I wish to take issue with is the assumption that the fact that human beings are *natural* beings can be abstracted from for the purposes of political theory. Accordingly, as already mentioned, the first premise of this book is that humans are a part of nature. If that ought to be uncontroversial for theorists of ecological values, the second would also be uncontroversial for many political theorists – this is the premise that one cannot reasonably or realistically assume that people are generally motivated to do other than what they take to be in their own interest.

The theoretical basis of my argument, therefore, depends on being able
to reconcile these two assumptions. Of course, it is certainly not
unheard of for political theorists to accept both assumptions, at least as
so baldly stated. So in what follows I shall briefly try to clarify how I am
interpreting them, and indicate what is distinctive about the conjunction I am proposing.

2   The argument from the first premise: humans as natural beings

Humans are a part of nature; we are natural beings. Despite widespread and deeply ingrained habits of talking about nature as something 'out there' and 'other' or radically different from 'us',[6] my
assumption is that there is nothing in the world – at least of which we
are or could be aware – which is non-natural, so humans are not in any
politically relevant respect 'non-natural'. Humans are not 'part nature'
and 'part something else', be that something else rationality, sociality
or whatever; rather, they are natural beings who have certain capacities
which some, or perhaps all, other natural beings do not have. These
capacities may set humans apart in some ways from other natural
beings – as any characteristic of a species might set it off from others –
but they do not set them apart from nature.

Non-reductive naturalism

Nevertheless, while it might be granted that human capacities, including perhaps even rationality, are in some sense natural, it may be
objected that there remains a sense in which some matters of concern to
humans – and most centrally, in the present context, the concerns
of political beings whose social relations are governed by abstract
norms that constitute an ethical life – may meaningfully be thought of
as non-natural. For there is a sense, it may be argued, in which social
phenomena are not natural, and this is precisely the sense in which
social sciences are distinguished from natural sciences. My reply to this
is that there is indeed a lot of sense in distinguishing between the
respective objects of natural and social sciences: failure to do so would
be to allow naturalistic reductionism into social explanation. Yet to
say that one cannot explain social phenomena by means of natural
scientific concepts and methods is only to say that social phenomena
differ from those studied by the natural sciences (Bhaskar, 1989);

but this is not because the former are unnatural, it is simply because we happen to reserve the name of 'natural sciences' to those that consider the physical, chemical or biological properties of natural phenomena: the mere fact that we use this nomenclature does not tell us anything about what *other* properties natural phenomena may or may not have.

Social relations, social norms and so on – like individual beliefs and ideas – do not have a tangible material existence, but this does not mean that they do not emanate from purely natural processes the way that more tangible phenomena do; in fact, there is a sense in which they are perfectly tangible – namely the sense in which we do actually apprehend them: for it is meaningful to speak of social phenomena precisely when we have good reason to credit their reality. If social science and understanding are possible, it is because there are real social phenomena. And I have said that I am assuming that whatever is real is natural.

But then with such a broad definition of 'natural', does the term not lose any purchase precisely where it is supposed to have some critical edge? In particular, if everything humans are and do is natural, can this fact have any normative implications at all? Certainly, if the question is understood as asking what direct substantive normative implications the simple fact of humans' natural being has then the answer I wish to give is, quite simply, none. 'Nature' or 'naturalness' are not criteria that can give any guidance to the content of norms: any attempt to invoke them for ethical or political ends is liable to be ideological. Furthermore, little or no normative guidance is to be found by looking at how affairs are regulated within nonhuman nature: to suppose the contrary, I shall argue, is a fallacy of certain, quite dominant, versions of ecologism.

Various hypotheses and prescriptions have been put forward by normatively oriented ecological theorists who have sought to derive values from 'nature' or 'naturalness'. Among the variety of such theories, the common aim is to have human action not guided by human interests, but to have it in some way 'follow nature'. My position is that to the extent that 'following nature' is an intelligible and feasible ambition, it does not mean trying to draw lessons from the ways nonhuman beings behave and relate, but to understand the nature that we humans are, in its specificity as a socially and culturally impregnated sort of nature. A defensible form of naturalism therefore accepts that the emergent properties of social and ethical life cannot adequately be explained in terms of properties at other levels of emergence: thus while ethical life is not autonomous of 'nature' as such, it still has to be understood in terms proper to it. The starting point for gaining such an understanding, therefore, must begin, immanently, within ethical life itself. This means, I contend, beginning with a critical analysis of how humans perceive their own interests; and this is to take a different approach from that which has hitherto been prominent in environmental ethics and ecological thought more generally. My argument against mainstream ethical and political theory, though, is that it goes astray if it assumes that the fact of our natural being can be abstracted from.

The assumption of humans' naturalness in political theory

There are three main areas in which the assumption of humans' naturalness enters political theory with distinctive implications.

1   Humans have *natural capacities*, as individuals and as members of the species. These condition possible forms of individual development and social cooperation; they constitute the limits to possible adaptation to changed environments; they constitute the parameters within which humans can have cognitive access to the rest of nature. They are relevant to characterizing the good life. Of course, natural capacities are always socially and culturally inflected, both in their workings and in our interpretations of their workings, so they do not determine a unique thoroughgoing conception of the good. They do, though, establish some parameters within which it may be sought.

2   Correspondingly, there are *natural limits* of both 'internal' and 'external' sorts to human development: there are limits to what the human organism, including its mind, can achieve or tolerate; there are limits to the demands humans can place on natural resources. These limits have not only to do with defining the good life, but also bear on questions of justice. Beings whose possibilities of internal and external development are more limited than their aspirations are beings who find themselves in what Rawls, following Hume, has called 'the circumstances of justice'. Furthermore, these circumstances, of limited resources and limited sympathies, are intensified by the depletion and deterioration of natural resources; and it is conceivable that the moderateness of resource scarcity that makes justice possible may not persist indefinitely into the future. As natural and finite beings in a natural and finite world, therefore, humans must heed this finitude, and not assume that distributive principles can be developed in abstraction from it.

3 The most distinctively ecological idea is that of *natural relations*. These are of numerous kinds: there are natural relations of biological kinship between humans, on which familial and social relations are supervenient; between humans who are not kin, too, relations are naturally mediated, for instance in the sense that reproductive and productive activities occur in a natural medium; such activities normally involve modifying the natural environment in some way, and all humans, individually and collectively, have relations to their environment. Moreover, humans not only *have* an environment, they themselves *are* the environment of other beings – this is the case for humans individually (as hosts for various micro-organisms), socially (as beings whose practices and institutions provide an anthropogenic environment) and as (populations of) a species, to the extent that they participate in ecosystemic relations as organic beings. Finally, and perhaps most strikingly, there are among other natural beings many, especially animals, with whom humans have work and leisure relations, forms of co-operation and communication, that are more like relations with other humans than with their environment.

To sum up, then, the assumption that humans' natural being is of political significance has three important corollaries for normative political theory. It places constraints on, and provides some determinations for, accounts of the good; it places constraints on accounts of justice or the right; and it places constraints on humans' dealings with nonhuman nature. Full recognition of each of these corollaries is necessary to an adequate political theory under contemporary conditions, and sufficient to distinguish such a political theory, informed by what we might call the political philosophy of ecologism, from other political philosophies. Certainly, other political philosophies may, in some versions of them, take on board one or both of the first two corollaries, since these can be seen as extensions of, rather than radical departures from, more traditional concerns with the right and the good: thus most coherent theories of the good life ought to be able to accommodate the fact of natural capacities and needs; and theories of justice ought in principle to be able to extend their traditional concern with conditions of scarcity to include the idea of natural limits. This helps explain the plausibility of claims to green credentials by certain liberals, socialists and conservatives.[7] However, in such cases we still only have to do with a green tinge, so to speak. Only when the third corollary, the idea of natural relations, also figures does the idea of human beings as one natural species among others come to have constitutive significance for political theory.

But if the idea of natural relations is the most distinctive feature of the political theory being proposed, its meaning and the constraints it places on normative political theory need to be carefully delineated. Like natural capacities and natural limits, natural relations operate in some ways to enable, and in others to constrain, humans in their pursuit of their own good; their specific difference is in introducing the idea that beings other than humans also have capacities, and face limits, as beings with their own 'good' – that is, as beings that can, for instance, live or die, flourish or languish. But is normative regulation of natural relations other than for human benefits desirable, possible or even conceivable? That is, how can 'quality of ecological relations' be considered other than as they benefit humans? This is the question upon which I reflect critically in part I of this book, taking issue with what I dub the 'two dogmas of ecologism'.

Critique of 'two dogmas of ecologism'

Prevalent in the literature on ecological values are what I consider to be misunderstandings about its normative commitments and, in the two chapters of part I, I criticize in turn two ways of characterizing them which I think are misleading (and which constitute an obstacle to appreciating how ecologists and political theorists can enter a dialogue within a common conceptual framework). One of these is the idea that an appreciation of ecological values involves a commitment to the 'intrinsic value of nonhuman nature'; the other is that one must be committed to a rejection of anthropocentrism. Although the basic impetus behind these ideas is essentially correct, its formulation in these terms allows for some avoidable confusion that can prove counterproductive in quite significant ways.

(1)   On many accounts of ecological values, one thing which is supposed to be distinctive about them is a normative commitment to the *intrinsic value of nonhuman nature*.[8] The idea is invoked to oppose the assumption that humans need have no regard to the effects on nonhuman nature of their activities. Of course, humans seldom if ever completely disregard the effects of their actions on nonhuman nature, but the point is that the concern must be for nature's 'own sake'. Nevertheless, there are two sorts of problem here: One concerns the

locus of intrinsic value – which kind of entity is to be deemed to have this sort of value, whether it be individual organisms, populations, species or entire ecosystems, for instance – and most of the debate within environmental ethics concerns precisely this question. The fact that what is good for one constituency might be bad for another is obviously a deep problem. But the other problem, and one which environmentalists tend to neglect, is the more basic conceptual question concerning what it actually means to predicate intrinsic value of anything at all. This is the problem I focus on in chapter 2: I argue that environmental ethicists have not offered a convincing account of what intrinsic value actually means when applied to the nonhuman world; and by analysing their use of the term, I seek to diagnose the reasons why a satisfactory account is in principle impossible. (Having due regard to the good of nonhumans is a defensible, but quite distinct, principle.)

My purpose, in removing this dogma, is to remove a source of counter-productive criticism of those who pursue ecological policies 'for the wrong reason'. (Indeed, the possibility is admitted of ecological politics being pursued for the reasons supplied by an enlightened self-interest, which has the considerable political advantage of admitting as 'truly ecological' many conscientious 'reformists' whom more radical greens would want to chastise as too shallow, or maybe not even ecological at all.)[9]

(2)   Another central tenet of many accounts of green theory is that it crucially involves the *rejection of anthropocentrism*.[10] However, while accepting the view that humans should not restrict moral consideration to their own kind, but have regard to the goods of nonhumans, too, I consider it unhelpful to refer to this as rejecting anthropocentrism. For there are also senses in which human-centredness is unavoidable, un-objectionable and even desirable. Firstly, taking a human perspective on the world is in some ways unavoidable if humans are indeed a part of nature and not unbounded, all-seeing beings potentially separable from the rest of nature. Secondly, objections to anthropocentrism miss their mark to the extent that they see the problem as humans having concern for other humans (if but they did!) rather than a lack of concern for nonhumans. Thirdly, humans having concern for their own kind may actually be a precondition of concern for nonhumans: if as bounded beings we have to learn what it is to care, and we learn this

from our nearest and dearest, then we can only transfer it to other beings once we have learnt it. To claim otherwise would be to assume that humans can transcend their humanness, which would be to go directly counter to the core assumption of ecologism.

What can be rejected is the assumption that it is acceptable for humans to be *exclusively* concerned with their own kind. This can be rejected, though, without any reference to the highly ambiguous idea of anthropocentrism. The arbitrary preference for members of one's own species over members of others is aptly described as 'speciesism', a term which designates a form of injustice. So to avoid potentially counterproductive confusions the obvious solution is to deny, as we quite consistently can, that rejection of anthropocentrism is a necessary feature of ecologism. It is not only not wrong to be human-centred; it is in important respects right and desirable to be.

Without these two dogmas, the political philosophy of ecologism can guide consideration of nonhuman nature by observing a distinction, taken as a central organizing principle of this book, which derives directly from a basic premise of ecological science.

The ecological distinction between organism and environment

Ecology studies organisms as environmentally interrelated: it therefore has two fundamental and constitutive concepts, that of organism and environment. An implication of this is that concern with the environment can be distinguished from concern with other organisms (cf. Hayward, 1997b). Certainly the environment of an organism is also constituted by other organisms, and this fact is only bracketed off to draw attention to a conceptual distinction and not to deny its importance. It makes a difference to how we view an ecological relationship depending on whether we view it from the point of view of the organism, or from the point of view of its environment. From the standpoint of any organism, the environment can be seen as an ensemble of enabling or threatening conditions for its own continued existence and flourishing; from the standpoint of an ecological totality (be this an ecosystem, biotic community, or whatever), an organism can be seen as either a beneficial or disruptive constituent. If we imagine what proto-normative judgements might be made from the two standpoints, it is easy to see how they would differ: from the standpoint of an organism, the environment 'ought' to be maintained or modified according as how it best serves to maintain the organism's flourishing existence;

from the standpoint of the totality, the organism's flourishing is a matter of almost complete indifference: if the organism contributes to the integrity and stability of the ecosystem then it is good; if it does not, then the organism can and should be treated as expendable. (This is why disputes arise between environmentalists and animal liberationists, for instance.)

Now a difference between humans and most, if not all, other organisms, is that they can think not only as organisms, but also from other standpoints. (This is what makes ecological ethics necessary and possible: we face choices about whether and when to preserve an environment at the expense of some of its inhabitants or vice versa.) Thus, on the one hand, they can view their environment in a functional, instrumental, fashion. Some, indeed, would maintain that the only appropriate concern of environmental ethics is to keep the environment in good condition to serve as humans' life-support system. A more expansive view of environmental concern, however, corresponding to a more 'enlightened' conception of human interests, would see the environment not only as a life-support system, but also as a source of meaning and fulfilment for humans as aesthetic, creative, recreational and spiritual beings. Nevertheless, this could be viewed as a merely sophisticated type of functionality. In starker contrast is the view of those humans, including some deep ecologists, for instance, who think to transcend the standpoint of a human organism so that neither their own organic existence, nor indeed the existence or flourishing of other humans or any organisms with whom they might have special relations, have any privileged claim to ethical concern. For reasons connected with my critique of the two dogmas of ecologism, though, I think the latter view is untenable as an ethical view.

Nevertheless, there remains the question of the relation between humans and nonhuman organisms. One way of conceiving this relation is as exactly the same as that of a human to its environment – indeed, to conceive of organisms as nothing other than constituents of the environment; morally no different from its abiotic constituents. However, as was noted above, organisms and environments have different 'standpoints' that can be distinguished, and I shall be arguing that this has moral significance. Given the fundamental ecological distinction between organism and environment, an ecological ethic has to be responsive, in the guidance it gives to action, to the difference between effects on environments and effects on other organisms. Concern for the environment can be treated as a matter of human self-interest; to the extent that it requires ethical advances over the crude instrumentality of our current normative regulation, this is in terms of *enlightened* human self-interest – no more and no less. Concern for nonhuman beings, however, is different: to the extent that these beings can be considered as bearers of interests – in some sense of the term – including an interest in the maintenance of their own conditions of life and flourishing, then there is a case, I shall argue, for respecting those interests, too. However, prior to establishing this case, it is necessary to examine the nature of human interests and the possible connection with nonhuman interests. This is the programme for part II.

3   The argument from interests

The preliminary analysis of ecologism has been developed primarily on the basis of the premise that humans are organisms and that organisms are conceptually and also ontologically distinguishable from environments. The constructive part of the account rests with equal weight on a second premise, namely, that humans are motivated primarily by their own interests.

The aim of the second part of the book is to identify the ecological values that are implied by or are consistent with human interests. To achieve this aim, though, I do not want to start from any exorbitant assumptions about the nature, extent or generality of human interests. Indeed, one cannot ignore reasons for scepticism about the very existence of any *human* – as opposed to individual or group – interests, or the associated problem that humans' interests can conflict. Accordingly, I start, in chapter 4, from the least controversial (and least ambitious) of assumptions about human interests – namely, that individuals are generally self-interested. The idea of self-interest, though, while frequently invoked as a premise in political theory, is not entirely adequate to the role (whether descriptive, explanatory or normative) assigned to it: for people have many and varied interests, and it is necessary to analyse the apparently simple idea of 'self-interest' into more nuanced categories, attending to the subtleties and complexities – conceptual and empirical – involved in its formation. Unpacking the view, it is revealed to be misleading: for, of the various interests human individuals have, few, if any, can be reduced to an egoism sufficiently pure to substantiate the standard claim; for this reason, I also therefore argue, it is neither necessary nor appropriate to invoke altruistic motivations to oppose it. Instead, I suggest, interests can be distinguished according to how narrow or wide, restricted or enlightened, they are.

These themes are developed in chapter 5, where I turn to consider how human interests bear on ecological values, focusing in particular on how rational self-interest and enlightened self-interest can be harnessed to environmental ends. The first consideration is that while many environmental problems are attributed to the prevalence of narrow, essentially private and economistic, interests, there are also reasons to think that rational economic self-interest can, in some circumstances, be harnessed to solve them. Even as manifest in market behaviour, the pursuit of rational self-interest is not necessarily anti-ecological. Hence in environmental policy-making there is a role for market-based approaches. But this role has to be carefully delimited, since there are also strong objections that can be made to basing environmental values on individual preferences or purchasing power. Accordingly I go on to examine an alternative approach to the evaluation of environmental goods, on which they are seen as a matter for political deliberation rather than economic calculation. This approach can yield more enlightened conceptions of people's interests and thus underpin environmental policies that go beyond the constraints of market-oriented interests. Still, I point out, to the extent that it is likely to be effective or legitimate, this deliberation must still be based in interests, albeit enlightened interests revealed in discursive will-formation. I argue that some of the leading proponents of deliberative approaches to ecological policy-making overstate the case against environmental economics, and understate the difficulties with their own, because they pit environmental values directly against economic preferences, instead of recognizing that what is at issue is degrees of enlightenment of *interests*.

Where the enlightenment of interests appears less likely to suffice to yield adequate values, however, is in relation to those parties with intelligibly attributable 'interests' who cannot directly compete in market valuations or participate in discursive fora: this is the case with future generations of humans, and with nonhumans. There is no institutional arrangement that can directly guarantee their adequate representation. In chapter 6 I focus on this issue as it applies to nonhuman beings, and ask whether they have any moral claim on us at all. The answer I develop is that if humans have an interest in respecting themselves and one another *as* humans, then they have no reason to withhold respect from nonhuman beings. This argument runs counter to the view that the reasons humans respect one another are bound up with facts about what it is to be a human being as opposed to any other kind of being. Of the various characteristics lacking in nonhumans that are appealed to in ruling out moral consideration of them, those which have a sufficiently direct connection with features of moral respect to be non-arbitrarily singled out can be grouped under the rough heading of rational autonomous moral agency. However, my argument that respect is not due exclusively to rational moral agents proceeds in three stages, focusing on agency, rationality and moral accountability, respectively, as criteria of worthiness of respect. I show that none of these criteria can successfully be appealed to as a basis for withholding respect from nonhuman beings. In fact, I argue, if humans respect themselves as rational moral agents, then fulfilling the demands of mutual self-respect requires them to view rational moral agency as a source of responsibility in relation to their cohabitants on this earth, rather than as a mere privilege.

Conclusion

Having outlined the case for dealing with ecological concerns in terms of interests, the final chapter discusses some of the implications for political theory of doing so. I focus particularly on the question of what it means to integrate ecological values into the basic institutions of society. Some environmental values are already recognized at the constitutional level: it is already recognized as appropriate to have constitutional rights in relation to some environmental social goods, and the question has become how to make these justiciable. Certainly, one would not expect environmental rights themselves to be a panacea for all ecological and social challenges, but they have an important role in opening up debate about the foundations and institutional design of an ecologically sustainable polity. Not all interests could readily be framed as (justiciable) rights, and it would probably be not be desirable always to attempt to do so, but there is a more general case for assimilating classes of human interest in ecological values to categories of primary social goods, whose distribution is a question for a general normative political theory. In that chapter I also draw attention to related descriptive and explanatory issues that I believe should be at the heart of the research agenda for the political theory of a sustainable society.

Part I

Critique: Two Dogmas of Ecologism

2

Intrinsic Value in Nature: Analysis and Critique of a Misleading Idea

Introduction

On many accounts of ecological ethics, one thing that is supposed to distinguish it from more traditional, humanistic, ethics is a normative commitment to the *intrinsic value of nonhuman nature*.[1] The impulse behind this commitment, as I understand it, is a conviction that the good of nonhumans should be given moral consideration; and this means not merely considering how realization of their good may affect humans, but considering it *for their own sake*, irrespective of how it bears on human interests.[2] Yet while I wholly support the view that ethics should not restrict the range of morally considerable beings to humans, what I am sceptical about is whether anything is contributed to the advancement of such a view by invoking the idea of 'intrinsic value'. In fact, the notion of intrinsic value cannot achieve the purposes environmental ethicists intend for it, I shall argue, and, furthermore, the polemical and intended critical force of the idea of 'nature's intrinsic value' is based on a mistake about humanistic values, about what these allow for humans and deny to nonhumans. When this mistake is corrected, the claim that beings other than humans are morally considerable can be stated and defended in its own terms, without any reference to the idea of intrinsic value.

In the first section I briefly survey the purpose of invoking the idea of nature's intrinsic value in environmental ethics, and, by raising some critical questions, indicate some initial reasons for scepticism about their likely accomplishment. In the next two sections I go on to analyse the concept of intrinsic value to reveal that it has two features –

nonderivativity and objectivity – both of which are in principle necessary to achieve environmentalists' aims. However, I show that these features cannot be preserved in the transference of the idea from the realm of human ethics to that of nonhuman nature. In the fourth section I argue, furthermore, that even if my analysis were mistaken, and the concept could be deployed, it could still not, in principle, achieve the required ends. In section 5, however, I show that while it is not possible to conceptualize ecological values that are *absolutely* nonderivative or *strongly* objective, this is not a reason to subscribe to a pragmatist or subjectivist position that would also remove the possibility of talking about values as *relatively* nonderivative and *weakly* objective. In conclusion, I indicate why the central problem is to provide an account of human obligations with regard to nonhumans, and why this can and must be addressed in its own terms without the illusory short cut held out by the idea of intrinsic value.

1 Nature's intrinsic value: preliminary observations

To begin with, I wish to consider a little more closely the reasons why the idea of intrinsic value is invoked in ecological ethics at all. To see why anyone would wish to claim that nature, the natural world, some features of it, or some nonhuman natural entities, have intrinsic value, it is necessary to understand how the category of intrinsic value functions in ethics generally.

The category of intrinsic value, like all ethical categories, is used to give agents guidance as to what they should and should not do. To say something has intrinsic value is to signal that it ought to be taken into account by an agent in a particular sort of way. Theories of intrinsic value, though, are not directly theories of obligation; nor are they only theories explaining what items ought to be taken into account when considering what obligations one has.[3] Rather, their role is to explain what it is that moral obligations should be aimed at achieving: thus when something is attributed intrinsic value it is the equivalent of saying that, *ceteris paribus*, the world is a morally better place when that something exists in it than it would be if it did not exist. Hence the idea that something has intrinsic value can be equated with the idea that this something is intrinsically good.

However, a complete theory of intrinsic value in the world also has to explain *how* good the items possessed of it are. One question to take a view on is whether there is any item that is *absolutely* good, such that no action tending to destroy or undermine it could ever be justified for

any reason whatever, and probably such that there would be an obligation overriding all others to protect it, and, perhaps, also actively to
promote it. Within traditional ethics, the idea of absolute goodness
attaches to rather few and exceptional candidates, such as God, or
perhaps the Kantian 'Good Will'; within ecological ethics a candidate
for such a value might be Nature itself, for I take it that ecological ethics
has a constitutive commitment to the proposition that it is better that
Nature exists than that it should not. Nevertheless, this proposition is
indeterminate as a ground of moral obligation: for given that it is in no
agent's power of action to bring it about that Nature should cease
to exist, no action whatsoever could be either required or unjustified.
So the question whether Nature in its totality is an absolute good can be
set aside for practical purposes.

Environmental ethics is in fact concerned rather with the question of
which, among the states that it is possible for Nature to be in, are better
and which worse. It thus has to say which states of affairs human
actions ought to aim at promoting and which they ought to avoid
bringing about. This means evaluating how much good the various
possible states of affairs in nature have in relation to one another. It is
in principle possible that some states of affairs will be attributed positive intrinsic value and others neutral or even negative intrinsic value;
actions in pursuit of such states of affairs would then be, respectively,
obligatory, morally indifferent or prohibited. The more difficult, and
practically crucial, question arises for the agent who is faced with
a choice between two or more actions, each of which would lead to
intrinsically valuable, but different, states of affairs. How can she do the
right thing if in pursuing state A she fails to pursue state B which is
(also) morally obligatory? If a theory of intrinsic value is to answer this,
it must be a theory of a type of value that admits of *degrees*. If the agent
knows that state A has more value than state B then she has clear
guidance for her action.[4]

Theories of intrinsic value, in general, then, have the task of supplying the values to be entered into a sort of moral calculus. They bring in
substantive considerations about features of states of affairs that make
one of them better than another. I shall not even attempt to indicate the
range of features that might be taken to confer intrinsic value, though,
for my question is why the idea of *intrinsic* value is invoked to fulfil this
task in environmental ethics: why not simply say that states of affairs
have more or less *value, tout court*?

One basic reason for wishing to impute intrinsic value to features of
the nonhuman natural world is to counteract what is claimed to be
a defect of humanistic ethics – namely, that it attributes intrinsic value

to states of affairs only when, and only insofar as, they are good *for humans*, so that whatever condition the rest of nature is left in is a matter of moral indifference except insofar as its being in one condition rather than another conduces to what is intrinsically valuable for humans. Now there is, of course, a formal sense, in which any value attributed or apprehended by humans is necessarily a value 'for them'; but one can distinguish this formal sense, in which necessarily all and only those things held valuable by an agent have value 'for' that agent, from a substantive sense in which things have value for an agent, contingently, because they contribute in some way to her own well-being. Yet not all humanistic ethics are by any means oriented exclusively to yielding direct benefits for their addressees, and indeed they often, even typically, prescribe obligations that are not 'good', in this sense, for the agent who has to carry them out. Perhaps the key point, though, is that the obligations on agents to disregard their personal interests are justified by reference to the interests of other agents, or of other humans more generally: part of the force of the appeal to intrinsic value in nature, accordingly, would reside in a claim that reference should be made to the 'interests' (using the term for now in a theoretically noncommittal way) of nonhuman beings too. But to say this is only to say that nonhuman beings are 'morally considerable'. So the question remains: what is the specific role of the concept of 'intrinsic value'? To try to answer this, then, to ascertain what kind of consideration it is that humans tend, wrongly, to withhold from nonhumans, let us examine what intrinsic value means within human ethics.

To begin with, as far as I am aware, no traditional ethic has claimed that human beings themselves have intrinsic value. The proposition sounds somehow strange. Indeed, if it is glossed as meaning 'human beings are intrinsically good' it is either straightforwardly wrong or else of indeterminate meaning. It is wrong if it is taken to mean that they can't be or do bad, since the fact that they can and do is precisely the reason why ethics, on most accounts of it, is necessary. But if it is understood to mean that, no matter how bad they sometimes appear, humans are nevertheless 'essentially' good, then it is problematic in respect both of its truth and its implications: its truth will be denied by anyone who believes, say, in Original Sin, or takes a materialist, perhaps Hobbesian, view of human nature; but even those who think it true may disagree on its ethical implications, since on the question of how to view and/or deal with people who are *actually* bad (assuming, still, that it makes any sense to think of people as good or bad), the belief that they are *potentially* good has no determinate bearing, or at least makes no answers mandatory that could not also be arrived at on the basis of quite different assumptions about human nature.

Perhaps rather than focus on the actual or potential moral qualities of particular human specimens, the idea that 'human beings are intrinsically valuable' could be taken to refer more generally to the *existence* of human beings, so that, *ceteris paribus*, it is better that there be human beings in the world than that there not. An ethical implication of this is that no human being ought to be arbitrarily killed.[5] An ecological ethicist might well want to say the same regarding members of any other species as well. Notice, though, that no statement of such an obligation can be supported by an appeal to the intrinsic value of those beings, since such an appeal would be tautologous. Therefore, if one wants to ground obligations regarding nonhuman nature in the idea of intrinsic value, it must be interpreted as meaning something other than this.

In fact, in the human case, too, intrinsic value is not appropriately attributed to the mere existence of human beings. For to say that the existence of the human species is good, or that the existing members of it have a prima facie 'right' to continue in existence, is not to say that the existence of each and every human being is an intrinsically good thing. Indeed, there are reasons *not* to say this. On the one hand, there is serious reason to doubt whether the existence of an unlimited number of humans would be a good state of affairs. On the other hand, simple existence, unaccompanied by certain further requisites of a meaningful life *as* a human being, is not uncontroversially something of value either: if a human being is leading a miserable existence, perhaps suffering a terminal degenerative illness, for instance, there is at least room for debate about whether 'they ought to exist';[6] it is certainly arguable that any human ought to do more than just 'exist'.

So, if not of their mere existence, is intrinsic value appropriately predicated of certain qualities they possess? Obviously we do value certain personal qualities, and some human virtues and excellences may strike us as intrinsically valuable; but it is also obvious that these are not displayed by all humans in like measure. The moral force of attributing intrinsic value to certain human qualities would be to exhort emulation; it would not necessarily mean claiming that preferential or privileged treatment was due to their bearer – and if it were, the idea would certainly not be suitable for uptake in environmental ethics. But in any case I do not think we would wish to say a person had intrinsic value only contingently in virtue of these qualities. Nor, though, would I want to say, and am not even sure what it would mean to say, a person 'has value' apart from these qualities. Such a proposition is one I feel it inappropriate either to affirm or deny.

Why, though, do I find it odd and difficult to speak of a person as 'having value'? Why, when I may value a person in their deeds, in their dispositions, and so on, does it none the less strike me as inappropriate – somehow arrogant or disrespectful – to say that I value *them*? Part of the reason, I think, is that the practice of valuing in general admits of degrees of value – this, after all, is why we engage in it; but the sort of respect I believe to be due towards human beings is not the sort that admits of degrees: I would find it intolerable to say that one human being, qua human, had greater value than another, even if one may exhibit finer characteristics, contribute more to human existence in terms of its richness or happiness, and so on. A 'value' that admits of no degrees, that is thereby somehow placed beyond any value judgement, is perhaps not appropriately referred to as a 'value' at all, but as something else.

This observation brings us to consider a central issue which is sometimes confused with the question of intrinsic value. I have said that I find it inappropriate to speak at all of a particular person, or indeed of humans in general, as 'having value', but what I do not find odd is the idea that human beings are appropriately treated in some ways rather than others – in particular, that they should not be treated as mere means to my ends. To treat another as not merely a means to my ends is to treat them with due regard. This means not only refraining from valuing them merely for their contribution to my life experience; it means refraining, in an important sense, from *valuing* them at all. For there is a respect in which other persons are literally *beyond* value. The basic reason is that human beings are the sort of being *for whom* things have value: when I think of a particular person as a person, rather than under some particular description such as colleague or plumber, I do not think of them as an object of valuation at all, but rather as a subject of valuation. The person's 'value' is literally not in question – just as my own, qua valuer, is not: I think of them not as a being to be judged good or otherwise, but as a being who '*has* a good', a being for whom other things can be good. Furthermore, I would note, I think this way also of human individuals who might not qualify for 'personhood' in some of its technical senses. What has intrinsic value for humans, then, is 'their good'. This involves no direct claim that humans *are* intrinsically good, but rather a recognition that certain states of affairs are intrinsically good *for* them. Theories of intrinsic value or goodness for humans typically alight on such things as pleasure, happiness, integrity, dignity, autonomy or rationality as appropriate candidates for bearing it.

Similarly, then, it would be a category mistake to speak of non-human *entities* as having intrinsic value.[7] It is not nonhuman entities that can intelligibly be attributed intrinsic value, but their *good*. Theories of intrinsic value in or of nonhuman nature would thus seek to modify the characterization of the capacities involved in 'having a good' so as to include ones that are not so humanly specific as autonomy or rationality, or to focus on ones whose application can more readily be extended to nonhumans (such as sentience, autopoesis, and so on). To do this is to specify what the good of the entity consists in. It seems to me quite plausible and correct to say, in general, that the full and untrammelled development of whatever capacities an entity has is intrinsically good for the entity in question. But whether this is equivalent to saying that its good 'has intrinsic value' in an ethically meaningful sense has yet to be determined.

To appreciate why intrinsic value might meaningfully be attributed to the good of nonhuman entities, it is again appropriate first to consider why it is, or can be, attributed to human goods. When we speak of goods, as I have been doing, in terms of conditions of flourishing, even of humans, we are speaking of goods in a *nonmoral* sense. For example, 'happiness' is not itself a moral quality; its goodness can be fully described without reference to any moral concepts. Morality, however, must always at some point relate to actions: thus happiness attains moral relevance in the case that one subscribes to a morality according to which those actions tending to promote and/or not hinder happiness are to be judged morally good actions. So while it is morally good for an agent to act with due regard for the other's happiness, it is not a *morally* good thing simply *that* the other is happy.

The moral judgement that pursuit of their happiness is morally good thus rests on a premise that needs to be stated – namely, that it is morally good that beings capable of happiness be allowed, *ceteris paribus*, to realize it. We simply assume, or have a conviction, that happiness is a (nonmorally) good thing for everyone capable of it; we also assume that everyone is 'equally entitled' to realize their happiness.[8] This is why we should have due regard to the good of others.

Going now beyond humans, an analogous proposition would be that some or all nonhuman entities have, as Arne Naess (1989) puts it, an 'equal right or entitlement to flourish and blossom'; given, though, that phrases like 'right' or 'entitlement' carry inconvenient conceptual baggage with them, it could more simply be said that they are 'morally considerable': with this phrase I mean that their good is to be taken as a reason telling for or against a proposed action when that action is liable to affect it.

Now how and why would one make this judgement? Ultimately, it rests, as in the human case, on a conviction or intuition. In our day, there is a quite general conviction – manifest, for instance, in the widespread acceptance of human rights – that all humans are equally morally considerable. There is not such a general conviction that nonhumans are. One of the aims of environmental ethics, I take it, at least and especially on many versions of it that appeal to intrinsic value in nature, is to produce such a conviction.

But does use of the notion of intrinsic value help either in conceptualizing or motivating the relevant change? As I understand it, it is supposed to do both; I shall argue, however, that it can do neither. The big issue is 'who counts?', that is, 'which entities are morally considerable?' Once this is established, what is intrinsic value theory supposed to add?

2   Intrinsic value as nonderivative value

Part of what it means for something to have intrinsic value can be understood by contrasting this with what it means to have extrinsic value. The contrast is illustrated by G.E. Moore's distinction in ethics between 'the question what things are good in themselves, and the question to what other things these are related as effects' (Moore, 1903: 27). For Moore, the former sorts of things have intrinsic value, and the latter sort have only extrinsic value. Whereas something with extrinsic value is 'good as a means', something with intrinsic value is 'good as an end' or 'good in itself'.

Before thinking about possible substantive interpretations of what it means for something to be 'good in itself', though, it is to be noted that the extrinsic–intrinsic contrast can be analysed under a formal aspect. The form of relation between intrinsic and extrinsic values is of one-way entailment: that is to say, within a given evaluative framework (or, more neutrally, wherever the contrast can be applied), items with intrinsic value necessarily have that value, but items with extrinsic value have the value they do only contingently – that is, if and only if they contribute in some way to the realization of intrinsic value. Hence one can think of extrinsic value as derivative in relation to intrinsic value. Intrinsic value, by contrast, is a type of value which is *nonderivative*.

The formal feature of nonderivativity, I therefore wish to suggest, is necessary for any conception of intrinsic value that can meaningfully be contrasted with nonintrinsic types of value.[9] But it is not sufficient, because the formal contrast can be drawn between other types of value which, for substantive reasons, might not appropriately be called intrinsic or extrinsic. For example, when Karl Marx contrasted 'exchange value' with 'use value' he showed how the latter is nonderivative with respect to the former (Marx, 1954: 43–88): the possibility of commodities having value in exchange presupposes that they have some use value; but no analysis of their exchange value can reveal their use value, because this is value of a more fundamental and nonderivative type. Yet it would not seem to be appropriate to describe this contrast as one between extrinsic and intrinsic values: for while there is a sense in which a commodity's value in use has to do with its intrinsic qualities, we would not usually think of this value as intrinsic, since it can in turn be analysed to reveal a dependence on more fundamental human purposes. Now in traditional human ethics, it is often the fulfilment of these human purposes, or what humans ultimately aim at – such as happiness, flourishing, or what Aristotle called *eudaemonia*, for instance – that *is* credited with intrinsic value. Of course, on some accounts, human fulfilment itself may in turn be analysed to reveal a dependence on sources of meaning and value that transcends it. In that case, its value would in turn be derivative. But here, I think, we also transcend appropriate talk of 'intrinsic value' and move to the realm of what we might refer to as 'absolute' value. So one might say that intrinsic value is more fundamental than use value, but less fundamental than absolute value; attributions of intrinsic value are nonderivative in relation to use values, but would be derivative in relation to absolute values, should such exist. Nevertheless, whether or not one takes there to be such transcendent values, the meaning of saying that human ends have intrinsic value, so far as implications for action are concerned, will be the same: since whether some human fulfilment is aimed at for its own sake or, say, for God's, it is aimed at the same.

Let us now turn to consider the sense(s) in which 'intrinsic values in nature' can be nonderivative. In the literature of ecological ethics, the contrast between intrinsic value and use value – or *instrumental* value, as it is more usually called in that context – is routinely noted, and, in fact, intrinsic value is sometimes even defined as non-instrumental value (cf. O'Neill, 1993). The sense of this contrast is generally illustrated in the following way: for instance, if the integrity of an ecosystem is valued because it provides a life-support system for human beings, and only for this reason, then it can be said to be valued instrumentally; if, on the other hand, the integrity of the ecosystem is held to have value independently of that instrumental function, and regardless of any benefit it has for humans, then it has intrinsic value. (The feature of nonderivativity is thus treated not just as a formal feature but as if it were the basis of a substantive contrast with instrumental value.) Nevertheless, this idea is not sufficient to account for (the supposed force of) what it means to say something has intrinsic value. Firstly, simply to say that the value something has is noninstrumental value is not in itself to say what sort of value it does have. To deny an object the applicability of one predicate (here the having of instrumental value) is not in itself to affirm the applicability of any other particular predicate – unless, that is, the other predicate is defined as a negation of the former. Obviously a merely definitional negation would be uninformative without a substantive definition of one of the terms. However, even with a substantive definition of instrumental value, its negation might be indeterminate, and therefore not much more informative. So if instrumental value is defined, as it normally is, in terms of being useful to some further purpose, then one way of defining intrinsic value as its negation would be as *not* useful to some further purpose: but this definition clearly does not suffice to capture what intrinsic value is intended to mean – since something that is not useful to some further purpose could also not be independently valuable either! An alternative focus for negation might be the idea that the something is not useful to some further purpose, but, rather, is 'useful to itself': but this does not seem a very cogent or informative idea; and, in any case, it fails to fit the definition since the item's intrinsic value is now defined in terms of, and not in contrast to, its instrumental value. It therefore appears that we have to identify a criterion of value that is distinct from usefulness. A second problem that then faces us, though, is that criteria of nonintrinsic value other than usefulness have no plausible connection with instrumentality:[10] for humans can and do value nonhuman nature for all sorts of benefits it yields them, including those of aesthetic, cultural and spiritual kinds. Hence not all nonintrinsic values are instrumental values, and, therefore, not all noninstrumental values are intrinsic values.

Instead of restricting the contrast to instrumental value, though, the general point underlying it might be that there is a kind of value in the nonhuman natural world which does not consist in any contribution the item bearing it makes to human goods – be that contribution instrumental, aesthetic, spiritual or whatever. It would be nonderivative, accordingly, in relation to *any* human ends or purposes. Now it was noted earlier that within human ethics it is possible to speak of transcendent values that are nonderivative in relation to human ends, in the sense that the value of those ends is derivative from them: do values in nature have a value that is nonderivative in this sense – that is, in the sense that the value of human ends derives from them? I do not think there could be any good reason for supposing they do. It is one thing to entertain the idea that the value of nonhuman goods does not derive from the value of human goods, but it is quite another to say that the value manifest in nonhuman natural items was fundamental while that manifest in human goods was derivative: this would be no less arbitrary and ethically no more acceptable than saying the converse. So there appears to be no warrant, in principle, for saying that intrinsic human goods stand in a derivative relation to the intrinsic value of any particular nonhuman goods.

A more tenable claim, therefore, is that the values of human and nonhuman goods are mutually nonderivative (which means the value human goods have is independent of the value nonhuman goods have, and vice versa, regardless of whether or not the value of both were ultimately derived from an absolute or transcendent source such as 'Nature' and/or 'God'). But if we then assume that among the various values within Nature there are some which are nonderivative with respect to others, then the very significance of the initial contrast is lost. In other words, I want to argue, the feature of nonderivativity does no work in explaining what it means to say values in nature are intrinsic.

To see why that is so, let us return to the work it does within the sphere of human values. This can be illustrated by reference to the approach adopted by Moore, which I shall call the *non plus ultra* approach. Here, one begins by identifying things one actually holds to be good, and then asks *why* they are good: reasoning typically pursues a chain of purposes, as one continues to ask what something is good *for* until no further answer can be given. Once we reach something of which we can no longer say why it is good, but simply *that* it is, then this something has intrinsic value. Here we come to rest at an intuition which is simply present and strikes us as incorrigible: concerning the claim that something has intrinsic value 'no relevant evidence whatever can be adduced'. On Moore's account, to say of something that it has intrinsic value is to attribute to it a simple, unanalysable, nonnatural property.[11] But this intuition is the culmination of a process of reflection, not its starting point. So is there a comparable process of reflection that would yield an intuition about intrinsic values in nature? Moore's own will not. His candidates for intrinsic value are 'certain states of consciousness which may be roughly described as the pleasures of human intercourse and the enjoyment of beautiful objects' (Moore, 1903: 188). On this account, what is intrinsically good is what people value most highly: value thus inheres squarely in the experience of agents, and its mode of existence is subjective. He does not think to find intrinsic value 'out there' in Nature: but that is precisely where environmental ethicists want to locate it. The problem, then, is that if the idea of intrinsic value is cogent on Moore's account this is precisely because the chain of purposes can stop at some human good. Yet the whole point of appealing to intrinsic value in Nature is to argue that items other than human states have this sort of value too. But if they do, how can we conceive of it? We cannot employ the *non plus ultra* approach to identifying them, for whereas human intrinsic values can be identified by analysing the 'chain of purposes', we cannot assume that any chain of purposes leads from human values to intrinsic values in nonhuman nature. The identification of such values cannot be achieved by the *non plus ultra* approach of human ethics, since human purposes do not lead to these values. In other words, then, these values have a different *source*.

But this takes us entirely outside the parameters of nonderivability – for it has precisely to do with the source from which their value is derived – and brings us, instead, to the question of whether values in nature, in being independent of human values altogether, are *objective* values.

3   Intrinsic value as objective value

Within environmental ethics, there are good reasons for wishing to conceive of value as objective: for if 'values in nature' were necessarily to be related to a valuing human subject, then any values which humans did not happen to acknowledge would be considered not to be values. Of course, it is trivially true that any values a subject does not acknowledge cannot be *considered* values anyway, if the consideration in question is the cognitive activity of a subject. The point, however, is to claim that subjects should not assume that the only values there are are the ones they happen to recognize, or that values are constituted by subjects; rather, they can in principle be discovered.

Now the idea of objectivity in values can be understood in various ways, but in order to highlight what I take to be the salient issues, I shall focus on the distinction between weak and strong objectivity as drawn by John O'Neill (1993), although the following definitions slightly modify the terms he uses.[12]

Weak objectivity: values that exist in the absence of evaluating agents. Strong objectivity: values that can be adequately described with no necessary reference to a valuing agent.

I shall now argue that, regarding values in nonhuman nature, the case for strong objectivity fails, and the case for weak objectivity is *too* weak to provide the requisite support for theories of intrinsic value in nature.

O'Neill offers an argument to suggest we can think of intrinsic values in nature being objective in the strong sense, claiming that evaluative utterances about the natural world in fact provide the clearest examples of such values. O'Neill introduces this argument by contrasting two distinct senses of the phrase 'X is good for greenfly'. 'It might refer to what is conducive to the destruction of greenfly, as in "detergent sprays are good for greenfly", or it can be used to describe what causes greenfly to flourish, as in "mild winters are good for greenfly"' (ibid.: 19). In the first use the term 'good for' refers to what is instrumentally good for the gardener; in the second, what is instrumentally good for the greenfly, quite independently of the gardener's interests. 'This instrumental goodness is possible in virtue of the fact that greenflies are the sorts of things that can flourish or be injured. In consequence they have their own goods that are independent of both human interests and any tendency they might have to produce in human observers feelings of approval or disapproval' (ibid.). O'Neill refers to such goods as the 'goods of X'; and these, he claims, are objective goods. Hence the existence of such goods, he maintains, tells for objectivism in values. But does it?

Essential to O'Neill's argument is the existence of a type of entity which 'has a good'. For some theorists (e.g. Attfield, 1987; 1995), the kinds of entity in question are the kinds or species of being that have a life; O'Neill thinks that goods of collective entities, human and non-, including colonies, ecosystems and so on, can also have a good. Without entering into the merits of this suggestion, the point to note is that whatever types of entity are included, for this argument to work, they must be the sort of entity that can 'have a good' in the above sense; that is, that they have developmental capacities, and so are the sort of entity to which it can be discerned to make a difference whether their life unfolds in one way rather than another, that they flourish rather than be harmed.

However, there is a problem which O'Neill notes, when criticizing consequentialist approaches to environmental ethics, but without appearing to appreciate how it actually tells against his own argument.

This problem is that '[i]t is possible to talk in an objective sense of what constitutes the goods of entities, without making any claims that these ought to be realized' (O'Neill, 1993: 22). O'Neill does not accept the assumption that 'Y is good' entails 'Y ought to be realized'. Yet without this assumption, then just to the extent that the good of X, where X is not a human moral agent, can be specified without reference to an agent, that good need not figure *as* a good from the agent's standpoint. In this case, there is no necessary link between these objective goods and any possible *moral* value. Thus the existence of these objective goods does *not* tell for objectivism *in ethics*; at least not for a strong version.

This does not rule out the possibility of weak objectivity, however, which O'Neill shows need not involve exorbitant philosophical claims. He likens this sort of value to 'secondary qualities' of objects.

> Secondary qualities are dispositional properties of objects to appear in a certain way to ideal observers in ideal conditions. So, for example, an object is green if and only if it would appear green to a perceptually ideal observer in perceptually ideal conditions. It is consistent with this characterization of secondary qualities that an object possesses that quality even though it may never actually be perceived by an observer. Thus while in the strong sense of the term secondary qualities are not real properties of objects – one cannot characterize the properties without referring to the experiences of possible observers – in the weak sense of the term they are. (Ibid.: 17–18)

So, in the kingdom of the blind, he writes, the grass is still green. By analogy, objective values are properties of objects that would produce feelings of moral approval in an ideal observer in ideal conditions, whether or not particular real observers happen to detect them. Clearly, there are questions one might raise about this suggestion, including those of whether and how these are real properties of objects; but we can afford to remain neutral on such questions here, since, precisely to the extent the analogy works, it yields too weak a conception of objective value to support a claim that intrinsic values in nature can be spoken of without making at least implicit reference to (human) subjective estimates. The reason this is a weak interpretation of objective value is that it does require evaluating subjects (the analogue of ideal observers) to get it started. The very notion of 'greenness' is inextricably linked to the perceptual characteristics of real observers, and can only be said to inhere in nature where there are such observers who are included in the description of it. The category of colour itself is arrived at through an analysis of the conditions of humans' phenomenal experience. Analogously, therefore, not only would particular values be traceable to judgements of real human valuers, the very category of value depends on their existence.

Certainly, if human subject-agents can have intersubjective relations of some sort with nonhuman subject-patients, and thus have cognitive access to the 'goods' of nonhuman beings, I do not rule out the possibility of these being considered as having 'objective' value, provided only that humans are prepared so to consider them. This proviso, however, clearly undercuts the mandatory force intended by environmental ethicists' appeal to intrinsic value as objective in the sense of being entirely independent of human estimates.

4   Intrinsic value as objective and nonderivative value

The arguments so far suggest that to assert that the good of a nonhuman being has intrinsic value adds nothing to the assertion that the being in question is morally considerable. If it were to add something meaningful to this, it would have to be about the sort of consideration the being ought to be shown. In other words, it would play a part in supplying a determinate guide to action. So the question I wish to consider is, if we accept the possibility of weak objectivity in ecological values, can this be combined with nonderivativity in such a way as to give a meaning to intrinsic value which exceeds the meaning of moral considerability? I shall suggest that it cannot in principle do this, even on the most carefully thought-out accounts of intrinsic value in environmental ethics, which I shall take to be exemplified by that of Robin Attfield (1987; 1995).

Attfield's account of intrinsic value conforms to the definition I have given: it is predicated not of entities but of the goods of entities that have a good; the intrinsic value of such states as flourishing is a kind of value that is both nonderivative and objective.

Regarding the objectivity of values, Attfield claims, plausibly enough, that we can, with existing knowledge about other living beings, arrive at some quite reliable judgements about what is good for them; and while these judgements are of course *nonmoral* judgements, Attfield argues, we can also make the further presumption – and moral consistency actually requires us to – that, other things being equal, we should judge our actions right if they tend to promote that good and wrong if they tend to diminish it. A problem, of course, is that moral judgements typically have to be made in situations where other things are *not* equal, and then one needs to decide how much weight to give the good in question. Attfield believes an objective solution to this can also be given, though, along the lines that the more an entity stands to gain or lose as a consequence of one's action, the greater should be the weight of that consequence in one's deliberation. Thus, for instance, vital needs in general take precedence over non-vital needs; and the needs of more complex life-forms take precedence over less complex life-forms.

If one accepts this account of values as objective, the question then is whether the claim that they are also nonderivative lends them any particular weight when it comes to guidance for action. The force of the question is shown by considering the possibility that states with greater intrinsic value need not be valued in practice more highly than states with lesser intrinsic value. Suppose that values of simple states of affairs are ranked from A through to Z, so that the intrinsic value of A is greater than that of B, that of B greater than C, and so on down to Z whose intrinsic value is infinitesimal compared to A. Suppose, too, though, that Z also happens to be a necessary condition for the existence of A: we then face the question of whether Z is still less valuable, all things considered, than states $B \ldots Y$. For while in point of its nonderivative value it is, we have to decide how to view the derivative value it has in virtue of being a necessary condition of A. If we will the ends, 'A', we presumably should will the means, 'Z', even if this may mean a relative devaluation of one or more of states $B \ldots Y$: yet that means precisely that the nonderivative status of the latter is not decisive for the purposes of action. The basic issue here is that of how one is to choose between different possible states of affairs when they each have the same aggregate weight of value. Attfield does devote a good deal of attention to this question, and I am not here concerned to evaluate his complex answer to it.[13] I merely wish to point out that whatever reason might be given for preferring one complex state of affairs to another, it can have little to do with the nonderivativity of the various constituent values. To say the value of something is nonderivative, I therefore wish to claim, is to say nothing of consequence except when that value is specifically related, critically, to a value which is derivative from it: for while it is clearly meaningful to say that any given end has a more fundamental value than any particular means to achieving it, at least where various means are available, ends that are not linked in such a 'chain of purposes' cannot be chosen between without introducing reasons of a different sort. In other words, if intrinsic values are to be related to one another, and thus to serve any purpose at all in guiding action, the whole burden of the theory must thus fall on the substantive, objective, part of the account, which is intended to supply the different weightings of different values.

But can an account of the objectivity of value yield reasons for preferring one state of affairs to another? My answer is that it could only succeed by rendering the claim to objectivity too weak to do what is required of it, namely, to provide the basis for relativizing claims of humans *vis à vis* nonhumans, because there is no sense at all in which different combinations of goods with the same aggregate value can be decided between on an objective basis. The only way this problem can be made tractable is through the exercise of judgement. And the sense in which judgements can be objective is constrained: certainly, when Attfield explains what he means by objectivity, he speaks of it in terms of intersubjective agreement about objectively good reasons. Yet in the event of nonagreement, there is no further resource of objectivity available to call upon.

To see this, let us ask how Attfield's value theory would persuade a human chauvinist of its general correctness. The human chauvinist[14] has to be persuaded to adopt the kind of moral view according to which important human concerns are only relatively more significant, and trivial human concerns are less significant, than many vital nonhuman interests. If this cannot be achieved by appealing to the nonderivative value of the latter for the reasons given, then to what can appeal be made? To the objective features of the various goods in question? That would not suffice because those features are *nonmoral* ones: the human chauvinist could agree to the accuracy of descriptions of these nonmoral goods, acknowledge the descriptive aptness of certain comparisons between human and nonhuman goods, and yet still ultimately deny that these comparisons have any moral significance. The human chauvinist, for whom being human is a necessary and sufficient condition for moral considerability, needs to be persuaded, in short, that nonhuman beings are morally considerable. If he were so persuaded, and if he were consistent, then he would in principle be open to entertaining the sorts of value comparisons Attfield would have him make. In this process of persuasion, however, not only can the nonderivativity argument play no part, nor can any argument for objective values; rather, what are appealed to are the principle of consistency in reasoning and the principle that beings other than humans are morally considerable. If we assume that a human chauvinist, qua ethical interlocutor, accepts the principle of consistency, what remains is to persuade him of the moral considerability of nonhuman beings. But as I pointed out earlier, this requires getting him to share a conviction or intuition. If there are any objective reasons why he should share it, they have to do with the objective conditions within which humans come to *any* shared convictions. There is no short cut to this. The short cut supposedly provided by appeals to intrinsic value in nature is in fact a dead end.[15]

5 Preserving relative nonderivativity and objectivity

I have argued that to fulfil its intended role in ecological ethics, intrinsic value has to be conceived of as a type of value that is both nonderivative and objective; but I have shown that these two properties cannot successfully be applied in combination to the practical evaluation of nonhuman goods. Accordingly, I think appeals to intrinsic value in ecological ethics deserve to be treated with extreme caution, if not outright scepticism, since they are liable to be taken to imply stronger claims about nonhuman values than could in principle be supported. Nevertheless, this is not to say that nonhuman values cannot be nonderivative and objective in more relative senses. Having already granted the possibility of weak objectivity in nonhuman values, in this section I wish to distinguish my position from one which denies any role at all to relative nonderivativity. This, I would suggest, is the problem with environmental pragmatism.

Environmental pragmatism (see Light and Katz, 1996) is a school of thought whose misgivings about the idea of intrinsic value are consonant with some of my own, and it also claims to provide a conception of value which is more coherent and more *ecological*. Yet its mistake, I wish to claim, lies in taking arguments which show one cannot expect to find *absolutely* nonderivative values as arguments against the possibility of *relatively* nonderivative values as well; as a consequence it deprives us not only of the critical purchase the latter can provide on some of our existing values, but of any firm criteria for value judgements at all; this, I further observe, is not a consistent outcome for a professed 'ecology' of values, since ecology is not without criteria.

A basic premise of environmental pragmatism is that for all practical purposes there is nothing of which intrinsic value can be predicated which does not also have extrinsic value. As will be recalled from the earlier discussion, I think there is reason to accept this premise. On its basis, the pragmatists develop a view of how different values relate to one another which contrasts with the linear, cause and effect, view which represents some (intrinsic) values as means and other (extrinsic) values as ends. 'The notion of fixed ends is replaced by a picture of values dynamically interdepending with other values and with beliefs, choices, and exemplars: pragmatism offers, metaphorically at least, a kind of "ecology" of values' (Weston, 1996: 285). Thus pragmatism pictures the relations between values holistically, as circular or weblike – indeed, as analogous to more tangible ecological phenomena. The web image also emphasizes the multiple adjacency of values; multiple circularities and feedback loops make up a 'map' of one's values. Just as any entity (at least, or especially, a living entity) always exists in a dynamic relation with others, and together they constitute their own environment, so with values. On such a view 'to justify or to explain a value is to reveal its organic place among others' (ibid.: 293). For instance, writes Weston, 'sometimes I value the mountain air because in it I feel (and am) healthy, other times I value health because it enables me to reach the mountains' (ibid.). To explain why one climbs mountains may take hours; the story is not a linear one leading to an end, rather, it is complete when the connections are all set out.

I agree that this picture of the relations between values captures features of those relations which are not captured in the linear picture conjured up by the *non plus ultra* approach. But I would also note that this picture is not inconsistent with (ultra-)weak objectivity of values, nor – and this is the point I am concerned to establish here – with relative nonderivativity of some of the values. Hence I wish to preserve the picture but challenge the pragmatic framing of it.

The real power of pragmatism, claims Weston, lies not so much in what it says as in what it does not say, in what it has removed the need to say. There is, he claims, no need for new arguments to establish ecological values; rather there is a need to remove unnecessary constraints that old ones are labouring under. 'We know that the experience of nature can awaken respect and concern for it. . . . These feelings are essential starting points for a pragmatic defence of environmental values' (ibid.: 298). Pragmatism does not ask, for example, 'Why should we value wilderness?' – which is too abstract a question, inviting unworkable general principles in response; instead it has us look at actual questions of normative ethics, case by case, looking at each case also in relation to other cases.

However, a problem I find with this approach is that it gives insufficient guidance regarding the question of *grounding* comparisons between values, resting content with particularistic or ad hoc judgements.[16] Yet even if value comparisons cannot, and do not have to, appeal to foundational or absolutely nonderivative values, there is nevertheless the need for some sort of justification for any particular value judgement. If value judgements as such require the assessment of competing value claims, then criteria of what makes one judgement better than another have to be invoked. This means that something has to be said about how values can be derived from others, even if that happens in a weblike and open way rather than a fixed and closed way. So for value judgements to be possible at all, some of the values in any shared value system must be nonderivative in relation to other values within it. If we assume that value judgements are possible, then, we must also assume it to be possible to identify some core values, even if they are not absolutely or exclusively nonderivative. Some values will be weightier than others, and the relative weights of different values can and should be critically examined: failure to do this leaves an indifferent empiricism in which values are not actually appreciated as values at all, but as mere preferences or opinions, incorrigible and not open to criticism.

If one is to take the existing values of one's ethical community as a starting point for developing stronger ethical view of values in nature, it is nevertheless only a starting point. Not only do different people even within a community think different things; they may think similar things for very different reasons, and vice versa; furthermore, some of the things they do think they would not think if they were presented with considerations against; and so on. In short, if we are to start from existing values, we need to carry out an immanent critique of them; and crucial steps in doing so are to reveal which value beliefs conflict, and the commitments that tend to prevail (as 'core' values) – whether because they are agreed to be weightier or because they represent values of socially dominant groups – when they do.

So if a problem with theories of nature's intrinsic value is that they abstract the question of values from human interests, it is not a satisfactory solution simply to accept human interests as unproblematically given. So while weak objectivity is established through the principle of reasoned agreement in judgement, part of what is involved in such judgement concerns the question of which values there is reason to take as nonderivative relative to which others.

Conclusion

I have argued that intrinsic value, understood as a kind of value which is nonderivative and objective, cannot successfully be predicated, as environmental ethicists wish, of nature or natural entities; and predicating it of their good is superfluous. I also believe that its employment is not necessary for them to achieve the ends they wish it to serve. The issue, I have argued, is that of establishing the moral considerability of beings other than humans; if and when this can be established, it entails an obligation to treat them with the kind of respect that the notion of intrinsic value obliquely aims for anyway. This is for the reasons I elaborate on later, in chapter 6.

For now, I wish to emphasize that it is not the case, as some environmental ethicists appear to believe, that in denying intrinsic value to nonhuman nature one is denying something allowed of humans: for our reasons for treating humans in one way rather than another cannot be captured in terms of their intrinsic value anyway. The strongest claims for ethical protection of humans do not attempt to show that each and every human being 'has value', but, rather, they seek to place humans beyond the scope of value inquiry altogether. Being subjects of values, there are constraints on the ways they can be treated as 'objects'. Thus the polemical force of the environmentalists' use of idea of intrinsic value is to say that not only humans, or rational beings, are subjects of valuation. This is just another way of saying that it is not only they who are morally considerable. When I, as an agent, recognize that some other being has a good, I recognize that there may be moral constraints on me with regard to how I consider and treat them. These constraints are identified with reference to their good; but nothing is added, either conceptually or in practice, by saying their good has intrinsic value.

3

Anthropocentrism: A Misunderstood Problem

Introduction

The term anthropocentrism is widely used in ecological ethics and politics to criticize attitudes, values or practices which promote human interests at the expense of other species or the environment. However, I shall argue that this usage is misleading and counterproductive. For while anthropocentrism can be criticized as a mistaken ontological or cosmological view of the human place in the world, attempts to conceive of it as an ethical error involve conceptual confusion. I shall point out that there is no need for this confusion because a more appropriate vocabulary already exists to refer to the defects the ethical 'anti-anthropocentrists' have in mind. My argument is not just about semantics, though, but engages directly with the politics of ecological concern: blanket condemnations of 'anthropocentrism' not only condemn some legitimate human concerns, they also allow ideological retorts to the effect that criticisms of anthropocentrism amount to misanthropy. My argument, therefore, is that a more nuanced understanding of the problem of anthropocentrism allows not only a more coherent conceptualization of environmental ethics, but also a more effective politics.

In the first section I shall argue that the appropriate objection to anthropocentrism refers to an *unenlightened* view of humans' place in the world, but that whether or not that view is taken has no direct ethical implications. The remainder of the chapter then critically examines the case against 'anthropocentrism' specifically in ethics. The second section notes some ways in which anthropocentrism is not objectionable. In the third section, the defects associated with anthropocentrism in ethics are then examined: I argue, though, that these are better understood as instances of speciesism and human chauvinism. In order to explain why it is unhelpful to call these defects anthropocentrism, I note, in section 4, that there is an ineliminable element of anthropocentrism in any ethic at all, and, in the fifth section, that the defects do not typically involve a concern with human interests as such anyway. Because of this last point, I also argue, the rhetoric of anti-anthropocentrism is not only conceptually unsatisfactory, it is counterproductive in practice.

1   What it can mean to overcome anthropocentrism

Anthropocentrism literally means human-centredness. But what exactly is to be understood by this is not self-evident or unproblematic. One can distinguish, firstly, between a cosmological or ontological interpretation and an ethical one.

Cosmologically or ontologically, it is an anthropocentric error to take 'Man' to be (at) the centre of the universe, as 'the measure of all things', and thus fail to see that 'the way things are in the world takes no particular account of how human beings are, or how they choose to represent them' (Bhaskar, 1989: 154). Refraining from anthropo-centrism, then, would mean viewing humans as one part of a greater order of being. Humans can overcome anthropocentrism in this sense by becoming more enlightened about their place in the world. This enlightenment, moreover, can be arrived at by either a scientific or a mystical route.

Anthropocentric assumptions are challenged by findings of modern science, which undermine humans' erstwhile views of themselves as the centre of the universe, or the purpose of creation, and show them instead to be a product of natural evolutionary processes, to have considerable affinities with other creatures, and to have a vulnerable dependence on ecological conditions of existence. The evolutionary view also tends somewhat to undercut claims for the uniqueness of certain human faculties and characteristics. In this sense, over-coming anthropocentrism has been part and parcel of the Western Enlightenment.

This may seem paradoxical in the light of some of the more extreme ecological criticisms of Western, especially Enlightenment, thought. The developments in modern science which have led to this cognitive displacement of human beings from centre stage in the greater scheme of things have been made possible by just that kind of objectivating knowledge which some proponents of ecologism hold to lie at the root of an attitude toward the natural world to be condemned as anthropocentric. For what the rise of objectivating science has done is bring with it the idea that humans can in some ways stand apart from the rest of nature: the achievement of objectivity carries with it an enhanced view of the power and autonomy of subjectivity; and this is at the heart of a set of attitudes which privilege human faculties, capacities and interests over those of nonhuman entities. There thus appears to be a paradox: the overcoming of anthropocentrism in science has been brought about by just those developments which are now seen by many as lying at the root of unacceptably anthropocentric attitudes and values. However, this only seems paradoxical if one expects to find a necessary correlation between cosmological and ethical anthropocentrism. Yet there is no good reason to expect this: even if humans do not in fact occupy a privileged place in the natural order, this need not prevent them from trying to act as if they did, to 'dominate nature', wherever and whenever it seems to them they can get away with it.

Nevertheless, it is not only modern Western science that challenges an anthropocentric cosmology. A non-anthropocentric worldview is also present in some Eastern forms of enlightenment, and these may seem more congenial to the ethical aims of contemporary ecological 'anti-anthropocentrists'. Certainly, the worldview or cosmology of Buddhists, Hindus, and Jains, for instance, combine a humbler estimate of the human place in nature with a greater solicitude for other living beings. Thus contemporary ecologists, especially deep ecologists, often appeal to a more Eastern, and mystical, worldview in the development of their philosophy (cf. Fox, 1995, ch. 8). Yet as at least some of the deep ecologists acknowledge, their own philosophy, like some of those they emulate, cannot itself be considered an ethical doctrine (see discussion in Dobson, 1995: 48–61) and to the extent that it can provide any guide for action, it is as a form of *human* enlightenment.

In this sense, then, the Eastern and the Western forms of enlightenment point in the same direction. Common to both is the basic idea that the right way to live is to seek to progress, through the development of greater insight, from a narrow, self-absorbed perspective to a wider, more open, perspective. While this wider perspective might bring with it a greater solicitude for the well-being of nonhuman beings, this would in some ways be a merely fortuitous result. Certainly, on the understanding of science as striving for detachment and objectivity, it has a tendency to be dispassionate as opposed to compassionate, whether in regard to humans or nonhumans. The detachment from worldliness of a more mystical non-anthropocentrism can be similarly dispassionate about the fate of people and other worldly beings too. Of course, there are also mystics, as well as scientists, who believe in the 'inherent value' of all beings. My only point is that this view is no more entailed than is a contrary one by the rejection of an anthropocentric cosmology. For these reasons, the critique of 'anthropocentrism' in ethics has to be addressed in its own terms.

According to the ethical criticism, anthropocentrism is the mistake of giving exclusive or arbitrarily preferential consideration to human interests as opposed to the interests of other beings.[1] Now while cosmological anthropocentrism is consistent with, and may even seem to support, the ethical view that only humans are of ethical value, it does not strictly entail it; conversely, one could hold onto that ethical view without subscribing to an anthropocentric ontology. Therefore, the reasons there may be for refusing an anthropocentric ontology do not necessarily have any direct bearing on anthropocentrism in ethics; and so criticisms of the latter cannot borrow force or credibility from criticisms of the former. An independent account is required of why anthropocentrism in ethics is wrong, and, indeed, what it could *mean* to overcome anthropocentrism in ethics.

2   What is not wrong with anthropocentrism

The idea of anthropocentrism in ethics generally derives its negative normative force on analogy with egocentrism (Goodpaster, 1979): just as it may be thought morally wrong to be self-centred in the individual case, it is wrong to be human-centred in the collective case. Nevertheless, anthropocentrism cannot simply be equated with human-centredness if it is to perform the critical function envisaged for it, since there are also respects in which human-centredness is unavoidable, unobjectionable or even desirable. It is important to recognize these if one is to attain a precise idea of what is wrong with anthropocentrism.

To begin with, there are some ways in which humans cannot help being human-centred. Anyone's view of the world is shaped and limited by their position and way of being within it: from the perspective of any particular being or species there are real respects in which they *are* at the centre of it. Thus, as Frederick Ferré for instance points out, to the extent that humans have no choice but to think as humans, what he calls 'perspectival anthropocentrism' would appear to be inescapable (Ferré, 1994: 72). It would also appear to be unavoidable that we should be interested in ourselves and our own kind. There may

indeed be respects in which human-centredness is unobjectionable –
for humans, like any other beings, have legitimate interests which there
is no reason for them not to pursue. As Mary Midgley (1994: 111)
observes, 'people do right, not wrong, to have a particular regard for
their own kin and their own species'. She points out, moreover, that
human-centredness may in some respects be positively desirable: for
just as the term 'self-centred' has been used figuratively in the past to
describe well-organized, balanced people (ibid.: 103), so being human-
centred can mean having a well-balanced conception of what it means
to be a human, and of how humans take their place in the world – the
sort of conception bound up with normative ideas of 'humanity' and
'humaneness'. Furthermore, human-centredness may be positively desirable: if, as various philosophers and psychologists have pointed out
(cf. Hayward, 1995: 54–62), self-love, properly understood, can be
considered a precondition of loving others, so, by analogy, it could be
maintained that only if humans know how to treat their fellow humans
decently will they begin to be able to treat other species decently. In
sum, a positive concern for human well-being need not automatically
preclude a concern for the well-being of non-humans, and may even
serve to promote it.

These considerations do not amount to a claim that anthropocentrism is not a problem at all; they do, however, indicate why one
needs to spell out carefully what is supposed to be *wrong* with it.

3   What is wrong with anthropocentrism in ethics

What is objected to under the heading of anthropocentrism in environmental ethics and ecological politics is a concern with human interests
to the exclusion, or at the expense, of interests of other species. In this
section I shall suggest that the various illegitimate ways of giving
preference to human interests are adequately captured by the terms
'speciesism' and 'human chauvinism'. Although these terms are
sometimes treated as equivalents of anthropocentrism in the literature,
it is important to distinguish between them since they are not equivocal
and misleading in the ways I shall go on to show anthropocentrism
to be.

SPECIESISM   A term coined on analogy with sexism and racism,
speciesism means arbitrary discrimination on the basis of species
(Ryder, 1992: 197). However, if it is possible to discriminate between
human and nonhuman interests for non-arbitrary reasons, as I believe

it must be, then it is possible to promote the former without being speciesist: that is, one can take a legitimate interest in other members of one's own species without this necessarily being to the detriment of members of other species; or, if detriments do arise from any particular course of action, they need not be distributed in speciesist ways.

Humans can appropriately be accused of speciesism when they give preference to interests of members of their own species over the interests of members of other species for morally arbitrary reasons. So, for instance, if it is wrong in the human case to inflict avoidable physical suffering because humans are sentient beings, then it would be morally arbitrary to inflict avoidable suffering on other sentient beings. That is why cruel and degrading treatment of animals can be condemned as speciesist. The purely instrumental consideration of nonhumans more generally falls into this category: as long as they are considered in terms of their instrumental value to humans, they are not considered 'for their own sake' – that is, in terms of their own good or interests. It is worth noting here, though, that the problem lies not with the giving of instrumental consideration as such to nonhuman beings, but in according them *only* instrumental value. In and of itself, instrumental consideration of other beings need not be opposed to their well-being. Consider, for example, in the human case, that a doctor may well need to give instrumental consideration to a patient's physiology in order to improve her well-being. This is not only not objectionable, it is necessary and positively desirable. What is also necessary, though, is that the doctor remember the patient is also a person, a being of dignity and worthy of respect, not simply an object to be manipulated. The question which follows, though, is whether (some, any or all) nonhumans are also beings of dignity and worthy of respect.[2] If they are, then denying them such consideration must be speciesist. However, the problem here is that the judgement that a being is 'of dignity and worthy of respect' is itself a value judgement, and not an independent fact to which one can appeal. Therefore to answer the question one has to move to the level of metaethics and explain what it is that constitutes a being's dignity and worthiness of respect. It is at this level that the problem of human chauvinism can be identified.

HUMAN CHAUVINISM   This is appropriately predicated of attempts to specify relevant differences in ways that invariably favour humans (Routley and Routley, 1979). What counts as 'being worthy of respect', for instance, might be specified in terms which always favour humans. Thus a human chauvinist could quite consistently accept that the moral arbitrariness of speciesism is always wrong and yet persist in denying claims of relevant similarities between humans and other species. For instance, other animals may not be deemed 'worthy of respect' because they allegedly lack certain features – typical candidates being rationality, language and subjectivity – which define beings worthy of respect. Such denials, in themselves, cannot be objected to as speciesist in the event that the factual claims about the animals' capacities and the normative assumptions about worthiness of respect are well supported. But if, when evidence is produced that tends to undermine these claims and assumptions, the response is to seek to refine the definition in such a way as to exclude nonhumans once more, then there is a case for thinking this is a human chauvinist response. The case, however, will not always, if ever, be watertight. Human chauvinism, then, is essentially a disposition, and as such requires a kind of hermeneutic to uncover. Thus whereas speciesism can be conceptualized as a clear-cut form of injustice, human chauvinism involves a deeper and murkier set of attitudes.

Partly for this reason, I think, it is important to observe the distinction between speciesism and human chauvinism. It is inappropriate to label as speciesist a systematically developed argument to the effect, for instance, that animals lack a morally relevant feature necessary for worthiness of respect. For what is actually at issue here concerns precisely the criteria in terms of which discrimination might be claimed to be arbitrary or otherwise. Therefore to counter such an argument one must either show that the animal in fact does possess the relevant feature, or else provide reasons why the feature is not a necessary condition of worthiness of respect. Yet it may often be difficult to present a definitive and incontestable argument of either of these sorts. For this reason, suspicions of human chauvinism may be hard to prove conclusively. Ascriptions of human chauvinism depend on judgement, and are liable to be controversial. Nevertheless, they are appropriate when there is evidence that redefinitions of moral considerability do not simply make more precise the 'rules of the game', but actually involve a progressive shifting of goal posts in humans' favour. Although it is often likely to be difficult to distinguish between the two cases, evidence of bad conscience and spurious argumentation may sometimes make it less so. The main point I want to make here, though, is that confounding human chauvinism and anthropocentrism merely compounds the lack of certainty. Even if actual ascriptions of human chauvinism may often be contestable, the idea itself is quite clear, and it is not equivocal in the way that the idea of anthropocentrism is.

What is involved in overcoming the defects misleadingly associated with anthropocentrism, then, is the overcoming of speciesism in normative ethics and of the human chauvinist disposition which tends to reinforce speciesist reasoning.[3] What this means, at least in principle, can therefore be stated quite straightforwardly: overcoming human chauvinism requires primarily a degree of good faith and the development of a sympathetic moral disposition; overcoming speciesism requires a commitment to consistency and nonarbitrariness in moral judgement combined with the development of knowledge adequate to ascertaining what is and is not arbitrary in our consideration of nonhuman beings.

Nevertheless, if we know in principle what would be involved in overcoming human chauvinism and speciesism, in practice there are some limitations on how fully it can be achieved. It is important to be clear on what these limitations are if they are not to be confused with those aspects of anthropocentrism which are ineliminable, but unobjectionable.

4   An ineliminable element of anthropocentrism in ethics

There is an ineliminable element of anthropocentrism in ethics as such which needs to be recognized, in order both to formulate goals accurately and to secure the advances made within ecological ethics against external criticisms. To these ends, it will be useful first to explain why speciesism, by contrast, is *not* ineliminable in the way that anthropocentrism is. Afterwards I shall also explain why human chauvinism is not ineliminable either.

My claim that speciesism is avoidable can be made vivid by referring to the analogy with racism and sexism: thus while a white man cannot help seeing the world with the eyes of a white man, this does not mean that he cannot help being racist or sexist. There is the possibility, of course, that despite his best efforts he exhibits attitudes a black woman could criticize: but precisely because she could specify what makes these attitudes racist or sexist they are, in principle, corrigible. Speciesism, I am claiming, is likewise, in principle, corrigible. Nevertheless, there is in practice a significant disanalogy between speciesism and racism or sexism in that, to put it bluntly, whereas black women can articulate their criticisms in a language which white men ought to be able to understand, there is scope for misunderstanding the interests of beings for whose interests humans, quite literally, do not have the ears to hear. Thus however good their intentions, humans can never be sure of being completely free of speciesist attitudes. What this consideration shows, however, is not that speciesism is completely unavoidable, but only that avoiding it is more difficult than is the case with sexism or racism. The practical difficulties with avoiding speciesism, I shall argue, can be differentiated from the *impossibility* of avoiding anthropocentrism.

The difficulties with avoiding speciesist arbitrariness in one's value judgements are due to the contingent limitations on the degree of knowledge available at any particular time – thus one might not yet know, for instance, whether a certain species of animal does or does not have a particular capacity which might be affected by a particular action, and so not know whether that action should be allowed or not. This sort of limitation, though, can progressively be overcome: for instance, if angling is claimed to be permissible because the fish do not suffer when caught, then to invalidate that particular claim it suffices to show that fish do in fact suffer when caught. In practice, of course, the overcoming of speciesism can only be fully accomplished within the limits of currently available knowledge: and however consistent one is at a given time, it may subsequently prove that one was in error in one's judgements. Nevertheless, the progressive overcoming of speciesism is a clearly defined project, and there is no reason in principle why it should not be fully accomplished according to the standards of knowledge available at a given time.

But if the project of overcoming speciesism can be pursued with some expectation of success, this is not the case with the overcoming of anthropocentrism. What makes anthropocentrism unavoidable is a limitation of a quite different sort, one which cannot be overcome even in principle because it involves a non-contingent limitation on moral thinking as such. While overcoming speciesism involves a commitment to the pursuit of knowledge of relevant similarities and differences between humans and other species, the criteria of *relevance* will always have an ineliminable element of anthropocentrism about them. Speciesism is the arbitrary refusal to extend moral consideration to relevantly similar cases; the ineliminable element of anthropocentrism is marked by the impossibility of giving meaningful moral consideration to cases which bear no similarity to any aspect of human cases. The emphasis is on the 'meaningful' here: for in the abstract one could of course declare that some feature of the nonhuman world was morally valuable, despite meeting no determinate criterion of value already recognized by any human, but because the new value is completely unrelated to any existing value it will remain radically indeterminate as a guide to action. If the ultimate point of an ethic is to yield a determinate guide to human action, then, the human reference is ineliminable even when extending moral concern to nonhumans. So my argument is that one cannot know if any judgement is speciesist if one has no benchmark against which to test arbitrariness; and, more specifically, if we are concerned to avoid speciesism of *humans* then one must have standards of comparison between them and others. Thus features of humans remain the benchmark: as long as the valuer is a human, the very selection of criteria of value will be limited by this fact. It is this fact which precludes the possibility of a radically non-anthropocentric value scheme, if by that is meant the adoption of a set of values which are supposed to be completely unrelated to any existing human values. Any attempt to construct a radically non-anthropocentric value scheme is liable not only to be arbitrary – because founded on no certain knowledge – but also to be more insidiously anthropocentric in projecting certain values, which as a matter of fact are selected by a human, onto nonhuman beings without certain warrant for doing so. This, of course, is the error of anthropomorphism, and will inevitably, I believe, be committed in any attempt to expunge anthropocentrism from ethics altogether.

But is admitting this unavoidable element of anthropocentrism not tantamount to admitting the unavoidability of human chauvinism? My claim is that it is not. What is unavoidable is that human valuers make use of anthropocentric benchmarks; yet in doing so, they may find that in all consistency they must, for instance, give priority to vital nonhuman interests over more trivial human interests. For the human chauvinist, by contrast, interests of humans must always take precedence over the interests of nonhumans. Human chauvinism does not take human values as a benchmark of comparison, since it admits no comparison between humans and nonhumans. Human chauvinism ultimately values humans *because they are humans*. While the human chauvinist may officially claim there are criteria which provide reasons for preferring humans – such as that they have language, rationality and sociality – no amount of evidence that other beings fulfil these criteria would satisfy them that they should be afforded a similar moral concern. The bottom line for the human chauvinist is that being human is a necessary and sufficient condition for meriting moral concern. What I am pointing out as the ineliminable element of anthropocentrism is an asymmetry between humans and other species which is *not* the product of chauvinist prejudice.

To sum up, then, what is unavoidable about anthropocentrism is precisely what makes ethics possible at all. It is a basic feature of the logic of obligation: if an ethic is a guide to action; and if a particular ethic requires an agent to make others' ends her ends, for the purposes of action, then they become just that – the agent's ends. This is a non-contingent but substantive limitation on any attempt to construct a completely non-anthropocentric ethic. Values are always the values *of* the valuer:[4] so as long as the class of valuers includes human beings, human values are ineliminable. Having argued that this is unavoidable, I also want to argue that it is no bad thing.

5   What is wrong with 'overcoming anthropocentrism'

The argument so far would suggest that the aim of completely overcoming anthropocentrism in ethics is at best of rhetorical value, since all that can actually be achieved is to draw attention to problems which are in fact better conceptualized in narrower and more precise terms. I shall now argue, though, that even as rhetoric the critical employment of the term can be unhelpful, and even counterproductive.

Proposals for the 'rejection' of anthropocentrism are unhelpful because they cloud the real problem they think to address. The problem has to do with a lack of concern with nonhumans, but the term anthropocentrism can all too plausibly be understood as meaning an excessive concern with humans.[5] The latter, however, is not the problem at all. On the contrary, a cursory glance around the world would confirm that humans show a lamentable lack of concern for the well-being of other humans. Moreover, even when it is not other humans whose interests are being harmed, but other species or the environment, it would generally be implausible to suggest that those doing the harm are being 'human-centred'. To see this, one only has to consider some typical practices which are appropriately criticized. Some examples would be: hunting a species to extinction; destroying a forest to build a road and factories; animal experimentation. In the case of hunting a species to extinction, this is not helpfully or appropriately seen as 'anthropocentrism' since it typically involves one group of humans who are actually condemned by (possibly a majority of) other humans who see the practice not as serving human interests in general, but the interests of one quite narrowly defined group, such as poachers or whalers. A similar point can be made regarding the destruction of the forest – for those who derive economic benefit from the destruction oppose not only the human interests of indigenous peoples whose environment is thereby destroyed, but also the interests of all humans who depend on the oxygen such forests produce. The case of animal experimentation, however, brings to the fore a feature which looks as if it could more plausibly be said to be anthropocentric: for if we suppose that the benefits of the experimentation are intended to accrue to any and all humans who might need the medicine or technique experimented, then there would seem to be a clear case of humans benefiting as a species from the use and abuse of other species. But the 'if' is important here. A reason why I am inclined to resist calling this anthropocentrism is that the benefits may in fact not be intended or destined for humans generally, but only for those who can afford to pay to keep the drug company in profit. As in the other two cases, it is unhelpful to cover over this fundamental point and criticize humanity in general for practices carried out by a limited number of humans when many others may in fact oppose them. There is in any case no need to describe the practice as anthropocentric when it is quite clearly *speciesist* – it is not the concern with human welfare per se that is the problem here, but the arbitrary privileging of that welfare over the welfare of members of other species. So a reason why critiques of anthropocentrism are unhelpful is that the problems the term is used to highlight do not arise out of a concern of humans with humans, but from a *lack* of concern for *non*humans. I earlier explained why this lack of concern is not appropriately termed anthropocentrism; I now add the further consideration that practices manifesting a lack of concern for nonhumans very often go hand in hand with a lack of concern for other humans too.

Taking this line of argument a step further it becomes evident that anti-anthropocentric rhetoric is not only unhelpful, but positively counterproductive. It is not only conceptually mistaken, but also a practical and strategic mistake, to criticize humanity in general for practices of specific groups of humans. If the point of anti-anthropocentric rhetoric is to highlight problems, to make them vivid in order to get action, then misrepresenting the problem is liable to make solutions all the harder. Something particularly to emphasize is that when radical critics of anthropocentrism see themselves as opposed to defenders of human interests they can be seriously in error. From what has just been said about the specificity of environmental, ecological or animal harms merely being disguised by putting the blame on humans in general, it should be evident that those who are concerned about such harms in fact make common cause with those concerned with issues of social justice. The real opponents of both sorts of concern are the ideologists who, in defending harmful practices in the name of 'humans in general', obscure the real causes of the harms as much as the real incidence of benefits: the harms seldom affect all and only nonhumans; the benefits seldom accrue to all humans.[6] Yet by appearing to accept the ideologists' own premises, anti-anthropocentric rhetoric plays right into their hands: by appearing to endorse the

ideological view that 'humans in general' benefit from the exploitative
activities of some, the anti-anthropocentrists are left vulnerable to ideological rejoinders to the effect that challenging those activities is merely
misanthropic. The opposite is in fact nearer the truth, I believe, because
it will more often be the case that challenging such practices is in the
interests of humans more generally.

Having shown why criticisms of anthropocentrism can be counterproductive, I should briefly make explicit why criticisms of speciesism
and human chauvinism are not. Criticisms of anthropocentrism can
be counterproductive in failing to distinguish between legitimate and
illegitimate human interests; criticisms of speciesism, by contrast,
apply precisely in those cases where species criteria are illegitimately
deployed: there is, by definition, no legitimate form of speciesism to
safeguard or defend. So while any particular speciesist attitude or
practice might well promote a sectional interest rather than interests of
the human species as a whole, this fact does not weaken the criticism:
for, given that the arbitrary deployment of species criteria is already
illegitimate, the fact that it does not even serve the interests of the
whole human species does not dilute the objection. Indeed, if anything,
the criticism is strengthened by the consideration that the attitude or
practice is doubly arbitrary. For similar reasons, criticisms of human
chauvinism, too, are not counterproductive. Criticisms of speciesism
and human chauvinism, then, focus on what is wrong with particular
human attitudes to nonhumans without allowing in unhelpful and
counterproductive doubts about humans' legitimate concerns for their
own kind.

A further question, however, is whether criticism of speciesism and
human chauvinism is adequate to capture all the respects in which
humans' concerns for their own kind are illegitimate; for if this were
not the case, there might appear to remain a role for more general
criticisms of anthropocentrism. In reply to this question I shall show
that for the same reason that criticisms of anthropocentrism are equivocal in relation to what is and is not legitimate in human-centredness,
alleged alternatives to it are indeterminate.

A basic reason why criticisms of anthropocentrism are equivocal is
that it is not self-evident what exactly it means to be human-*centred*:
where or what *is* the 'centre'? The idea of anthropocentrism is typically
understood as analogous to egocentrism: but just as the latter is anything but unproblematic, if it implies a simple, unitary, centred ego, so
too is anthropocentrism – for the human species is all too at odds with
itself. If the project of bringing humanity to peace with itself, of constituting itself *as* a body which is sufficiently unified to be considered

'centred' is anthropocentric, it is anthropocentric in a sense I have suggested should be applauded rather than condemned. To be sure, what attitude such a body has towards nonhumans cannot be predicted before the event, but there is good reason to think that such a unified and peaceful body is more likely to be considerate – or at least guided by a far-sighted and ecologically enlightened conception of its self-interest – than one which is riven by internal strife.

Posing the question of 'where and what is the centre' not only allows this constructive perspective on anthropocentrism, it also reveals the indeterminacy of alleged alternatives to it. One alternative often referred to in the literature is 'biocentrism'.[7] However, if biocentrism means giving moral consideration to all living beings, it is quite consistent with giving moral consideration to humans; biocentrism in this sense is actually presupposed by my own rejection of human chauvinism and speciesism, and thus appears to be a complement of, rather than an alternative to, anthropocentrism. Another perspective, however, which purports to offer an alternative to either anthropocentrism or biocentrism, is ecocentrism.[8] For ecocentrism, not only living beings, but whole ecosystems, including the abiotic parts of nature, are deemed worthy of moral consideration too. The ecocentric claim is particularly significant in the present context in that it purports to stake out a role for the continued use of anthropocentrism as a term of criticism. From the perspective of ecocentrism, the critique of speciesism would not be adequate to capture all aspects of environmental concern, for while it serves to counter the arbitrary treatment of species and their members, ecocentrists would nevertheless argue that other sorts of entity, including abiotic parts of nature, are also worthy of concern. It is here, they claim, that a distinction between human-centredness and eco-centredness reveals its force: for in disregarding ecosystemic relations humans may not be disregarding the interests of any particular species, but they are nevertheless doing ecological harm. In reply to this claim I would argue that no harms can actually be *identified* without reference to species-interests of one sort or another. This is to return to the question of the lack of any determinate 'eco-centre' – that is to say, to the problem of identifying the loci of ecological harms. One ecocentric response might be that whole ecosystemic balances, which can be upset by human interventions, should be preserved. But this response gives rise to a host of further questions, concerning, for instance: which balances should be preserved and why; whether unaided nature never 'upsets' ecological balances, and some activities undertaken for human purposes do not sometimes 'improve' them; whether humans should, *per impossibile,* seek simply not to influence ecosystems at all. In short, it leaves open the question of what criteria there are, for telling whether one balance is preferable to another, which do not refer back to anthropocentric or biocentric considerations. In fact, to my knowledge, the best, if not only, reason for preserving ecosystemic relations is precisely that they constitute the 'life-support system' for humans and other living species. Still, another ecocentric response might be to claim there is independent reason to take as morally considerable abiotic parts of nature – such as rocks, rivers, and mountains, for instance. But while one clear reason to value these is that they provide habitats for various living species, it is not so clear what reason there is to insist on their continued undisturbed existence for its own sake.[9] In fact, arguments in favour of these parts of the natural world almost invariably appeal to spiritual or aesthetic reasons, and while these may be good reasons, they cannot, it seems to me, be disentangled from specifically human-centred concerns – namely, those of spirituality or beauty. In short, the attempt to pursue a radically ecocentric line is more likely to reintro-duce objectionably anthropocentric considerations – such as unrecog-nized prejudices about what is beautiful or spiritual – than a position that recognizes, on the one hand, that aspects of anthropocentrism are unavoidable, but, on the other, that speciesism is not. My claim, then, is that ecocentrism is radically indeterminate and therefore provides no basis from which to launch an all-encompassing critique of anthropocentrism.

Conclusion

The aim of overcoming anthropocentrism is intelligible if it is under-stood in terms of improving knowledge about the place of humans in the world; and this includes improving our knowledge about what constitutes the good of nonhuman beings. This kind of knowledge is significantly added to by objectivating science. There may also be a role for other kinds of knowledge – for instance, kinds characterized by empathetic imagining of how it might be like to be a member of another species (Cassano, 1989: ch. 1); but here one must always be cautious about unwittingly projecting human perceptions onto beings whose actual perceptions may be radically different, since this would be to reintroduce just the sort of error that characterizes ontological anthropocentrism.

The need for caution is all the clearer when it comes to attempting to gain a non-anthropocentric perspective in ethics. Indeed, it may be that anthropocentrism in ethics, when properly understood, is actually less harmful than harbouring the aim of overcoming it. At any rate, a number of the considerations advanced in this chapter would tend to suggest this view. I have noted: that the ethical impulse which is expressed as the aim of overcoming anthropocentrism is very imperfectly expressed in such terms; that there are some things about 'anthropocentrism' which are unavoidable, and others even to be applauded; furthermore, the things which are to be condemned are not appropriately called 'anthropocentrism' at all; that the mistaken rejection of anthropocentrism misrepresents the fact that harms to nonhumans, as well as harm to some groups of humans, are caused not by humanity in general but by specific humans with their own vested interests. For these reasons, it is my suggestion that discussions of environmental values would be better conducted without reference to the equivocal notion of anthropocentrism.

Part II

Reconstruction: Human Interests and Ecological Values

4

The Enlightenment of Self-Interest

Introduction

The reconstructive part of this book begins with a critical analysis of the idea of individual self-interest. The assumption that individuals are primarily motivated by self-interest is widely accepted as a conceptual starting point in modern liberal political theory; and it is an assumption that can claim both some descriptive adequacy, in terms of empirically verifiable motivations of individuals, and some normative legitimacy, in the sense that the idea of self-interest provides criteria for some of the sorts of individual rights that are deemed worthy of protection against the imposition of political measures intended to secure collective goods. However, the prevalence of self-interested motivations, and the legitimation of them, also constitute a problem for normative theory in general, and for ecological ethics in particular, since part of the purpose of ethics is to combat the anti-social, and anti-ecological, effects of self-interested behaviour. The assumption that individuals are primarily motivated by self-interest in their social and political behaviour, then, is one that there is reason to wish to resist. Nevertheless, a merely moralistic rejection of it would not only be practically inefficacious to the extent that such motivations do in fact prevail, it would also be ethically unwarranted to the extent that such motivations can claim justificatory legitimacy. But if the assumption is one which cannot simply be rejected, there is also no reason to accept it uncritically, I argue, because it is only partially accurate as a description of real motivations, and the normative justification for it is only partially adequate. To show this, though, I shall not directly appeal to empirical evidence about people's motivations or engage in substantive normative argument about the legitimacy of them; rather, I shall engage in conceptual analysis of the idea itself.

The self-interest assumption is usually taken, by those who accept it as well as by those who reject it, to be relatively unproblematic as an idea;[1] yet as I try to show in the early sections of the chapter, this is not the case. In the first section I indicate that while any substantive account of what specific sorts of good individuals generally are supposed to pursue for themselves will quickly collapse under the weight of exceptions to it, any sufficiently general and open account will become so formal and tautologous as to lose any descriptive or normative purchase. I then address the basic thought that self-interestedness equates with egoism, a notion that can quite meaningfully and relevantly be contrasted with altruism: I show, in section 2, that the meaning of self-interest simply cannot be reduced to egoism in a sufficiently substantive sense; and in the third section I indicate why, correspondingly, altruism can no more meaningfully be conceived of as the negation of self-interest. In section 4 I expand on this latter thought to explain why self-interest and altruism are descriptively and normatively indeterminate terms of limited usefulness in social and political theory; I argue that self-interest is often inseparable from an interest in others' good, and that this fact only seems surprising if one takes a peculiarly restricted view of individuals' interests. Indeed, I argue, the whole contrast between self-interest and altruism functions on further assumptions that hold good only within an atomistically individualistic horizon; against this, in section 5, I introduce communitarian and universalistic considerations which point to an interest in solidarity.

The thrust of the argument as a whole is to show that 'self-interest' can, in fact, be *enlightened*. Moreover, humans actually have an interest in enlightening their self-interest, I claim in section 6, and this – which stems from a fundamental interest in integrity – is the soundest, and perhaps only, basis for developing social and ecological values.

1   The self-interest assumption: pro and con

The self-interest assumption I take to consist, essentially, in a belief that human individuals are in general primarily motivated to pursue what is good for themselves while remaining indifferent to the good of others. There is no need to subscribe wholeheartedly to this belief, however, to appreciate reasons to accept the assumption for the purposes of political theory:[2] it would seem more prudent to assume individuals to be self-interested in this sense than to assume the converse; it would seem unrealistic and dangerous to base political theory or practice on assumptions of widespread altruism or benevolence, or to design institutions depending on the existence or efficacy of these dispositions. Moreover, this assumption seems to provide a useful basis for the analysis of typical economic, social and political behaviour; and part of the reason for the prevalence of this assumption is its explanatory power. The success of its use in rational choice theory, for instance, illustrates this: various 'free-rider' problems – including 'The tragedy of the commons', which neatly captures important features of the problem in an ecological context – are cogently analysed in terms of individual self-interest prevailing over the common good.[3]

As well as having descriptive purchase, the idea can also be claimed to have a certain ethical force. Most modestly, a thoroughly self-interested individual, who is indifferent to the weal and woe of others, is as little concerned to do them harm as to do them good: in this respect, the steadfast pursuit of one's own interests can be taken to represent an advance over more malicious or spiteful behavioural traits (cf. Holmes, 1990). Historically, indeed, when praise for the 'virtue' of self-interest began to be heard (cf. Hirschman, 1977), this was closely linked to the idea that in going about one's business in a dedicated fashion one was making a net contribution to the common good – a thought captured in Adam Smith's observation that '[i]t is not from the benevolence of the butcher, the brewer or the baker that we expect our dinner, but from their regard to their own interest' (Smith, 1986: 119). It is also worth observing that historically the focus on individual self-interest served as a foundation for democracy: in the context of contesting a hierarchical political system, the emphasis on the right of individuals to pursue their own interests is a progressive and liberating one. So while these considerations stop somewhat short of attributing self-interest an intrinsic ethical value, they do point up an indirect value it has in virtue of its social and economic consequences. The productive efficiency of self-interested behaviour, when harnessed in a capitalist market economy, may not have a direct ethical value, but it does make possible the development of institutions that would foster more ethical values: ethical neutrality in economic behaviour makes possible the efficient production which in turn makes possible ethical institutions and practices. This, I take it, is the kernel of an archetypically liberal democratic view of the place of self-interest in political theory.

Nevertheless, the descriptive adequacy of the self-interest assumption can be challenged on the grounds that as a matter of fact many kinds of action and behaviour occur that are not obviously self-interested. For instance, between friends and within families, in particular, it may frequently be the case that behaviour is not purely self-interested; in other forms of association and community, too, non-self-interested behaviour may be quite usual. Indeed, in such contexts, the very idea of individual self-interest, as distinct from the interests of family or community as a whole, starts to break down. Now one standard line of reply to this argument would be that the spheres of life where self-interest is not necessarily predominant are distinct from those with which political theory has properly to deal: thus non-self-interested behaviour is held primarily to occur in the context of essentially private relations, whereas the political sphere is one constituted by public relationships. Within the latter, accordingly, even where there exist groups of individuals bound by common interests – be they households, trades unions or whatever – these groups confront one another, and other individuals, as bearers of what might be called a 'corporate' self-interest. In this sense, then, the assumption of self-interest does not need to be abandoned, but merely qualified to allow for 'corporate selves'. Still, something to query in this reply is the assumption that the political as such can be defined in terms which include certain 'public' relations and exclude certain 'private' ones: if individual self-interest really is the mainspring of types of social interaction, it is inconsistent to disregard the individual's motivations as a participant in intimate and intermediate associations, and it is inconsistent to defend *individual* self-interest with reference to corporate behaviour. This sort of inconsistency appears to have gone unnoticed even by some of the most sophisticated contemporary political theorists, including Rawls: for while taking individual self-interest as the starting assumption of his theory of justice, in elaborating that theory he has had to introduce among his mutually disinterested individuals 'heads of household', thereby allowing families to be considered as what I've termed corporate selves. He has been criticized by feminists on this score, for covering over the fact that (usually male) heads of households may have a self-interest which does not coincide with the interests of other family members (cf. Okin, 1990). That critique can be taken a step further,[4] though, since, as stated, it is quite consistent with the view that all individuals are still primarily self-interested, with the problem being that patriarchal power relations allow men's self-interest to prevail over the self-interest of women. What I want to suggest, rather, is that members of households – and not just their heads, if any – have interests as members of households; and, more generally, that members of all kinds of association have interests as members, which cannot intelligibly be reduced to individual self-interest.

What these points lead me to observe is that the very idea of self-interest needs some unpacking. Until that is done we cannot even begin a normative assessment of the idea.

2 Unpacking self-interest: from solipsism to solidarity

When self-interest was first invoked as a basis for political theory by philosophers such as Hobbes or, later, Bentham, it was defined in terms of certain substantive dispositions – these being for Hobbes an overriding desire for self-preservation, or for Bentham the pursuit of pleasure and avoidance of pain. Yet in assuming that the self to be preserved is a mere organism, not the type of entity that could see its interest, for instance, in preferring death to dishonour, Hobbes's substantive considerations seem at best only partially to fit the facts of human behaviour; likewise with Bentham – since numerous people quite manifestly and quite routinely act out of motives other than personal pleasure-seeking. So without multiplying examples, I think it can be appreciated why more recent theorists have tended to avoid substantive definitions of self-interest. Contemporary utilitarians and rational choice theorists, for instance, tend to define individual self-interest merely formally, in terms of the pursuit of an individual's preferences, whatever those preferences happen to be. When the self-interest assumption is defined in this way, though, it becomes irrefutable, since even if an individual 'prefers' to act for the good of another, this is still the individual's own preference; for the same reason, the assumption appears to be vacuous. Sometimes, though, to sustain the substantive force of the idea, self-interest is equated with that of egoism, which in turn may be defined, not merely formally, as an individual's taking an exclusive interest in their own good, without any concern with the good of others except insofar as it contributes to the individual's own good.

Nevertheless, it seems to me, there is no warrant necessarily to equate self-interest with egoism in this sense. In what follows, I shall show that significantly different types of 'self-interest' can be distinguished, some of which are inherently more 'other-regarding' than others, so that they in fact span a continuum from egoism to altruism.

SOLIPSISM   It is possible to conceive of an individual lacking any interest at all in any other person and being completely self-absorbed. The complete solipsist would not even acknowledge the independent reality of any other being 'outside' the self: qua solipsist, this individual is constitutionally incapable of considering the needs of others, or even to consider others in a merely instrumental or calculating fashion, and hence is trapped in immediacy. In a pure form, solipsism can hardly even be termed 'self-interest': certainly, any interest in others is excluded, but any intelligible interest in the self is also excluded, for with no apprehension of an other to contrast with self, and no sense of self as a self among others, a basic 'division' of the part with interests and the part that assesses them is missing; no interests as such are differentiated, and there is mere immediate impulse.[5] As soon as interest in one's self *as* a self begins, some interest in others – even if only a calculating one – must begin too.

RATIONAL SELF-INTEREST   This is the name usually given to the kind of calculating attitude and disposition which is most typically understood as self-interest by social and political theorists. Motivated by this sort of self-interest, individuals calculate what course of action is likely to bring the greatest net satisfaction of their own preferences; that is, they select the most efficient or effective means for achieving their own given ends. The carrying out of such calculations does involve at least some 'instrumental' consideration of others' interests, though, since it has to be recognized that others, in pursuing them, can help or thwart that satisfaction. Thus the things others wish for and are likely to do have to be brought into the rational calculations; and sometimes it will be calculated that helping them may be the best strategy. They will not be helped, though, for their own sake, or because it might be an intrinsically good thing to do.

Now it should be evident that the more fully one calculates, the more one's interdependence with others must assume a central role in one's thinking. Indeed, I would suggest that the consistent pursuit of self-interest necessarily involves cognitive development – development which takes the agent an increasing distance from the cognitive deficiency of solipsism. As calculating self-interest undergoes this cognitive development it begins to look increasingly 'selfless', since the more one appreciates how one's own well-being is bound up with others, the more one has occasion to pursue paths other than one's own immediate gratification. Of course, whether one's actions actually benefit others may remain a matter of indifference, in terms of one's motivations, and the form of self-interest so far described can not yet be equated with a virtuous disposition; nevertheless, once calculating self-interest has developed beyond seeing a merely contingent connection with others' interests, so that the latter become a primary datum along with the datum of one's own interests, the difference is qualitative.

ENLIGHTENED SELF-INTEREST   This is the term I use to refer to motivations based on the recognition not only that in pursuing one's interests one needs, contingently and strategically, to heed the interests of others, but also that others' interests play a part in shaping one's own interests, and indeed that others' interests are partly constitutive of them.[6] One's own personal interests cease to be a sole primary datum. With the realization that the very substance of one's interests is at least in part the product of one's interdependence with others, self-interest itself is, quite literally, thrown into a critical condition. Furthermore, once one's own interests are no longer taken as simply given, transparent and self-evident. One actually finds oneself with a new interest – a sort of meta-interest, perhaps – namely, that of discovering what one's real interests actually are.

This is an 'interest in the self' which is radically different from self-interest of the pre-enlightened sort. It is in part a purely cognitive interest: one seeks to discover what exactly one's interests, as a self-among-other-selves, are. It is also a motivated interest, though, in that the reason for seeking this knowledge is, at least in part, motivated by the need to secure one's identity. But given the recognition that one's identity is constituted through relations with others, it is at same time a motivated interest in those others. Here, I want to suggest, is the basis of solidarity.[7]

SOLIDARITY   This arises when one is drawn to take the other's perspective, to see their cause as one's own, and so to develop an interest in others which appears to comprise an element of altruism: for the more one looks outside one's own immediate interests, and as one becomes increasingly absorbed in others' concerns as well as one's own, one develops interests regarding others, some of which take on a 'life of their own', so to speak. Nevertheless, on the account I am offering, the interest in others is only possible as long as there is still a substantial self that is now interested in others. Solidarity involves expanding one's own sense of self and world: it does not mean the abandonment of self-interest but, rather, the enlightenment of it to the point of recognizing that different individuals' interests are in significant ways mutually constituting.

The position I am seeking to develop, though, is to be distinguished from any which would involve simply substituting the assumption of self-interest by an assumption of altruism.

3 'Altruism' is no less problematic

There are three main reasons, I believe, why altruism is no less problematic than self-interest as a starting assumption for political theory, and quite possibly is more so.[8] One is simply the lack of empirical evidence for sufficiently widespread altruism to warrant an assumption that people are generally altruistic. Secondly, it is in any case not entirely clear what could count as evidence. If, on the one hand, altruism is defined in opposition more specifically to egoism, then my argument is that any assumption about its prevalence or otherwise cannot be meaningfully applied. If, on the other hand, though, altruism is thought of as the converse of self-interest, and if the latter is susceptible of various interpretations, then so too must altruism be: in this case, the idea of altruism would be simply too indeterminate to admit of a definition which is both unequivocal and substantive. The third problem concerns the normative valency of the term: there is a widespread assumption that altruism is a virtue, or virtuous, but this assumption I shall show to be erroneous.

Regarding the first problem, of lack of evidence for altruism, there is little I wish to say here. I take it most people would accept that as an empirical claim about people's most prevalent dispositions, altruism is even harder to take as a starting assumption than self-interest. The assumption of prevalent altruism almost invariably requires auxiliary hypotheses about a 'better world': that is, given the apparent lack of widespread altruistic behaviour in the world as we know it, those who would claim people 'really' are altruistic – in some deeper sense than that accessible to empiricists – have to offer some explanation of how that altruism is stifled under existing conditions. But in the nature of the case, this counterfactual altruism cannot, under existing conditions, be put to the test.

The reason it cannot be put to the test is not merely contingent, though, because of the second problem noted. It is seldom, if ever, appropriate to say that a *person* is egoistic or altruistic. Such descriptions can at best be treated as shorthand expressions meaning that egoistic or altruistic motivations tend to prevail in the individual's usual character as manifest in her acts and behaviour. Yet it can happen that when faced with just a situation which calls for the greatest moral commitment an individual responds in such a way that her minority tendency manifests itself with greater strength than the more habitual one. Thus an individual who from day to day does many minor kindnesses may become uncompromisingly selfish in a major crisis, and, conversely, someone who might be described as a habitual egoist may prove capable of supreme self-sacrifice in that same situation. So not only would it be objectionably presumptuous to describe any individual as egoistic (except perhaps sometimes in the shorthand way mentioned above), one could anyway not always, if ever, be certain of the accuracy of the description.

Nevertheless, it might be thought possible at least to say that an individual was habitually egoistic or altruistic in certain spheres of activity, or in certain aspects of their behaviour, and that here is a role for the employment of the terms. For that to be the case, the acts which make up the behaviour would have to be so classifiable. But can any *act* be classified unequivocally as altruistic or egoistic? If considered objectively, as an event with effects, it obviously cannot: for not only may one and the same act appear in a different light depending on external circumstances, the question in any case gets no purchase here, since an act could only be judged altruistic at all if it is other-regarding; and therefore the question can only be answered by reference to the agent who is or is not doing the regarding. If it is considered from the subjective side, as the execution of an agent's purpose, then the question can get a purchase, but just to the extent it does we have to do with the *motivations* behind it. The problem then is that any real-life act may comprise various motivations – each of which would have to be investigated for its own degree of egoism or altruism. As far as any particular act is concerned, it therefore follows, egoism and altruism need not be mutually exclusive: some acts may appear to involve strong egoism *and* strong altruism (consider, for instance, how one would classify acts involved in getting married or having children); conversely, of course, other acts may involve little of either (a vast number of daily actions would fall under this heading).

In my view, it is unlikely, to the point of practical insignificance, that any act will derive from a pure set of either altruistic or egoistic motivations (cf. Mansbridge, 1990a). For this reason, the idea of altruism as the negation of self-interest is also problematic. If altruism is thought of as the negation or opposite of self-interest, as it often is, then what it is taken to mean will depend on which interpretation of the latter is being negated, so that there is a corresponding variety of meanings.

'PURE' ALTRUISM AS SELF-ABNEGATION At the other extreme from pure solipsism is a pure altruism which would be a complete absorption in the concerns of others and mean the abnegation of any concern with self. Adopting this attitude would be as unsatisfactory in its way as solipsism. Firstly, it would be ethically unwarranted, since there is no good reason why one self – whichever one it is – should be deemed less worthy of consideration than any or every other self. Secondly, it would be not only unwarranted but also ethically undesirable: if denigrating any being worthy of consideration is wrong it is no less wrong in one's own case, and there may even be reasons for considering it more wrong. Thirdly, self-abnegation shares with solipsism the epistemic defect of not appreciating the interdependence of self and others. For these reasons I do not consider pure altruism to negate the defects of egoism; it merely mirrors them – they are, so to speak, two sides of one false coin. If the *substantive* negation of solipsistic self-interest is a better appreciation of the self's interdependent relations with others, the same remedy has to apply to self-abnegating altruism.

ALTRUISM AS SELF-SACRIFICE Whereas extreme self-abnegation is probably not what is generally intended by writers on the subject, the idea of altruism as self-sacrifice sometimes is.[9] The idea of self-sacrifice differs from that of self-abnegation in that concern with self is not precluded at the outset, rather, it is considered and then overridden: the agent is prepared to act in ways which promote others' interests at the expense of her own. Clearly, there are different degrees of intensity of self-sacrifice: at one extreme, one might sacrifice one's life for the benefit of another; at the other extreme, one might sacrifice relatively insignificant personal interests. It is to be observed, however, that the degree of intensity of the sacrifice varies along a different dimension from the dimension represented as a continuum between egoism and altruism. Certainly, the ultimate forms of self-sacrifice might appear tantamount to denying one's own interests altogether, but in fact, for reasons I shall return to, that need not be the case; conversely, sacrifice of relatively insignificant interests might seem to involve very little sacrifice at all, but may in fact represent a purer loss in terms of self-interest. The point I shall want to make on this basis is that action guided by the principle of setting another's interests over one's own may or may not be virtuous or praiseworthy, and whether it is will depend not on the following of that principle, but on independent reasons for valuing the pursuit of the other's interests in preference to one's own.

SUPEREROGATORY ACTS   What is often meant when speaking of the virtues of altruism are the sorts of consideration and action which involve not the abnegation or sacrifice of self, but a sort of 'overflow': virtues of kindness, generosity and magnanimity, for instance, come to mind. Here altruism seems to have a less equivocal meaning and a clearer connection with virtue. With supererogatory acts, in the sense I am using,[10] the agent does more for an other than is strictly required of her as a duty; the other benefits from a strong and balanced self which shares its bounty, so to speak. Here there is more clearly a 'net gain' in terms of virtue, since both self and other benefit with no sacrifice on either part. It will be noted, though, that the virtuousness here has as much to do with considerations of self-interest as of altruism. Indeed, this description makes reference to what was given as the criterion of 'healthy' self-interest. Supererogatory acts may well be morally praise-worthy, but they are precisely the sorts of act where the altruism *vs* egoism distinction seems to break down: for they involve as much a spontaneous overflow and expression of one's own powers, self-love even, as a moral concern with the well-being of others. These would seem, in short, to be just the sorts of act that would follow from the sense of solidarity outlined in the previous section.

On my view, then, solidarity stops as far short of pure altruism as it goes beyond pure egoism. It is important to emphasize this given the not uncommon view that morality requires one to try to progress as far as possible from solipsism in the direction of altruism. Which brings us to the third problem noted.

4   Altruism is no virtue

In the moral philosophy of the last two centuries, as Neera Kapur Badhwar notes, 'altruism of one kind or another has typically been regarded as identical with moral concern' (Badhwar, 1993: 90). However the kind of 'altruism' that can be equated with moral concern more generally is not the kind that has any particular connection with virtuousness.[11] Moreover, it has also been noted that excessive concern for either self *or* other is generally bad, and that 'pure' altruism would in its way be a pathology just like solipsism, since a pure altruist would be fixated on others to the point of forgetting self and thereby becoming as incapable of doing real good as the solipsist. So the kind of altruism that does have a connection with virtue, it appears, might do so just because it also involves a significant degree of concern with the self. These considerations give us reason to think altruism is as little a criterion of virtue as self-interest is, but I now want to make the stronger claim that *altruism cannot conceivably be a virtue* because to attempt to conceive of it as such involves a category mistake. Furthermore, it is not appropriate even to assume that altruism, if not *a* virtue, is necessarily virtuous.

To think of altruism as a virtue is to make a category mistake because the sorts of entity or phenomenon of which altruism and virtuousness can be predicated belong to quite different orders. Virtues are dispositions of character, tendencies of behaviour or qualities of action that are judged ethically desirable. Virtuousness, then, can be predicated, first and foremost, of the character or disposition of persons; it can also intelligibly be predicated of their actions and behaviour. Altruism, however, like egoism, for the reasons noted previously, cannot be predicated of a person's character or actions, but only of motivations – and, indeed, of only one aspect of them. Any adequate discussion of virtues will involve a richer and broader set of considerations than those involved in contrasting altruism and egoism, since this is quite literally one-dimensional, restricted to considering the *direction* of interest or concern: it does not take into account questions about the *nature* of concern, the *strength* of concern, the *grounds* of concern or the fact that real-life concerns and interests are generally *complex*. Altruism therefore cannot be a virtue, for it could at most be an element of virtuousness.

Yet if altruism can be virtuous, it is not necessarily because self-interest is excluded. When one examines any canonical list of virtues one finds that some of them can be categorized as primarily other-regarding (such as kindness or generosity) and others as primarily self-regarding (such as courage or temperance). I have said 'primarily' in both cases since it is only a matter of degree, and it will often – even perhaps typically – be the case that primarily self-regarding virtues are also 'good' for others, and other-regarding virtues 'good' for the self. Indeed, it is probably a criterion for the identification of virtues as such that in exemplifying them one 'makes the world a better place', in principle, for everyone. So if virtues involve elements of altruism, they also involve elements of self-regard.

This point has been put more strongly by Badhwar, who claims that in the absence of the right kind and degree of self-interest, altruism would not be a virtue at all (Badhwar, 1993: 116). She makes this claim in a commentary on some studies of the motivations of rescuers of Jews in Nazi Germany. The rescuers, in harbouring Jewish families for no reward and at considerable risk to themselves and their own families, seem to provide an exemplary illustration of strong altruism. When questioned, though, the rescuers typically reported that they felt they had no option but to do what they did: their actions appear to have sprung from deep-seated dispositions which formed their identity and character. Badhwar claims these studies reveal '*a more fundamental interest*: the interest in being true to oneself and affirming the values central to one's sense of oneself, i.e., the interest *in integrity and self-affirmation*' (ibid.: 101, emphasis added). This interest is manifest in an undivided desire for their own good and others' good.

While persuaded by the substance of Badhwar's argument, I would wish to qualify an aspect of her presentation of it: for having identified a fundamental and undivided interest in pursuing both their own and others' good, she analyses the rescuers' interest as a combination of altruistic and self-interested motivations; but I shall suggest that if the interest identified is actually more fundamental than either of these sorts of motivation that analysis is not entirely appropriate. On Badhwar's interpretation, 'the self-interested desire to affirm their altruistic identity was necessary to make their acts wholeheartedly altruistic' (ibid.: 115). In the absence of the right kind and degree of self-interest, altruism would not be a virtue at all, Badhwar claims, and so there is a kind of virtue which is both self-interested and altruistic. I want to suggest this puts things the wrong way round, though, and what is more correct to say is that virtue requires, in particular circumstances, acts which may appear as both altruistic and self-interested. I speak of *appearance* here advisedly: Badhwar's account retains a role for two distinct sets of motivation, but I do not think we can consistently hold them distinct. She wants to hold them distinct, I take it, so as not to slip into the argument that altruism is merely a sophisticated form of self-interest. Yet her own analysis would seem to render the reference to altruism redundant since 'the right kind and degree of self-interest' would be sufficient to account for the virtues she describes. Indeed, she does claim that self-interest has a moral quality because she believes, like Aristotle and others, that it is implausible to suppose a person can lack concern for her own character and still consistently be good: a sense of the importance of one's life is at the core of *self-respect* and *integrity*; so, she says, someone who lacked this sense would also lack self-respect and integrity, and this would be a moral lack (ibid.: 116). On the other hand, however, it should be evident that the moral quality does not reside in self-interest per se either. My claim, accordingly, is that the interest in self-respect and integrity is more fundamental than either self-interested or altruistic motivations, and that it is this which is the spring of virtue.

A further consideration which I believe supports this view is prompted by the fact that, in the case of some of the rescuers, their own families were put at risk for the benefit of those being rescued.

Badhwar's own explanation of how some rescuers could fail to be altruistic towards their own families preserves the distinctness of altruistic and self-interested motivations but stands in tension with her own acceptance of a more fundamental interest manifest in an undivided desire for their own good and others' good. The view she advances is that the rescuers' normal hierarchy of values – which would put family first – is transformed: that interest, she writes, 'was not only *subordinated* to their interest in saving innocent lives, it became *irrelevant* in arriving at the decision to help' (ibid.: 103). But this claim undermines the argument she accepts about basic dispositions being at the root of action: for actions cannot be rooted both in one's disposition and in a radically transformed set of values unless that value transformation also springs from the disposition. Certainly, with a given disposition and novel circumstances, even quite fundamental values might in principle be transformed, but is this an explanation of the rescuers' actions? Surely, it cannot be that their basic interests became either subordinated or irrelevant, as Badhwar claims.

Rather, I would suggest, there are various elements of contingency and indeterminacy which prevent us from knowing whether the acts through which a basic disposition will manifest itself will appear as altruistic or otherwise. That appearance depends on factors other than the motivations themselves. Ultimately, these appearances are as much products of moral evaluations made 'from outside' as intrinsic qualities of motivations. It is not possible to describe any disposition, action or even motivation as unequivocally altruistic or egoistic. So to refer to them is not to *describe* them, but to employ a shorthand way of expressing a certain sort of approval or disapproval of them. This point is reinforced by considering that the favourable and unfavourable evaluation of an act itself can be no less equivocal. Actions always take place not only in the context of the actor's identity, but also in a social context. Depending on the context, performance of one and the same action, with the same motivations, may be subject to either praise or blame. One might think of various cases which illustrate this: for instance, where a lone woman struggles for women's rights in a hostile environment where other women 'don't want the boat rocked' she might be called egoistic; but if her struggle were endorsed and supported by others, then her personal cost would be noted and she called an altruist. One and the same act, one and the same actor, can be judged altruistic or egoistic depending on the context and on broader considerations of what is good and right.

Something these considerations point up, I would suggest, is that the very assessment of actions or motivations in terms of egoism and altruism is conducted within the limited horizon of atomistic individualism. They are therefore of limited usefulness within any theory that aspires to a social perspective, as social science in general and political theory in particular do. Assumptions of either self-interest or altruism are ultimately assumptions about human nature; and no assumption about human nature which is insensitive to social determinations is likely to be adequate for social or political theory.

So it is not possible, empirically or conceptually, to assume that individuals are generally altruistic. Moreover, it is as morally unnecessary and inappropriate as it is unrealistic to do so. Thus even accepting the self-interest assumption for the purposes of political theory does not mean accepting that individuals are irredeemably egoistic. Self-interest comes in the variety of forms noted previously, which are more and less 'enlightened'. A question then is how strong and prevalent is an interest in enlightening one's self-interest.

5   The human interest in solidarity

Accordingly, I wish to focus on the fundamental individual interest in self-respect and integrity, the interest in being true to oneself and the values central to one's sense of self. I shall ask whether this can ground an interest in solidarity with others, and whether there is any reason to believe that individuals in general have such an interest. If one refrains from taking an atomistic perspective on the question, I shall argue, reasons for affirmative answers to both questions do appear. This means adopting first a communitarian argument establishing grounds of concrete relations of solidarity; but considering limitations of this will lead to recognizing a universalistic element; and this element in turn will be seen to be rooted in an interest in integrity.

THE COMMUNITARIAN ARGUMENT   The fundamental interest Badhwar identifies is also an interest in shaping the world in the light of one's values and affirming one's identity. No individual can shape the world, even their own small corner of it, without a basic recognition of the relationships that in good measure constitute it. This involves recognizing the interchangeability of perspectives and the fact that others are both different from and like oneself; it also involves recognizing that without others, I would not be me, or at least not the me I am, since relationships with others are partly constitutive of my own identity. The interest I am speaking of here is an interest in the 'situated self'; it entails an interest in the self's situation; and, because the interests of others are partly constitutive of the situation, it entails an interest in these too.

At root, this is a fundamentally different presupposition from those involved in what is aptly named the 'possessive individualism' which has continued to pervade so much modern political theory (Macpherson, 1962). It does not involve denying altogether the existence of narrow, 'rational', self-interest, but relativizes it and puts it in its place. Theories based on a possessive individualist conception of self-interest mistake a part of human motivation for its whole; in doing so, they also to some extent misrepresent the part. The connections between self-interest, individualism and possession can be loosened if one recognizes *belonging* as a more fundamental and important category of relationship: in possessive mode, we say that objects belong to us; but this is only possible because *we* belong to a community which underwrites these particular claims to possession. Our belonging to the community is logically, phylogenetically and ontogenetically prior to the possibility of anything belonging to us as a possession. One can belong to various local and global communities and associations, from family and work circles to the human species as such. A sense of belonging is important to identity development; the fact of belonging is indispensable to it. Maintaining my belonging is not a question of asserting egoistic rights – it involves constantly renewing my own eligibility; that means treating the others who belong in ways that foster the reciprocal belonging. That is not altruism, but nor does it need to be. The idea of altruism is invoked in opposition to narrow self-interest, but it shares with the latter its limitedness within an individualistic horizon.[12] The distinction between self-interest and altruism is beside the main point here, which is that even if I work to maintain a relationship to others for my sake, the relationship maintained only continues to exist *as* the relationship if I maintain it for the sake of the others, too. If they do not wholeheartedly participate the relationship crumbles; if I do not wholeheartedly participate, the relationship crumbles.

To say I have an interest in solidarity, then, seems to be quite straightforwardly true in the case of affective relations, where my personal contribution tangibly matters. A critical question, though, in the context of political theory, is whether this interest does, could, or should extend to other people with whom I have no affective relation.

SOLIDARITY BEYOND COMMUNITY   But aside from, and indeed prior to, the question whether one has an interest in universalistic solidarity, there is the question whether solidarity can be universal even in principle. There are two sorts of reason I shall consider why solidarity might be thought not to be universalizable in principle: one is that solidarity may be considered as essentially particularistic, in the sense of applying between people who have concrete dealings with one another; the second is that since various communities and allegiances may be in conflict with one another, solidarity with (members of) all of them would be self-contradictory. In response to the first point I shall argue that solidarity necessarily includes a universalistic dimension; if that can be established, then I think that an adequate response to the second point would be to say that while it is evident that one cannot concretely show solidarity, for instance, with all members of conflicting ethnic groups if they are intent on exterminating one another, one can nevertheless endorse a principle of solidarity with all oppressed humans, whatever their ethnicity.

Firstly, then, I would distinguish solidarity from immediate relations of care between people. Solidarity, as I understand it, combines the perspectives of care and justice.[13] In the political world, solidarity is manifest, paradigmatically, when one group of people is involved in a struggle for rights, recognition, justice or an end to oppression and when other people, who are not directly involved in the struggle, nevertheless feel that they want to side with those involved, take their part, and make the cause their own. There is here both an element of empathy or care and a sense of justice. Without the element of empathy, the second group might make an intellectual judgement that the situation of the first group is unjust and should be remedied, but this would involve no commitment to supporting their struggle to overcome it. On the other hand, though, it is only in situations where there is injustice, and thus where care or empathy are not arbitrary in their attachment, that solidarity as such is an appropriate response. Solidarity is called up in the face of *oppression* of others; compassion is called up by their *suffering*. Solidarity is therefore called up in situations which 'could be otherwise'. In situations where suffering has causes which cannot be traced to unjust or oppressive human actions, sympathy and empathy with the sufferer can certainly be appropriate, but solidarity is not.[14] The point I am seeking to emphasize, then, is that a more universalistic sense of justice is integral to solidarity in the sense that I am using the term.

So, on this understanding, solidarity can extend beyond affective relations within one's immediate community, but that leaves the question of why it would or should. To answer this it is appropriate to review what communitarian appeals to community entail under mod-

ern conditions. For one thing, the appeal cannot be directed to a traditional type of community, where this is understood as providing a
single comprehensive set of values, norms and practices which are fully
constitutive of one's identity. While the values and norms of a community with a hermetic existence may not admit of any norms relating
to intercommunal (or even generalized intracommunal) solidarity –
precisely to the extent it does not come into contact with other communities, such a community does not, because it cannot, come within
the purview of our political theory. By contrast, in modern societies,
few individuals, if any, belong to a single community (Plant, 1974); any
community is itself a part of society, and relates to and overlaps with
other communities. Furthermore, there are few communities of whom
one can specify that all and only certain identifiable individuals are
members: one neighbourhood shades into another; one family has all
kinds of complex relations with other families, and so on. The upshot
of this is that communities are not self-subsistent any more than an
individual is.

One implication is that each individual therefore may be unique, in
belonging to a unique set of communities. Another is that any individual's concrete loyalties will be quite peculiar to that individual; she
may experience conflicting loyalties between her communities – as, for
instance, in the conflict between loyalty to neighbours who work in an
environmentally damaging factory and loyalty to an environmental
group campaigning to close it. Now this consideration, rather than
support widespread solidarity, might seem to tell against even the
possibility of it. However, if each individual knows that each and every
individual can have a unique set of loyalties, and at some stage one
may potentially find themselves in direct or indirect affiliation with
individuals with any other set of loyalties, then there is a presumption
in favour of universalistic solidarity. This would be so on just the
pragmatic grounds that potential allegiances are always somewhat
uncertain. But to this instrumental or strategic consideration can be
added another more closely bound up with the conditions of ethical
life. Thus the presumption in favour of universalistic solidarity can be
reinforced by thinking through a communitarian insight into the role of
community in identity-formation. Individuals with plural community
membership and plural interests must have complex identities. If one
accepts with communitarians like Sandel (1982), as against Rawls
(1972), that there is no self prior to its ends, because each is 'constituted
by its ends', then it is constituted by – and as – a *problem*, since its ends,
in a pluralistic and complex society, are likely to stand in tension, even
in contradiction, with one another. If any individual has conflicting

loyalties, and perhaps uniquely so, they cannot get adequate guidance from the norms of their community since their very dilemma arises from their plural community membership. Reflexivity at both a personal and political level is required to make sense of, and to seek to unify, conflicting normative requirements. In conditions of multiple community membership and complex identities, the personal struggle for internal consistency requires a degree of reflexivity about one's values as an existential necessity. This is the 'meta-interest' I spoke of earlier in getting clear about one's interests; it means seeing these in relation to others' interests and viewing them from their standpoint, so that principles of reciprocity and generalizability are adopted quite spontaneously. Hence from reflexivity comes a degree of universalism. Of course, one can think universalistically without acting on it, but a convergence of thought and action *is* required for the maintenance of individual *integrity* as a human being; and this interest in integrity supplies the motivational force to support the normative presumption in favour of universalism. Or so I shall now argue.

6 A human interest in integrity

The most fundamental interest humans in general have, I am going to argue, is an interest in integrity – an interest in attaining it, preserving it, and where necessary recovering it.[15] I shall understand integrity in a wide sense as a state of being 'undivided, an integral whole' (McFall, 1987: 7). Integrity is sometimes thought of as a specifically moral virtue, or as a quality of character, but while it importantly is these things, they do not exhaust its meaning. Integrity, as I understand it, refers to wholeness, unity, and health in one's physical, mental, and spiritual being; it implies a unity within and between these spheres of one's being. Thus it includes, but is not exhausted by, the integrity that comes from steadfastness of character and moral rectitude. It also implies balance and harmony in one's bodily or somatic existence, in one's emotions, in one's thoughts and in one's actions. Integrity is disturbed by imbalance, be this physical, emotional, cognitive or moral. Bodily balance and wholeness are an inherent good for any embodied being, and disturbances lead to stress, illness and premature death. Emotional balance, likewise, is an inherent good for emotional beings: negative emotions, such as fear, anger and anxiety, are both cause and effect of imbalances that spill over into one's physical, phenomenological, cognitive and spiritual life. To the extent that being emotionally consistent involves coming to grips with conflicting ends, it also means being cognitively consistent. Psycho-physical integrity also requires an integrity of 'fit', or coherence, between thought and action. For there to be this fit on a sustained and enduring basis, there must be coherence *within* thought, too; and thought which is consistent with action must also be normatively consistent, so a person with integrity will be conscientious in striving for consistency, and this is what gives integrity its virtuous quality.

Now before taking this argument further, there are two critical questions to register. One concerns the connection between the psycho-physical dimensions of integrity and moral integrity: for while I am portraying them as interrelated and interdependent, the suspicion might arise that the alleged connection only appears because of an equivocation on the meaning of the word itself, since moral integrity is a sort of virtue, whereas physical and psychological integrity by contrast are more like functional *needs*. The other question concerns my characterization of moral integrity itself, and whether the virtues of conscientiousness and consistency are sufficient to account for its moral quality. In order to make clear how I am going to respond to these questions, I shall first flesh out a little further my 'integral' view of integrity, explaining how one can see a continuum of interrelated interests at biological, psychological, and moral, as well as social levels.

Given that humans are a part of nature, it is appropriate to begin an account of their interest in integrity with the most direct implications of this fact. A human's interest in integrity starts with their interest as an organism, which is manifest in its striving to persist in its own being.[16] The organism cannot achieve this on its own, though, as without the continuous influence of the environment the internal organic processes cannot sustain life for more than a moment. What is true of an organism – that its integrity depends on both internal integration (among its organic processes) and external integration (with its environment) – is true in its way of any whole of which integrity can be predicated: that is, any integral whole is composed of parts and is in turn an integrated part of a greater whole. This means that while integrity implies – in each of its contexts – a corresponding degree of self-sufficiency, it does not mean complete separateness. Thus it is that the integrity of an organism can be undermined either by internal disruption to its constituent organs or by disruptions in its environment. Just as humans' bodily integrity, which involves being integrally related to environmental conditions, is not a matter of pure self-sufficiency, nor is their psychological integrity.

Psychological integrity is experienced by an individual as something like a mental equilibrium that permits clear and reliable judgement and an ease of relationship with self, others, and world: one's mind is integrated with one's body, with the minds of others and with material reality. What I mean by this is not that one has to live in perfect harmony with self, others and world to have psychological integrity, for of course the world and others can often be experienced as hostile, and one can experience conflicts within the self as well; what I mean by mental equilibrium is that the relations are experienced as intelligible. Psychological integrity is undermined or breaks down when meaning is lost or distorted (not just when meanings are harsh or unpalatable, since intelligibility has also to be adequate to reality). Psychological integrity is perhaps most clearly manifest in good judgement, and this contains a cognitive component.

One has an interest in cognitive integrity, in the sense of having coherent beliefs about the world and one's place in it. Cognitive integrity has both synchronic and diachronic dimensions: at any given time, one has an interest in holding beliefs which are, on the whole, noncontradictory, coherent and true; one also has an interest in the coherence of one's beliefs across time, and this is connected to the need MacIntyre (1981) has noted for individuals to secure their identity *narratively*, through the narrative cohesion of how they tell their life's story.[17] Moreover, this narrative cohesion involves not only beliefs, but also motivations: beliefs and motivations together make up projects and commitments. With the appreciation of the value of commitments arises an interest in moral integrity.

A necessary condition for, and minimal definition of, moral integrity is that one stick to one's moral principles over time. Hence cognitive consistency and narrative coherence, which are necessary to formulate commitments, are brought together with *conscientiousness* in moral integrity. But this leaves the question of how far consistency, coherence and conscientiousness take us ethically: can a person with integrity not consistently and conscientiously do 'bad' things? If integrity means sticking to one's principles, surely it cannot mean sticking to just *any* principles? The description given so far thus does not seem sufficient to capture the meaning of *moral* integrity.[18]

Certainly I agree with those moral philosophers who insist that integrity requires consistent commitment to not just any principles. Thus I share the intuition, as articulated by McFall, that it is inappropriate to speak, for instance, of the pursuit for oneself alone, of pleasure, or wealth, or others' approval, as substantive commitments being true to which would count as having integrity. But given that many individuals, to all appearances, do pursue such things, does this not undermine my claim of an interest that includes moral integrity? I do not think so, because the intuition can be squared with the rest of my view. The objection to such pursuits is not, I take it, that they are inherently immoral, but that they are not inherently good – that is (with the arguable exception of pleasure – although see the observations of Williams, 1987: 112ff), these are not ends that could conceivably be intrinsically good, even nonmorally, for anyone, and so exclusive and unconditional commitment to them would be irrational, and go against cognitive integrity; and if that is not in place, moral integrity might not be possible; this does not deny an interest in it. So these are not the sorts of things one can have a *commitment* to pursue; moreover, such things are not interests; rather, they are *preferences* for particular means for satisfying interests. Preferences differ from commitments in having no necessary connection with narrative integrity.[19] Their exclusive pursuit would mean neglecting other important areas of one's life. In reducing commitments to preferences, rather than deriving preferences from commitments, there is a lack of narrative integrity. This means that a precondition of moral integrity is lacking, not necessarily that an interest in it is lacking.

Yet perhaps rather than resolving the question, this reply just pushes it back a stage to the question of why one cannot have a morally problematic narrative identity, in that the story one tells oneself about one's life squares away morally dubious features. To be sure, there are likely to be psychological constraints built into one's identity, too. It is surely true, as McFall (1987: 13) observes, that there are things we cannot do without self-betrayal and psychological disintegration. Nevertheless, the things that could have such a dramatic effect on most of us would include only particularly abhorrent actions or practices: so on this basis we might expect only a minimal set of moral principles to be generated, proscribing only the most extreme moral offences or atrocities. For the rest, it seems quite conceivable that psychological integration might be secured for an individual by refraining from too much concern about moral principles at all – thereby removing potential moral conflicts at source: so what is to stop the interest in psychological integrity yielding an interest in being *amoral*? To make matters worse, it is even conceivable that a person could maintain their psychological integrity only by participating in practices that we would want to condemn as unequivocally *immoral*. Is there any way of avoiding this conclusion?

Now in setting out this problem, I have accepted a tacit assumption on which this set of questions is premised, namely, that 'we' know roughly what would count as being moral or not, and, indeed, that we are liable to be disturbed by the prospect of people being motivated only to a minimal morality, or even being amoral or immoral. In the very appreciation of the problem *as* a problem, therefore, we can discern an interest in its being the case that people in general should be moral. If you and I did not have this interest, there would, bluntly, *be* no problem. Without labouring the point, then, I am willing just to assert that each individual has an interest in every other individual being moral; and this provides a context, a social context, for dealing with the problem. As social beings, we have an interest 'that there should be morality'; we also have some reasonably clear sense of the kinds of virtue and duty which constitute its core. So a problem that at first sight looked intractable, is now recognizable as just a 'free-rider' problem: that is, given that each has an interest in everyone else being moral, the only question remaining is why each does not have an interest in being moral herself. Considered as an isolated individual, in abstraction from any social relation, it might be hard – even impossible – to show this; but if individuals lived in isolation, there would be no occasion for, or possibility of, morality anyway. Considered as they are though, as individuals who are necessarily social beings, they have an interest in social integration; and from this fact it is far less difficult to supply good motivating reasons for being moral, or for at least acting in conformity to moral norms.

Yet the serious objection can now be made that, in saying morality comes from a motivation to integrate socially, my argument at most shows an interest in conforming to prevailing norms: and if prevailing norms are abhorrent then no distinctively *moral* integrity could come into play. What would I say, for instance, of an individual who consistently and conscientiously conforms to prevailing norms, when they are like the norms prevailing in Nazi Germany? I certainly do not claim that moral integrity merely means conforming to external norms. The conscientious Nazi's hypothetical claim to integrity is based precisely on conformity to certain culturally specific norms. Now the sorts of norms I am assuming we find odious are not the entirety of even that culture's norms: on the contrary, the Nazis gained the support they did, in considerable measure, by appealing to values which in themselves were not objectionable. So if the culture also embodies certain more usual virtues and norms, a person with integrity would have to be able to square these with the odious norms. Failure to do so would be a failure of coherence in normative commitment, factual belief and practical action. So while the Nazi could perhaps be 'true to himself' qua Nazi, he cannot also be true to himself, qua human person, unless he has a coherent account of why oppressive behaviour is appropriate towards certain outsiders and is not appropriate towards members of his own group. Without attempting to prove the point here, I would assert that any such account would involve some serious cognitive defect.

I think it is worth distinguishing, at this point, between the 'conscientious Nazi' and those less wholehearted supporters, or even simple non-objectors, who merely conform to or passively accept the external norms. Of the latter, one might be tempted to say that they lacked moral integrity – if, after all, they believed it was wrong, say, to withhold business from Jews, then surely they lacked integrity in doing so. My reply is that it is more accurate and appropriate to say that they lacked the requisite courage: for this can be said as a matter of simple observation, and carries no particular normative weight – unless you think that there is a moral duty to be courageous, a point I shall return to. What I want to say at this stage is that the existence of this passive conformity to external norms does not undermine my claim of a general interest in integrity, since in a society where the pursuit of moral integrity puts one at risk in one's psycho-physical integrity, one just cannot have complete integrity. But one can then quite reasonably be said to have an interest in a better society.

If we return to the case of the conscientious Nazi, it may well be that he precisely believes he is working for a better society, and that the practices we consider atrocities he considers as merely a price to pay for it. Of him, I would want to reaffirm the cognitive deficiency mentioned before. Failure to address this cognitive deficiency may in some cases be due to the psychological disequilibrium of some sort, hence the psychological integrity precondition is missing; but in other cases there is the possibility that the cognitive defect may not even be perceptible to the individual because it is suppressed in the ideological norms that construct his identity, and therefore his failure to overcome it might not be due to any particular lack of conscientiousness. This points, in fact, to a lack of something else. It is relevant to note that an archetypal way of transforming citizens into murderers and torturers in oppressive regimes is not only to convince them ideologically of value-relevant differences between their group and the oppressed group, but also to dehumanize and brutalize them. In short, the training usually works by removing their effective autonomy.[20] So before asking whether they have integrity, it is necessary to ask whether they have not been deprived of necessary preconditions for it – for example, autonomy. Here the question of personal integrity must be linked to its political dimensions. For if integrity involves the full development of one's faculties and powers, then the existence of a regime which systematically blocks any aspect of that development does not constitute a refutation of the human interest in integrity, but, rather, a practical obstacle to its realization.

But what about individuals in societies that allow considerable autonomy but who nevertheless defect from social moral norms when it is expedient for them to do so? How can they be said to have an interest in moral integrity? Defecting regularly would incur individual costs – especially, but perhaps not only, psychological ones. The greater part of morality, the 'everyday' kind, is what makes social integration possible. (Opting out of the morality is at the same time to opt out of social integration.) The extent to which one can get away with being a 'free rider' depends on the character of the society, the degree and nature of integration possible within it. My claim is that individuals have an interest in living in a society with a degree of social integration that would actually make significant or regular defection difficult and undesirable. If, by contrast, an individual lives in an anomic society, their interest in moral integrity may become attenuated, because the interest in social integration is insufficiently fulfilled.

At this point, however, I anticipate the objection that whatever it is I claim to have established individuals to have an interest in, it is not moral integrity. Integrity is a virtue whose presence or exercise does not wait on the achievement of ideal social conditions – indeed, an important part of what it means is sticking to one's principles precisely in adverse conditions – we would hardly have had occasion to formulate the idea if one's commitment to principles were never put to the test. Indeed, the point of departure for this whole discussion of integrity was the case of the rescuers who did just that. However, the reason the rescuers were singled out for attention in the first place is that they appeared to have done something exceptional and exemplary. So while I would affirm that a degree of courage is surely necessary in the maintenance of moral integrity, the precise kind and degree of courage required will depend on the principles an individual is committed to; and while principles requiring one to sacrifice one's life are certainly worthy of emulation, I think it would be an unduly strenuous conception of integrity that made such principles a necessary condition of it. A person who lives by such principles would, I think, strike us as a person not just of integrity, but also of some further quality, which we might call heroism, for instance. The kind of integrity I am talking about, though, is the kind that individuals can reciprocally expect from one another. This does not mean that an individual cannot live according to more demanding moral standards than she expects from others – and if she has certain religious beliefs, for instance, her integrity may require this of her – but this moves into the area of *supererogation*, in the full sense of the term, whereby what the person gives another is not only a generous overflow (as supererogatory acts were characterized in section 3) *from* herself, but, because of a faith in a transcendent sense, she gives *of* herself.

To perform supererogatory acts oneself is laudable; to place an expectation of them on others can actually undermine their integrity. Given human frailty and fallibility, we need a certain psychological resilience, and this is not fostered by setting ourselves unrealistic moral goals which we too often fail to live up to; or, perhaps worse, there is the risk that it *could* be fostered, but at the price of hardening us against the demands of morality more generally, thereby further inuring us against experiencing a sense of moral failure in those cases where our moral motivation is already somewhat flaky.

It is not in our interest to be crushed by every moral failure, I am claiming, but it is in our interest to do what we believe is morally required. In relation to this point there is one more feature of moral integrity that warrants comment. A necessary condition for moral integrity, claims McFall, is that one not only does what one takes to be the right thing but that one also does it for what one takes to be the right reasons. While I would not dispute this claim, I would emphasize that if it has any implications at all, these cannot include the alleged corollary, namely, that if one does the right thing for the wrong reason one is not acting with integrity. This is not because of the consequentialist consideration that what 'really matters' is simply that the right thing be done since – *ex hypothesi* – that might not be all that matters to the person concerned. Rather, it is because the sort of person to whom it matters – namely, one who generally strives to resist the temptation to follow inclination when it conflicts with duty – just will not be able to know, when they happen to coincide, whether she is not merely witnessing the normal operation of a temptation which, under less auspicious circumstances, she would in fact resist. I think, though, that a strenuously moral person is liable to make an excessively harsh self-judgement in that situation.

So I return to sum up the idea of integrity as an interest, and why it should be acknowledged to have this status in political theory.

In important respects, it should be noted, a fundamental interest in integrity is already widely recognized. To begin with, people's interest in bodily integrity is recognized and protected by internationally accepted human rights to be protected against the infliction of bodily harm; and human rights also cover at least the more extreme forms of psychological torment. Hence that humans have an interest in psycho-physical integrity is widely recognized. Furthermore, the protection of socio-personal integrity is, according to Habermas for instance, the very purpose of morality.[21] The sustaining of morality requiring social integration, one's general interest in there being morality is inseparable from one's interest in participating as a moral agent.

The broad political implications of this are clear. An individual's integrity can be threatened in any of its dimensions, and she has an interest in being protected in all of them: imagine being asked to choose to eliminate all but one of a range of threats which included torture, hunger, psychosis, profound alienation, solitary confinement, prevention from following one's religion, from speaking one's mind or associating with others. Clearly, actualization of any one of such threats would make the person less than they are or would wish to be.

It may perhaps be asked why political theory should focus on integrity as a fundamental political value rather than on better established alternatives such as autonomy or needs? If integrity is a formal virtue, then why should political theory focus on conditions favouring the development of this rather than, as it traditionally does, on autonomy? Certainly, there is good reason for autonomy to be taken as a fundamental political value. Autonomy is invoked as a primary good in political theory to establish the claim that a defensible political order is 'one in which people are able to develop their nature and interests free from the arbitrary use of political power and coercive relations' (Held, 1995: 151). It is therefore crucially important, but it is nevertheless valued, as that quotation makes plain, as a *means* to the end of developing one's nature and interests. So, certainly, autonomy is a necessary precondition for the development of certain aspects of integrity, but one's interest in it is derivative from those more fundamental interests.

What is true of autonomy is also true of needs; indeed, according to Doyal and Gough (1991), autonomy *is* one of the two most basic types of need, the other type relating to survival and health. Needs in general, like autonomy in particular, *are* needs just because they serve some further end: 'Whenever someone says "*x* is needed" it always makes sense (though it may be pedantic in some contexts) to ask what it is needed for' (Barry, 1965: 48). It is thus worth recalling that need is not of itself a justificatory principle in political theory, in the sense that no policy or normative implication follows directly from any statement about needs: 'no statement to the effect that x is necessary in order to produce y provides a reason for doing x. Before it can provide such a reason y must be shown to be (or taken to be) a desirable end to pursue. . . . To speak of needs, then, is to operate on a lower level of generality than that of the ultimate justifications for policies' (ibid.).

Indeed, Doyal and Gough themselves make the relevant point when developing their theory of needs: since 'the end state in relation to which basic needs take on their definition . . . becomes the final goal for all humans – the ultimate "*Y*" in "*A* needs *X* in order to *Y*" – it makes more sense to describe it as our most basic human *interest*' (Doyal and Gough, 1991: 55, my emphasis). They actually refer to this basic interest as avoiding harm, but the positive state of which harm is a negation, I am claiming, is best thought of as *integrity*.

Conclusion

The most fundamental interest humans have, I have claimed, is an interest in integrity, understood as wholeness, unity, and health in one's physical, mental, and spiritual being. All enlightened interests spring from this. Furthermore, no individual can have any reason to wish to deny others' pursuit of integrity. As Kitwood observes, 'to seek an inner truth and integration for oneself is of necessity to desire integrity on the part not only of a few close others, but of a much larger circle of friends, colleagues, and acquaintances. But if these, then why not all? At this point psycho-logic and moral argument flow together into a single stream.' (Kitwood, 1990: 211) So in desiring integrity for others one is desiring something that is good for them, but also good for oneself in one's dealings with them. To try to decide between 'self-interest' and 'altruism' here would be beside the point: the interest in integrity – like the reality of integrity – is deeper than such distinctions, more fundamental than any motivation that could adequately be described in terms of self-interest or altruism; indeed, it points to an interrelatedness that is more profound than the separateness of persons. The enlightenment of self-interest reveals that the self is part of a greater whole and related to all other selves, with no particular privileges or claims.

However, we have also seen that the effective pursuit of integrity requires conditions of autonomy; the problem then is that to secure these is also to secure the conditions of freedom for individuals to disregard the pursuit of integrity: conditions for the enlightenment of self-interest do not themselves guarantee its accomplishment. Other motivations compete. Indeed, if an individual maintains that their self-interest lies elsewhere than described, they can invoke traditional liberal arguments in justification. This issue will be a central one for the next chapter, where we turn to consider how these considerations about individual human interests bear on ecological values.

5

Human Interests and Environmental Values

Introduction

We turn now to the question of how human interests bear on ecological values. As noted in the Introduction to this book, a major obstacle to an ecological reorientation of political values or an ecological reconstruction of social institutions is that people often do not consider such changes would be in their interest. In this chapter, though, I expand on the thought that since humans have come to be aware of the ecological problems they are creating, they are also capable of realizing that it is in their interest to solve them. As noted in the previous chapter, human interests, being many and varied, include 'enlightened' interests, such as that in personal integrity and social solidarity, and from these, as I shall be showing, certain ecological norms can be extrapolated. Nevertheless, there is also reason to accept as a fact that not all humans would necessarily own the more enlightened interests, or at least not give them precedence if and when they conflict with self-interest of a narrower, paradigmatically economic, sort. Accordingly, the main focus for this chapter is on these two types of interest, on how they relate to one another and to ecological values.

In the first section I inquire how far rational self-interest – of a paradigmatically economic kind – can be harnessed to ecological ends. For while there is a strong current of ecological thought which locates the root of many environmental problems precisely in the prevalence of narrow, essentially private and economistic, interests, whose pursuit can permit or even encourage the despoliation or degradation of the natural environment, there are also reasons to think that rational economic self-interest can in some circumstances be harnessed to favour the perception of, and action against, ecological problems. Yet there are also limits to the extent this can happen, and in the second section I examine criticisms of approaches to environmentalism based on rational self-interest and the alternative view they lead to. On this view ecological problems are seen as a matter for political deliberation rather than economic calculation. Still, I argue in section 3, to the extent that it is likely to be effective or legitimate, this deliberation must still be based in interests, albeit enlightened interests revealed in discursive will-formation. I also note, though, in section 4, that some of the leading proponents of deliberative approaches to ecological policy-making do not clearly and explicitly recognize the connection with interests. This is partly because they do not attend sufficiently to the difference between interests and preferences, and so, in section 5, I elaborate on this distinction, offering a more detailed definition of interests as such. In section 6, I then indicate some ways in which interests can be enlightened, and how these bear on ecological values.

1   Rational self-interest and market-based evaluation of environmental goods

The basic question for this section is how far rational self-interest can be pressed into the service of environmental ends. Rational self-interest I take to be, paradigmatically, but not exclusively, the economic interest of individuals and businesses as manifest in market behaviour. There are a number of good reasons to explore the environmentalist potential of the interests implicit in economic rationality. Firstly, economic activity being a key feature of any society, the interests that sustain it are an important source of motivation for a very significant sphere of social life, and so accounts of economically rational behaviour can be taken as accounts of real powerful motivations: in modern market economies, the relevant behaviour is paradigmatically market behaviour. Secondly, these interests generate goods, and, arguably, by operating within market mechanisms, make for efficiency not only in the production of goods but also their distribution. Thirdly, and most important in the context of normative theory, these interests can claim some legitimacy. For if one starts from the assumption that, other things being equal, individuals have a right to pursue their own interests, as they understand them and as they see fit, then, other things still being equal, it is legitimate for individuals to pursue their own economic interests.

If private economic interests really do oppose the provision of environmental goods, then, this is a serious problem. However, reasons to think they do not, or need not, are provided by those who advocate some form of market-based solution to environmental problems.

Pros and cons of rational self-interest

Some environmental problems are problems that it is in people's rational self-interest to solve. This is the case, for instance, where they are perceived as presenting a clear and present threat to the quality of life, or even survival, of an identifiable group of human interest-bearers. Local environmental degradation, resource depletion, and so on, as well as the local effects of more global degradation and resource depletion, can bear directly on identifiable immediate human interests, and thus constitute problems that it is in those humans' rational self-interest to address. For any such rationally self-interested group the only issue for debate would be whether the benefits of solving the problems – assuming for the moment that solutions are available – outweighs the costs of doing so; the outcome, though, given rationality and adequate information, will be that the problem will be solved if, all things considered, it really *is* a problem for the group in question. In principle, then, there is a type of environmental problem that is straightforwardly a matter for humans' rational self-interest; and in practice, the harnessing of rational self-interest to environmental ends can be a potent motivating force for the pursuit of environmental policies.

Nevertheless, there are also reasons for caution about thinking that, in practice, policies will generally be lighted upon, or quite so straightforwardly, as a matter of rational self-interest. Apart from the questionable assumption that groups of human interest-bearers are generally rational and adequately informed, there are other, more specifically political, difficulties in the way of this. One is that groups of human interest-bearers do not always constitute a political unity: so while some environmental problems may affect a political region in such a way that its whole population has a general interest in dealing with them, many do not. Moreover, the costs and benefits of addressing acknowledged environmental problems will seldom affect, or be perceived by, all sectors of society in the same way, and hence a consensual view of the appropriate course of action may not be possible. This problem is even more marked at a global level, where the particular groups of humans who confront environmental problems *as* problems are not the same humans who are engaged in and/or benefit from the activities causing them. So the 'harnessing' of rational self-interest to environmental solutions is no straightforward matter when the rational group of interest-bearers that has some power to deal with the problem does not have a rational interest in dealing with it.

It is not a straightforward matter, but then nor are environmental problems, and there are reasons to think that rational self-interest does not necessarily entail disregarding these problems. Because many of the most significant environmental problems involve risks that are difficult to quantify or predict, it is often difficult or even impossible to arrive at reliable rational calculation of costs and benefits. Hence doubts about the applicability of a 'pure' rational self-interest view of environmental problems arise in a number of ways. For one thing, under conditions of uncertainty, there may be doubts about the reliability of quantitative assessment of costs and benefits, and therefore reason to err on the side of ecological caution rather than maximize immediate economic advantage: the increasing acceptance by governments of the 'precautionary principle' attests to the growing significance of this consideration. Furthermore, there is also uncertainty about where costs and benefits are ultimately likely to fall: ecological disturbances are no respecters of political boundaries, and the global spread of the economic practices causing them is matched by repercussions that can also become global in scope; moreover, even when ecological repercussions are not directly felt, adverse effects on others can have mediate effects by destabilizing political, economic and security relations. In short, it is becoming increasingly difficult, for a growing range of environmental issues, to think of these purely as 'other people's problems'.

Nevertheless, the fact that there might be a quite widely shared interest in solving these problems does not entail a corresponding interest in contributing to their solution: there are also likely to be individuals, communities, businesses and nations which have particular interests in resisting specific policies for providing environmental goods because of the more immediate costs involved for them. Hence one of the archetypal ways of characterizing ecological problems in general is in the familiar terms of the problem of how to secure collective or public goods when the means of securing them conflict with more particular or private interests. Indeed, this view of the problem, as a problem of choice for rationally self-interested individuals, has been captured in 'The tragedy of the commons' (Hardin, 1968). In essence, the problem, an instance of the sort of 'free-rider' problem familiar from rational choice theory, is that when resources are commonly owned, or not owned at all, individuals have an interest in exploiting them for maximum private benefit, and have little regard to the costs of doing so since these are distributed more widely and thinly.

Various ways of dealing with this problem have been discussed in the environmental literature. On one sort of approach, as advocated by Hardin himself, emphasis is placed on the need for coercive measures to ensure that the bearers of particular private interests cooperate in the provision of collective goods.[1] But there are difficulties with this: coercive agencies can be inefficient at devising and implementing appropriate policies (Dryzek, 1987), and this is partly because they are ineffective at motivating reluctant subjects, particularly when the latter do not accept the legitimacy of the coercive authority. Thus while there is an important place for coercive regulation in the environmental field, it is not the only, and not always the most effective or efficient option – especially in the context of capitalist economies and liberal politics, where the powers and motivations of regulators can be an uneven match for those of the industries they would regulate. Thus there is good reason to seek approaches to *harness* rational-self interest, rather than to suppress it, in the search for solutions to environmental problems.

That this can and should be done is the basic premise of the approaches to environmental problems that I now turn to consider. Because rational self-interest is taken to be paradigmatically manifest in market behaviour, these approaches advocate market-based solutions.

Market-based approaches to environmental values

Various market-based solutions have been proposed (see Jacobs, 1995, for a useful critical survey of these), but for present purposes it will suffice to compare and contrast two main types: one that relies on the 'free market' and another that requires regulation of the market, supplementing actual money values as revealed in real market transactions with values arrived at by other means such as the 'shadow pricing' based on preferences as elicited in 'willingness-to-pay' surveys.

What is common to the various market-based solutions is the assumption that environmental problems arise because environmental goods are free, or under-priced, which means that there is little or no economic incentive to refrain from their consumption or destruction; and accordingly their solution to this is to put a price on such goods so that their wanton use would be curbed. They differ on how best to achieve this.

FREE MARKET ENVIRONMENTALISM   The key claim of free market environmentalism (FME) is that if all currently unowned or commonly owned resources were privately owned, the owners would have a vested interest in protecting them from harm. FME is seen by some as potentially the most effective means of securing environmental protection, particularly in view of the problem dramatized in Hardin's 'The tragedy of the commons': when resources are owned in common, or not owned at all, everyone has an interest in exploiting them for their own benefit, with little regard to the harms and costs of doing so since these are distributed more widely. The problem here is that private interests compete in the exploitation of common resources. FME diagnoses this, though, as a problem arising not from the existence of market forces or the self-interested behaviour of economic agents, but rather from the absence of well-defined, universal, exclusive, transferable and enforceable private property rights in respect of common environmental assets (Eckersley, 1993: 4). The problem could be avoided, they claim, by making them all private property: this would remove the incentive to exploit resources wantonly, since to do so would no longer be costless. Thus if a common resource like a river, for instance, were parcelled out into private property lots, then each owner would have a definite interest in preventing others from polluting it. This would be a more effective and reliable anti-pollution measure than regulations which people have an interest in trying to circumvent. FME thus proposes that environmental problems can be solved by creating and enforcing tradeable property rights in respect of common environmental assets. Advocates of FME seek full privatization of environmental services and activities wherever possible.

A number of advantages can be claimed for this approach. One is that rational self-interest is harnessed in the service of the common (environmental) good: this is more efficient, effective and legitimate than regulatory alternatives. Another is that it can be held to depend on and support key normative principles and values like responsibility, democracy and freedom. *Responsibility* can be claimed as a value promoted by FME on the grounds that the more extensive is the system of rights, the more complete will be the system of corresponding responsibilities and liabilities to accept obligations: there are no 'free spaces' to dump one's rubbish and no free resources to exploit. This is held to contrast favourably with a regulative system of state control which may be run by bureaucrats who do not have to pay for the costs of their actions, who are insulated from the consequences of their advice and decisions, and who might be motivated purely by the narrow self-interest of personal advancement in their careers (cf. Eckersley, 1993: 6). FME is also claimed to be a *democratic* form of solution: whereas governments are imperfectly informed of people's preferences and may therefore impose inappropriate solutions, people's preferences are expressed directly in markets. For the same reason, FME is a respecter of individual *freedom*.[2]

Nevertheless, serious objections can also be levelled at FME, and each of the claims in its favour can be questioned. For one thing, there are many significant instances where privatization is simply not an option: in the case of 'pure public goods' like clean air, for instance, there appears to be no way of parcelling them out into private holdings.[3] For another, the responsibility argument assumes that the rational self-interest of property-owners consists in preserving their environmental assets into the indefinite future; yet there is no obvious reason why they might not rather consider it to be in their rational self-interest to discount the future benefits of doing so and instead attempt to derive maximum benefit from them in the short term, even to the extent of completely consuming or destroying them. Then again, the normative claims regarding freedom and democracy are vulnerable to serious objections: for it is clear that only people with money actually express their preferences in markets, which therefore cannot represent the interests of poorer people, let alone those of unborn people or nonhuman beings.

Still, while these are very serious objections, they are not necessarily objections to the *principle* of linking environmental protection to rational self-interest. They might be problems specific to markets which are allowed to operate in a manner that is totally unregulated.

ENVIRONMENTAL ECONOMICS   This approach recognizes that environmental decisions cannot be left to the unregulated market (cf. Pearce *et al.*, 1989). This does not mean rejecting market mechanisms, though, for the diagnosis of environmental problems is that they are often due primarily to 'market failures', 'such failures being, roughly speaking, a matter of existing market mechanisms failing to do what markets are generally good at doing' (Keat, 1994: 333). What markets are generally good at doing is 'maximising the total amount of preference-satisfaction for any given set of resources: markets, that is, are efficient' (ibid.: 334). What markets 'fail' to do is take into account the full environmental costs and benefits of economic activity; this is because environmental assets and services have not been properly valued, and, indeed, in many cases, have been exploited as 'free resources'. To address this, environmental economists recommend that governments correct market failure by imposing taxes or charges to enable environmental factors of production to be internalized as costs of production: they thus seek to modify the workings of existing markets, as, for instance, by means of the 'polluter pays' principle which ensures that total costs of production, especially including environmental 'externalities', are reflected in market prices. In contrast to FME, this is therefore not advocacy simply of a *free* market, but of the use of market-based instruments such as taxes, penalties, charges, tradeable permits and so on, which are designed to provide incentives for certain kinds of behaviour by directly or indirectly structuring the market place.

Furthermore, because environmental economics is not constrained to accept real market valuations, it can introduce different criteria and indicators of economic costs and benefits (Pearce *et al.*, 1989). To do this it employs various methods for simulating market conditions where real markets do not exist – such methods include 'shadow-pricing' and 'contingent valuation'. These typically involve conducting cost–benefit analyses (CBAs) of options for environmental policy so that the environmental impacts are translated into economic costs and benefits for rationally self-interested agents.

In this way, standard calculations of economic costs and benefits are expanded and modified: in particular, the concept of 'externalities' is expanded so as to include intangible costs and values such as people's aesthetic appreciation of nature, or their 'valuing' of wilderness, kinds of natural landscape, or the 'sheer existence' of certain living species, and so on. Keat illustrates this distinction between narrow and broad conceptions of externalities:

> Suppose a firm discharges its waste into a river, but that further down the river another firm makes use of this water for its own productive purposes. The effect of the first firm's discharges is that the second firm has to purify the river water before using it itself. This is a straightforward case of externalities: the first firm is imposing a cost on the second, but there is no mechanism by which it has to pay for this itself . . .

This is a standard kind of market failure.

> By contrast with this straightforward case, there may also, or instead, be people who attribute value to unpolluted river water: for instance, to the aesthetic qualities of sparkling streams or their ability to support various species of fish or plant-life. They may also regard such pollution as a desecration of nature, as something that it is inherently wrong or bad to allow . . . (Keat, 1994: 335–6).

In order to incorporate these less tangible, non-market, values into economic calculations of costs and benefits, various methods are devised for attributing them the equivalent of a market price. Typical of such methods are the 'willingness-to-pay' surveys which are designed to elicit from respondents how much value they place on specific features of the environment so that these valuations can then be set in relation to other, non-environmental, goods. Using the valuations thus arrived at, appropriate policies for market regulation can then be devised.

This sort of approach can be claimed to preserve the main advantages of FME, while overcoming the latter's shortcomings. Thus it still harnesses market motivations to environmental ends, but does so also in areas where the free market would fail to do so. Moreover, the normative claims made for FME are here better supported: it is clearly more democratic to take into account the valuations of ordinary citizens rather than allow only the effective demand of those with adequate property rights to count; and it thus also distributes more equitably the freedom to choose the environmental harms one is willing to bear. It also encourages a sense of responsibility in arriving at environmental values, for although the valuations individuals make are not tied to real property interests, the rigours of the market are nevertheless simulated by constraining individuals not just to say what they would like if they could have every environmental and social good they wanted, but what they would be prepared to forego in order to have this good rather than the other.

However, something that emerges from attempts at actually carrying out contingent valuation by doing surveys of real subjects, is that preferences are revealed that simply do not translate into market prices (cf. O'Neill, 1997). Rather, they point to evaluative estimates of environmental goods that seem to place these outside purely economic calculations. This is taken by critics as evidence to support an important objection to market-based approaches to environmental policy in general – namely, that environmental goods have the character of public goods and are not appropriately considered as questions of individual preference at all; decisions about the provision of public goods is appropriately a collective and political matter, not an individual economic one.

2 Political deliberation about environmental values

There is thus a contrasting view which challenges the assumption that attitudes and values appropriate to market behaviour are appropriate to valuing environmental goods at all. On this view, environmental goods have a kind of value that cannot be reduced to economic value or to preferences that can be attributed an economic price. The evaluative methods of environmental economics force the valuers into a rationally self-interested frame of mind; yet their real preferences do not neatly fit that frame of mind. This is partly because some of their preferences are more like commitments, and so to the extent that they correspond to interests, they are enlightened interests (for more on the distinction between commitments and preferences, and their relation to interests, see below). An associated objection is advanced against the principle of preference-aggregation used in environmental economics on the grounds that environmental goods are collective goods and so valuations of them should be based not on their effects on individual interests but on their contribution to the collective good. This would mean arriving at valuations by means of political deliberation in public fora rather than through economic calculations of private interests; it would involve collective deliberation about social goals, and not the mere aggregation of individual preferences.

Now the question of different types of good, on the one hand, and the question of individual preferences, on the other, are conceptually distinct, since individual preferences could in principle favour non-economic goods. However, in the critique of the practice of environmental economics there are reasons for seeing them as conjoined (partly because, of course, individuals are forced to place monetary values on the non-economic goods); it is when we come to consider alternatives that problems arising from their distinctiveness will have to be addressed.

Reasons for thinking that the attitudes and values of market behaviour are not appropriate in the evaluation of environmental goods are revealed from the work of environmental economists themselves, argues John O'Neill (1997), when they attempt to arrive at market valuations by means of 'willingness-to-pay' surveys. In these surveys individuals are asked how much they would be willing to pay in additional taxes to preserve some particular environmental good, but they are frequently bewildered by what they are required to do. Their bewilderment is plausibly interpreted as arising from a belief, intuition or conviction that some sorts of good are 'beyond price', and that environmental goods are of this sort. If a value is to be placed on them, therefore, it is reasonable to think this should be arrived at by the kind of process that other non-monetary cultural values are arrived at: valuing environmental goods is not a question of what individuals happen to prefer for their personal benefit, let alone what they would be willing or able to pay for their preferences, but, rather, a matter of properly informed public debate.

The idea that the valuation of environmental goods is a matter for citizens rather than consumers has been developed by Mark Sagoff (1988). He argues that appropriate decisions about environmental issues are not to be made on the basis of preference-satisfaction, but rather by reference to ethical, aesthetic, cultural, and political values. He thus insists on drawing a distinction between preferences and *values*, one which is systematically ignored from the economistic perspective of CBA, which treats values simply as a particular sort of preference. Sagoff claims that whereas preferences are simply a 'brute fact' about us, values are the kind of thing for which we can give, or be expected to give, some kind of reason or justification. Environmental decisions, then, are to be made by reference to values and not preferences; they involve one in one's role as citizen and not as consumer. As a consumer, says Sagoff, one is exclusively and properly concerned with one's 'private interests', and hence with the pursuit of preference-satisfaction. But as a citizen one is concerned with 'the public interest'. Deciding what is the public interest involves seeing oneself as a member of a political community; this in turn involves reflective debate with others about matters essentially concerning values.

The thrust of the critical arguments of O'Neill and Sagoff thus points to political deliberation as opposed to economic valuation as being the appropriate means for arriving at decisions regarding environmental goods.

A question that arises, though, is this: if environmental issues are to be seen as matters for political deliberation, as opposed to economic calculation, then how satisfactory a solution will this be to the original problem, namely, that if people can democratically choose, they will choose what is in their interest; and if it is not in their interest to choose environmental policies, then environmental problems will not be resolved. Some theorists have argued that it is unlikely to provide a solution at all: Goodin (1992), for instance, emphasizes that democratic procedures entail no commitment to substantive values at all; moreover, as Saward (1993) points out, even if democracy has certain 'self-binding' commitments, these are unlikely to include environmental values, since democracy is about relations between persons, not about relations with the environment or nonhuman beings.

Now a first line of reply to this argument is that it misses the intended force of the contrast between citizens and economic agents and the conception of democracy this implies, namely, a discursive or deliberative conception (cf., for example, Dryzek, 1987). Thus the appeal to citizenship is intended to highlight how, as citizens, individuals can and do bracket out concerns of immediate private self-interest in order to focus on common concerns with the provision of public goods. This is facilitated and encouraged when institutional arrangements are so designed as to embody the participatory values of deliberative or discursive democracy. For the idea is that the more citizens are enabled to participate in political decision-making, the more able and willing they will become to reason and act as citizens rather than as bearers of purely private interests. In other words, political deliberation allows the articulation of more 'enlightened' interests.

But this first line of reply leaves the questions of why individual citizens would or should set aside their rational self-interest; and of why, and in what sense, citizens' values would be more favourable to environmental goods.

On the question of why citizens *should* set aside their private interests, Sagoff's answer depends on seeing these as preferences as opposed to values. He does not accept that preferences necessarily have any legitimate claim to be satisfied, since preferences can be sadistic, envious, racist, or unjust; they can also be coerced or adapted to coercive circumstances, and so express not the autonomous choice of the individual but a process that pre-empts autonomy. Sagoff's argument, accordingly, is that preference-satisfaction is only good when what is preferred is itself good. The burden of his distinction between preferences and values is that, for the latter, reasons can and must be given. But what makes one reason better than another? Sagoff does not seek to lay down criteria for this, but takes instead a pragmatic line on values and rationality; a deliberative approach to social policy-making, he writes, 'need not depend on methods, theoretical underpinnings, or criteria laid down in advance. Rather, a rational approach emphasizes the virtues of clarity and open-mindedness in describing problems and finding ways to solve them' (Sagoff, 1988: 12–13). So, for Sagoff, political debates are to be conducted in accordance with certain *virtues*, with their outcomes not being determinable by the application of any specifiable methods. His view is that as citizens, as members of a community, individuals already have a set of values they subscribe to; so when they discourse with one another as citizens, these values will articulate themselves.

So reasons why citizens *should* set aside rational self-interest derive, on Sagoff's account, from reasons why they *would*. In this he expressly aligns himself with communitarianism. He believes that environmentalists should be communitarians because they 'would base social regulation on shared or public values, which may express not our wants and preferences as individuals but our identity, character, and aspirations as a community' (ibid.: 147). 'This is not a question of what we *want*; it is not exactly a question of what we *believe in*; it is a question of what we *are*' (ibid.: 17).

Nevertheless, this argument is vulnerable to criticisms made by Russell Keat (1994), who notes that even working within the horizon of a given culture – in Sagoff's case, that of the USA – it is an untenably selective account which maintains citizens' environmental values are more widely shared than the values associated with consumption, or the belief that what can be achieved through consumption is at least part of 'the good life for humans'; for while the activity of consuming may be chiefly a private one, at the level of the culture as a whole there is a commitment to the value of this for everyone. Indeed, Keat notes, the very existence of a competitive market economy is itself a public rather than a private good. He is therefore sceptical about Sagoff's view that if people detach themselves from their role as individual consumers with private interests, they will find themselves thinking as citizens committed to the shared value of the environment's preservation, since they will also find themselves committed to the value of consumption and will have to resolve the conflict between these shared, public, values. It is not that people value consumption as consumers and nature as citizens – rather, he claims, they value both as both – and the potential conflict between these values arises in both contexts. Hence the contrast between preferences and values cannot do the work Sagoff wishes it to. This is significant because it means that questions about rational – economic – self-interest cannot simply be set aside in citizens' deliberations.

So if a deliberative approach to environmental valuation is to be defended, it will have to be on a different basis from that supplied by Sagoff. It is appropriate, therefore, to correct three questionable assumptions Sagoff makes: firstly, that there is a 'we' with a homogeneous set of values; secondly, that those values are unproblematically worthy of endorsement; and, thirdly, that they are generally more environmentally friendly than individual preferences. I shall deal with the first two points together, and then consider the third separately, because, as will become clear, a reconstructed defence of deliberation can more clearly deal with the former than with the latter.

In claiming that as citizens, people would set aside their consumer preferences, and acknowledge (quite homogeneous) cultural values instead, Sagoff obviously assumes no serious conflicts of interest will arise. He sees political deliberation as a haven from the competition and conflict which continue to operate in the economic sphere. Yet in order to make this claim plausible he expressly assumes that basic needs are met (Sagoff, 1988: 100). It is on this assumption that very crucially depends his whole idea that citizens have a strong motivation to be liberated from being 'forced' to think like consumers, and to articulate what are in effect enlightened interests. This idea is illustrated when Sagoff endorses the view that '[t]he pursuit of private satisfactions, except for the committed hedonist, soon becomes disappointing or boring, and we look for some public cause, like saving the whales, that does not benefit us personally but appeals to our conscience' (ibid.: 116). This vision of the sated consumer turning with relief towards the pursuit of higher pleasures or nobler causes may have normative appeal, but it has limited descriptive adequacy in a world where not only are there also insatiable consumers, but also would-be consumers who lack the wherewithal to meet even their basic needs. The assumption that basic needs are met absolves him from having to deal with some serious problems. For given this assumption, one can also assume that whatever else people might like for themselves can be treated as a 'mere preferences' without undue worry that some serious interest might be at stake. Yet in the real world of political strife, what constitutes a genuine interest is often precisely what is a contested issue: conflicting interests will have more legitimacy if grounded in need than if taken as the expression of mere preference. If there is dispute about what are real needs and what 'mere preferences', then no appeal to 'shared values' – which, *ex hypothesi*, will be absent – can resolve it. The very question of what counts as a basic need, and of what satisfies it, is one to which an answer has to be agreed *within* the discursive fora.

So the enlightenment of self-interest is not automatically accomplished by a switch from a consumer to a citizen perspective. If the deliberative approach is to be defended, therefore, it needs to be reformulated in such a way that it does not depend on the problematic assumptions identified. We need to consider *why* public deliberation would yield 'better' values than those manifest in individual preferences, and also why citizens would be prepared to take decisions on their basis. This would require some transformation of perceptions of interest as manifest in preferences.

I would suggest that what would seem to be involved in deliberative processes is more adequately captured by Jürgen Habermas's characterization of the process of discursive will-formation that take place in discourse ethics.[4] Like Sagoff, Habermas methodologically refrains from moral exhortation, but is more consistent in that his discourse ethics does not rule out 'mere preferences' nor appeal to values which (perhaps just some members of) a community happens to uphold. Habermas shares the view that people's felt preferences do not have any automatically legitimate claim to satisfaction, but he does maintain that they are entitled to be heard: one of the conditions for discourse is that there are no restrictions on what can be talked about. He is also more careful to consider the conditions necessary to make discursive will-formation possible rather than place reliance on pre-existing shared values, for the moral values arrived at through discourse are not necessarily identical with those that are inherited within the community; rather they are those which can be agreed by participants in discourse, when this is itself conducted according to certain principles. Thus while the substance of ethical deliberation comes from the articulation of the needs and interests of previously socialized subjects, the deliberation itself involves processes of reflective argumentation among those subjects so that their needs and interests are themselves open to discussion and transformation. Habermas's view is that 'our basic moral intuitions spring from something deeper and more universal than contingent features of our tradition' (McCarthy, 1990: ix–x), and so although these intuitions are 'acquired in the process of socialization, they include an "abstract core" that is more than culture-specific' (ibid.: x). This core preserves the liberal principle that those who are to have duties should freely assent to the obligations they are to come under, but not the unreconstructed liberal interpretation of that principle which allows or assumes an empiricist view of assent whereby no distinction can be drawn between felt preferences and real interests, and no significance given to the possibility that people may sometimes misrecognize their own interests (cf. Offe and Wiesenthal, 1985). The Habermasian approach does not attempt to impute 'true' interests, of course, but rather requires that participants themselves come to a discursive clarification of their own perceptions. Such clarification can be expected to yield a more enlightened conception of interests where such is appropriate.

However, what this also means is that the principle of 'rational agreement' does not necessarily entail any substantive environmental commitments. Or rather, while one may expect discursive processes to yield enlightened interests in environmental protection, this may not be to the exclusion of other, less enlightened, kinds of interests, and it is not to be expected to yield 'disinterested' environmental values; or at least, while some participants in discourse may appeal to disinterested (for example, 'ecocentric') values, they will have difficulties getting general acceptance for them against others' interests because all the conceptual and practical problems associated with the two dogmas of ecologism may be expected to come into play against them.

Accordingly, the principles and procedures of deliberative democracy are not a panacea for the problem of arriving at environmental values. Certainly, in allowing the articulation of more enlightened interests, they are more conducive than approaches based on rational self-interest to seeing environmental goods as social goods, rather than a question of individual preferences; but we are still talking about interests here, and not about a leap from 'mere preferences' to 'disinterested values'. Moreover, there remains the problem signalled by Keat, that institutions favouring individual preferences – paradigmatically the market – are themselves, qua institutions, social goods. So, if we reason as citizens, we would not necessarily rule out a role for market valuations. A task for citizens would therefore be to decide how far individual preferences should be allowed to count and what would be reasons for overriding them. So if rational self-interest approaches cannot simply be ruled out as appropriate to environmental valuations, then, the critique of them needs to be reviewed and reformulated.

3   Environmental values as enlightened interests

The distinction between private preferences and public values, then, is not adequate to the purposes intended for it by those who invoke it in the critique of environmental economics. My argument is that rather than attempt to draw a stark contrast between preferences and values, one should recognize that normative propositions put forward in discursive fora must be assumed to be grounded in *interests* – interests that can be revealed to be more or less *legitimate* when discursively tested. It will of course be the case that the comparative legitimacy of interest claims will be assessed at least in part in terms of *values*, but these will be values that are articulated as such within the discursive forum, and, if they are accepted as values, this is because they are assented to by participants on an appropriately clarified and enlightened apprehension of their interests: there are no external or transcendental values to pit against mere preferences. I shall suggest that neither Sagoff nor O'Neill are sufficiently clear on this point; Keat, on the other hand, who is, introduces considerations that leave us uncertain whether discursive democracy should in fact be defended as an approach to (at least some) ecological valuations. In this section, I attempt to recast the critique of environmental economics, as it appears in these three writers, in such a way as to offer a qualified defence of the approach to it exemplified by Pearce *et al.* (1989): the qualification, which is not an insignificant one, though, is to shift the focus onto interests as opposed to preferences in the evaluation of environmental goods. In the subsequent section, I shall also spell out the significance of this shift.

Accepting with Sagoff and O'Neill that individual preferences are an inadequate basis for environmental decision-making does not mean they can legitimately be ignored. Preferences articulate all sorts of interests and values (as Keat argues against Sagoff). The question then is how to deal with them. If the rationality of rational self-interest is paradigmatically that of market behaviour, then the question can also be posed in terms of market boundaries: the pursuit of rational self-interest would be legitimate where markets are, and illegitimate as a basis for valuing goods whose distribution should not be left to markets. The critique provided by Sagoff and O'Neill, however, seems to deny any legitimacy at all to interests manifest in market behaviour when it comes to making environmental decisions. For this reason, both of their positions are problematic.

Sagoff's position is that market-based valuations are inappropriate for *any* social goods. This is clear from his radical separation of consumers' preferences from citizens' values. Yet while he maintains that environmental decisions – like other social decisions – should not be made on the basis of consumer preferences, he leaves consumerism unchallenged in its sphere. To this it can be objected that: (a) allowing consumerism at all is a political decision; (b) consumerism itself can have adverse environmental effects; and (c) the system of production and exchange underpinning consumerism can have adverse social effects. His complacency about the separation of economic and sociopolitical spheres matches his complacency about accepted values, and a more radical critique of consumerism and its capitalist premises seems appropriate.

O'Neill appears to be more consistent on this score, seeing processes of commodification themselves as the root of environmental as well as social problems. Yet this view is also the source of problems identified by Keat, who argues that while O'Neill is officially committed to a 'market boundaries' argument, whose aim is to 'keep markets in their proper place', his position is actually liable to collapse into a total rejection of the market, since his reasons for rejecting the extension of the market to the environment would, if generalized, imply that the market was a wholly inappropriate institution in any context of application at all: if markets are blind to the meanings of social goods, they should have no role in decisions about the provision of those goods. To prevent the position advanced from collapsing into a total rejection of markets, one would have to show there was something special about environmental decisions that made reason-blindness inappropriate for them but not necessarily for other cases. For instance, if an acceptable justification of reason-blindness is that it allows individuals to be the best judges of their own interests, this justification might be deemed not to apply to environmental goods, on the grounds that protecting these might not be in humans' immediate best interests, and that human individuals may not be the best judges of what is best for the environment. However, O'Neill cannot adopt this approach, Keat points out, because he does not appear to entertain the idea of any 'good' which is independent of humans' preferences (albeit the considered preferences revealed through public discussion about ends). If O'Neill does not see this as a problem, Keat suggests, it is presumably because he assumes that enlightened human self-interest will coincide with what is good for the environment in that living in a right relationship with the environment is itself a central and constitutive feature of human flourishing.

Now it seems to me that the assumption imputed to O'Neill is essentially correct: for the environment, qua environment, is precisely what it is in humans' enlightened self-interest to preserve (albeit with some qualifications about the nature of enlightenment of self-interest which I shall come to in section 5). Yet Keat claims that O'Neill is mistakenly anthropocentric on this score and that the value attributed to the environment cannot consist wholly in the part it plays in inter-human relationships. In saying this, though, Keat appears to be gesturing to the possibility of environmental values which are independent not only of rational self-interest or market values, but also of enlightened interests in social goods. This suggestion is made more explicit in Keat's discussion of Sagoff, where he argues that the latter fails to distinguish two different non-economistic ways of valuing the environment. On the one hand, a natural item like an unpolluted river, for example, can be valued for the contribution it makes to human individuals' own well-being, for instance through the opportunities it offers them for aesthetic enjoyment (that is what I would call 'enlightened self-interest'); on the other hand it could be held to have some value over and above any such contribution to humans' own well-being – by either contributing to the well-being of other humans or by being valuable 'intrinsically', or 'nonanthropocentrically' (Keat, 1994: 337). In similar vein, Keat says that what is missing in O'Neill is some notion of a 'right relationship with the environment' governed by 'some equivalent of the concern for the other person' that is characteristic of good human relationships (Keat, 1997: 140–1). Although he does not really flesh out what this might be, the suggestion seems to be, and it is reinforced by his critical emphasis on O'Neill's 'anthropocentrism', that it is 'intrinsic value of nature'. But if this is the case, then Keat would be inviting us to endorse what I have called the 'two dogmas of ecologism'. I therefore do not think the position he adverts to is a tenable one, for the reasons spelt out above in chapters 2 and 3.[5]

So if there are specifically environmentalist grounds for opposing markets, as all the authors under discussion agree, this is not because there are environmental grounds that are not also grounds of enlightened self-interest, but because there are specifically environmental *social* goods. On the view I would wish to defend, all environmental goods, qua environmental, are social goods. (It is of course necessary to distinguish environmental from interspecies concerns and recognize that we are only dealing with the former here.) All social goods are goods because they satisfy human interests; and because all social goods can be related, directly or indirectly, to human interests, all environmental values correlate in some way to human interests. An advantage for political theory in adopting this view is that, as social goods, environmental goods can be subject to principles of just distribution. This does not preclude the possibility that, like some other social goods, some environmental values might appropriately be left to market-based principles of valuation or distribution. The question is which and when.

If one is to establish criteria for establishing market boundaries for environmental and other social goods, I shall suggest, it is necessary to distinguish legitimate interests from mere preferences. But an account of legitimate interests is what is missing from the three authors under discussion, who are rather too chary to talk about the constructive role of interests at all.

4   Defining interests as distinct from preferences

The need to appreciate the distinctive role of interests becomes clear from the inconclusive outcome of Keat's criticism of Sagoff's preference–value dichotomy. Sagoff quite reasonably points out that not all preferences can claim the sort of legitimacy necessary to make respect for, or protection of, them mandatory. But, as Keat in turn points out, there is also no reason to treat preferences as automatically illegitimate, to set them aside as 'mere' preferences, in the sense of being based on poor or irrational judgements. For all one knows, he says, 'what neo-classical theorists represent as "mere preferences" might in fact be a good deal better than these terms would normally imply' (Keat, 1994: 346). But what does Keat mean here by 'better'? He presumably means something like preferences that 'are less narrowly self-interested'; or 'have a broader claim of legitimacy to their satisfaction'; or 'have a more worthy object'. Yet in each case one would be pointing to a *value* which can be contrasted, as it is by Sagoff, with the mere fact that it is someone's preferred value. Thus I think we can and should retain the idea of 'mere preferences', both to allow for the use that economists and rational choice theorists make of it, and also to allow for the objections, made by Sagoff and others, to its use in inappropriate contexts. To accommodate Keat's point about more laudable preferences, I shall suggest, it is necessary first to be clear about the difference between preferences and interests, and then see how different kinds of preference relate to different kinds of interest.

Accordingly, I aim to provide conceptual underpinning for the intuition that while a rational and reasonable citizen might be expected to understand why her mere preferences need carry no automatic weight in decision-making processes, as a general principle, when it comes to her interests, she could in turn expect at least a specific reason to be given. Central to my argument is the claim that while preferences – of any kind – do not have the sort of legitimacy necessary to make respect for or protection of them mandatory, interests *do* have this sort of legitimacy. To avoid any misunderstanding, though, let me emphasize that to say interests have the kind of legitimacy necessary to warrant respect for them is not to say it is also sufficient. Or, to put the point more precisely, and in terms I will in due course further explain, interests have a necessary claim to be *recognized*, but not necessarily *satisfied*. In what follows I shall elaborate on the contrast between preferences and interests, show how they are related, and how we can accommodate preferences of a more 'laudable' kind.

In everyday discourse it is clear that in claiming or ascribing an interest one is doing something different from stating a preference. A first difference is that one can have a preference for something one knows is not in one's interest – for example, smoking. The feature of interests this example highlights is that, unlike preferences, they have a necessary connection to one's good. The connection between one's good and preferences, by contrast, is contingent: for while what one prefers may most typically be what one believes to be one's good,[6] nevertheless, as is standardly noted, one can also have preferences that appear to be altruistic, masochistic or in some way ill-formed or misguided. So the first feature interests necessarily have, and preferences do not, is captured by saying that statements about A's interest in relation to X are not true independently of facts about whether the outcome of X is good in some way or other for A. Hence, A has an interest in X (where X is, say, a state of affairs or a policy to bring them about) when X is in some sense *good* for A.

However, the fact that X is good for A is not sufficient to establish that A has an *interest* in X. This is because, for one thing, while X might be good for A, an alternative – say, policy Y – may be better, so that it is in A's interest that Y be implemented rather than X. In this respect, an interest is like a preference, but there is another respect in which it is not: for the good to take the form of an interest it must be the basis for a potential claim to acknowledgement by others, and for such a claim to be meaningful, there must be some action/practice/proposal/ policy, actual or proposed, which affects (or threatens or promises to affect) that good for better or worse. In other words, the ascription of interests becomes meaningful just when one's good is 'at stake', that is, when it is liable to be advanced or thwarted by some action or proposed action of another,[7] when the fulfilment of one's good is set in some sort of competition with goods of others. In the ascription of an interest there is thus an element of assertion which includes a normative claim that the good merits protection or promotion. In this respect interests differ from preferences, since statements of preferences do not make any necessary reference to goods of others, and do not in themselves have this implicit normative force.

Still, while it is such a context that makes ascriptions of interests meaningful, and reveals that an interest embodies a normative claim, the very fact that the context is a 'competitive' one indicates that not all such normative claims can or should be redeemed (or, in the context, be considered justified or legitimate). For the interest to have sufficient normative force to warrant acting on, there must be some reason why it should have weight in the considerations of the actor(s) carrying out (or proposing) the practice or policy that may affect it. In this sense, claims of interest stand in need of, and are capable of, intersubjective verification.[8]

To explain what I mean by this it is helpful first to draw a distinction between the recognition and the satisfaction of a claim, which relates to two different types of interest. This is the distinction between saying, on the one hand, that A has an interest in – say – the outcome of a policy, because, whatever the outcome may be, A is liable to be affected by it, and, on the other, saying that A has an interest in the implementation of specific policy X, or that 'A's interests *are served by* policy X'.[9] The former interest I shall call a general interest, the latter a special interest.

The intersubjective verification of the existence of a general interest takes the form of recognition, and that only; a general interest is not the sort of interest that can be satisfied. Special interests, by contrast, can be satisfied, but they need not be unless their claim to satisfaction is independently validated.

Now the idea of a general interest has an importance that is evident in legal contexts: in deciding whose legal claims should have a hearing, or should be admissible, a general interest has to be established; once this is done, the merits of special claims can be assessed. Going beyond a specifically legal context we can say, accordingly, that the recognition of a general interest implies a prima facie assumption that the corresponding special interests do have some claim to satisfaction; whenever there is at least one general interest, then the special interests of at least one interest bearer should be satisfied. This is the sense in which I said interests necessarily have a kind of legitimacy. By contrast, there is no conceptual impossibility in imagining a world full of preferences, none of which are granted any legitimate claim to satisfaction.

So if the question then is what considerations give weight to the claim to satisfaction of (special) interests, the answer, given that (general) interests are established on the basis that the good of their bearer stands to be affected, is that the weight of the claim will be determined by the weight of those effects. In assessing effects on people's goods, we come very close to adopting a discourse of needs. Indeed, insofar as interests, unlike preferences, have a necessary relation to what is good for one, they do resemble needs.[10] They are similar in that statements about them have some objectivity and are in principle corrigible, where preferences are purely subjective and sincere statements of them are incorrigible.[11] Nevertheless, interests are also more subjective than needs: a person needs nutrition, but suppose the only nutrition available is a beef steak, and the person is a vegetarian, perhaps for religious reasons, then in such circumstances, her interest may be to preserve the integrity of her lifestyle and beliefs rather than fuel her body; or suppose a Jehovah's Witness will die unless given the blood transfusion which his body needs but his religion proscribes. If an individual in such a situation chooses death rather than defection from their beliefs, would we want to say they are mistaken about their interests? I think not: for in this sense their beliefs about their interests are like statements about preferences. They are incorrigible; for there is no dispute about the facts of bodily needs, and yet these facts have no influence on judgement about where their interests lie.

Interests thus appear to have features of both needs and preferences. So can their distinctiveness be captured more exactly? I have suggested that the interests of the Jehovah's Witness would not be served by being given a blood transfusion, and I feel confident in this negative assertion; however, I am not confident that I would want to say, in the affirmative, that the Jehovah's Witness's interests *are* served by being allowed not to have a transfusion. I feel a resistance to saying this because there is a connotation of the term 'interests' which strikes me as out of place here; it is a connotation that comes from seeing rational self-interest as the paradigm of an interest.

The standard sort of case where rational self-interest is at issue can be characterized thus: A has a (special) interest in (for instance, a policy) X when A stands to benefit (or maybe in some contexts just not to lose) from the outcome of its implementation; A has an interest in not-X when she stands to be harmed by (or incur costs from) X. In the standard case, then, the interest is arrived at by a cost–benefit calculation of a rational agent; his interests can be determined, quite straightforwardly, by identifying the best means to achieve his (pre-given) ends. But this assumes – as economists feel they have to assume – that individuals have just one set of ends, or at least that their ends can be subsumed within one parameter. However, as I argued in the previous chapter, any rational being necessarily has a range of interests including interests in bodily integrity and integrity of beliefs and lifestyle. When these conflict, there is no possible decision that fully captures their interests as a whole.

Hence, returning the case of the Jehovah's Witness, we can accept the negative proposition – that it is not in his interest to have the transfusion – while refusing the apparent affirmative corollary that it is in his interests not to have it. What he has an interest in is preserving the integrity of his religious lifestyle and belief; and when this conflicts with interests associated with bodily integrity he gives the former interest priority. This does not mean that it is in his interest, any more than it would be in anyone else's, to have to concede any aspect of his integrity if it could be avoided. When conceding one aspect of it becomes unavoidable, though, he prefers to preserve his religious rather than his bodily integrity.

Interestingly, then, what is decisive here is a preference as opposed to an interest. Note, though, that this is not a preference in the economist's technical sense: in saying one prefers to die rather than compromise one's values, one is expressing something significantly different from a 'mere preference'. The difference can also be illustrated by a type of case more clearly relevant to our concerns, such as, for instance, where A has an interest in the outcome of policy X (that is implementing policy X serves her interests), because it would directly benefit her, but prefers that policy X not be chosen; this occurs, for instance, when she takes account of considerations other than her rational self-interest and prefers to support policies relating to social goods whose provision is not in her individual rational self-interest. This can happen because rational self-interest is not the only kind of interest a rational agent might have. So while, in casual speech, we may say that someone prefers death to dishonour, or prefers to save lives rather than make money, or prefers to save wild habitats rather than exploit them for profit, such preferences are more aptly expressed in the language of 'commitment'.[12]

Commitments are distinguishable from preferences in that they are more deeply ingrained, in resilience and in temporal extension: commitments imply patterns of behaviour where preferences usually imply discrete actions; 'commitment' (in stemming from narrative identity (cf. chapter 4)) necessarily implies commitment *to the future*, whereas preferences do not necessarily operate beyond the here and now – in other words, commitment says 'not just I happen to prefer X now, but I have such good reasons for preferring X now that only very strong ones would get me to change my mind about it in the future'. Nevertheless, commitments are just as subjective as preferences – otherwise they would not be commitments at all (merely impulses that the agent has no investment in) – and they can be contrasted with interests in the same way. Hence, with commitments as with preferences, one is conscious of wanting it to be the case that, say, X be realized, whereas one can have interests without being conscious of wanting their corresponding object; and, again in contrast to interests, statements of both preferences and commitments are incorrigible. Furthermore, I would add, neither preferences *nor* commitments have the qualification for legitimacy that interests do – which is just as well, perhaps, given that commitments can sometimes be fanatical.

Hence the conceptual structure which contrasts preferences – laudable and otherwise – with interests is not undermined: preferences are more subjective than interests at whatever level of objectivity of interests we are dealing with; but when and insofar as one prefers to follow enlightened interests rather than rational self-interest, the latter ceases to be operative as an interest in the sense of being a decisive motivation. Nor does the subsumption of commitments under the general category of preference threaten my premise that all choices are ultimately motivated by interests, for the commitments that provide the motivation for allowing more enlightened interests to override rational self-interest are themselves motivated by the more fundamental interest, as described in the previous chapter, in integrity.

5   Ways of enlightening self-interest

It is appropriate to distinguish between two dimensions in which self-interest can be enlightened: on the one hand, in that of one's personal development; on the other, in that of one's social relations. On the basis of that distinction we can then pose the question of the relation between the enlightening of self-interest and concern for the good of nonhumans.

1   Enlightened self-interest considered as an individual's interest in self-development generally is part of an essentially *elevated* conception of one's own individual interests. It is arrived at by reflecting that one's immediate interests are not the only interests one has. It is a fact that many humans value aspects of flourishing – such as cultural, aesthetic, spiritual and so on – over and above the values associated with their economic interests narrowly understood; and an appreciation of 'nature' or natural beauty, harmony or integrity can be of this kind. Pursuit of 'higher' interests, though, is in principle consistent with extreme individualism: an individual aesthete, for instance, while highly refined in personal taste, need nevertheless own no interest at all in the well-being of other humans or nonhumans.
2   Enlightened interests of the second type, by contrast, include a social dimension. An individual who recognizes her interdependence with others will acknowledge an interest in social cooperation: this, in itself, can be arrived at on the basis of rational self-interest; this becomes 'enlightened' when the interest in cooperation is understood to entail an interest in social *justice*. This can be seen as a development beyond (1) inasmuch as one also recognizes that even purely personal capacities cannot be fully developed in isolation from others.

A point which is of some significance for my overall argument is that an interest in self-respect, as well as in integrity, entails both types of enlightened interests: (1) is necessary because it is the development of those capacities which make the self worthy of respect; (2) is necessary as a precondition of potential self-respect because one cannot even be a 'self' on one's own, and relations of reciprocity are necessary for *actual* recognition.

With these considerations in mind I turn to the question of whether, and if so how, it would be appropriate to think of a concern with the goods of nonhumans 'for their own sake' as an enlightened interest. To the extent that such concern can be considered as enlightened, it can be viewed either as a further enlightenment beyond the social perspective (2) or as part of the personal development (1). On the former understanding of them, such concerns would represent an extension of the sort of enlightenment that carries an individual from narrow self-interest to a wider social interest in solidarity to an even wider interest in solidarity with nonhumans; on the latter understanding, however, they could be subsumed under enlightened interests of type (1), with an appreciation of natural phenomena being essentially on a par with aesthetic sensibility. On the former understanding, these interests would represent a normative 'advance' over interests of type (2); on the latter understanding they would not.

The question of which understanding is appropriate raises an important issue, and is what is at stake in my worries about Keat's more radical 'anti-anthropocentric' critique of O'Neill. The issue is how legitimate are claims to be allowed to enjoy 'higher' interests (even in nature) when other humans suffer from inadequate fulfilment of 'lower', economic, ones? After all, it is not the poor and hungry who are pressing for the preservation of wilderness, and so on; those who press for values of wilderness cannot consistently press for this *against* the poor and hungry. If, on the other hand, concern for nonhumans represents a further extension of ethical concern in the direction away from narrow self-interest towards greater solicitude for all the other beings with whom we share the world, then the normative picture looks different. To conceptualize this difference, I therefore believe, we should bring to bear my earlier distinction between the indiscriminate 'critique of anthropocentrism' and the more justified critique of speciesism and human chauvinism. This distinction, which in turn is based on the basic ecological distinction between organism and environment, involves recognizing the difference between environmental goods as such and the goods of nonhuman beings – who also have an environment.

So, regarding interests in *environmental* goods per se, my argument is that there is a robust line that one can and should take, namely this: if, after appropriate deliberations, citizens decide they have generalizable interests in preserving items attributed such values as existence value, aesthetic value and so on, then fine; if they do not, then this is also fine. To see why it is fair enough one need only look from the other side – if people have vital economic interests, what other humans have a right to try to deny these? Whether or not one shares my view, as against Keat, that 'existence value' *is* what 'anti-anthropocentrists' want, it is right that whatever it is they want should be argued for in the face of other interests.

However, when what is at stake are interests of nonhuman beings – as opposed to putative 'noninterests' (or 'disinterested' values) – of (some) human beings, robustness of argument can be applied in quite a different direction. To the extent that such interests are admitted, then they have a prima facie claim to respect, and on the same grounds that human interests do. To make and defend this argument, though, in view of problems of speaking about interests of nonhumans at all, let alone of these being interests for humans as well, is the challenge of the next chapter.

Conclusion

In this chapter I have sought to show that the relation of human interests to ecological values is not a simple one, and that differentiating between types of interest and types of ecological values makes possible a constructive approach to the political furtherance of the latter, and makes for a more judicious assessment of policy options than is available either by taking an uncritical view of the 'sovereignty' of 'consumer' attitudes to environmental goods or engaging in an overly swingeing critique of market-based evaluations. The organizing distinction between rational self-interest and enlightened self-interest is intended to indicate a framework within which the relative legitimacy of different interest claims might be assessed. It was noted that in practice such assessment is most appropriately carried out in discursive fora, by participants, and from the standpoint of citizens; but certain general conclusions can – and I think must – be drawn from the standpoint of theory too.

In environmental policy-making, there is a role for the harnessing of rational self-interest in various market-based measures. Indeed, in practical terms, these are likely to remain among the most significant measures for the foreseeable future. Because rational self-interest involves selecting suitable means for given ends, it is neutral with respect to ends, and therefore has no inherent connection to any particular substantive value; it is not inherently either pro- or anti-ecological. Even as manifest in market behaviour, the pursuit of rational self-interest is not necessarily anti-ecological. As we have noted, there is a role for the harnessing of rational self-interest in the evaluation of environmental goods, and, correspondingly, a role for market-based approaches, both contingent valuation and even free market environmentalism. But this role has to be carefully delimited, since the critique of basing environmental values on individual preferences is also well-taken. Calculations of rational self-interest, which essentially involve the choice of appropriate means to given ends, are liable to seem more or less objectionable or problematic (from certain points of view) depending on the ends in question. In the evaluation of these ends, deliberative procedures are appropriate. These can yield more enlightened conceptions of people's interests and thus underpin environmental policies that go beyond the constraints of market-oriented interests.

Nevertheless, conflicts of interest are not straightforwardly between economic and environmental values, or between economic and political valuations. Few if any environmental interests can be neatly separated off from economic ones, especially when the 'economic' is understood less chrematistically than in conventional, non-environmental, economics.[13] It is not possible neatly to divide environmental goods or bads into those that affect people as citizens and those that affect them as consumers (or producers or exchangers). Apart from environmental issues that affect people's material welfare (resource issues), there are others that affect people's physical well-being and health; some affect their lifestyle (and psychological well-being) in other material ways (such as traffic congestion or high stress levels); some affect their spiritual well-being; others relate to (pure, as opposed to productive-technique orientated) scientific interests, or to people's cultural or aesthetic enjoyment. Many environmental issues will bear on more than one of these categories, and perhaps on others besides.

Therefore environmental issues are always liable to involve conflicts of interest and trade-offs, of which there are different types. Some issues involve trade-offs for an individual, and the limitation of preference-aggregating approaches is that they tend to focus only on these. Others involve trade-offs between different individuals or groups which may be competing either for access to a particular type of good, or for the provision of one type of good as opposed to another: the former clearly raise questions of distributive justice as well as allocative efficiency; the latter type of competition, likewise, can sometimes be left to markets, free or regulated, but should not always be. In relation to both, then, the question of what should be left to the market, and what not, is a political decision, and one involving considerations of justice: not only about the distribution of goods, but also about distribution of entitlements to decide what *count* as goods.

A quite separate issue, though, is that some parties with intelligibly attributable 'interests' cannot directly compete in market valuations or participate in discursive fora: this is the case with future generations of humans, and with nonhumans. Regarding future generations, the question hinges on relative benefits between present and future humans, and despite the various moral complications arising when dealing with non-existent but potentially existing people, this can nevertheless be addressed as a question of distributive justice. A different matter, however, is whether nonhuman interests can or should be addressed as a question of justice, since here the complication of identifying bearers of interests is of a different sort: for while we may suppose that whatever claims they do have, and whatever their actual compositions, future generations of humans would have interests – and prima facie rights – which are essentially the same as currently living humans, this, however, cannot simply be assumed to be the case with nonhumans, and in fact needs arguing. Hence a different sort of question arises in their case. It is to this that I now turn.

6

Human Self-Respect and Respect for Nonhumans

Introduction

The basic claim of this chapter is that if humans have an interest in respecting themselves and one another as humans, then they have no reason to withhold respect from (at least some significant classes of) nonhuman beings. This argument runs counter to the view that the reasons humans respect one another are bound up with facts about what it is to be a human being as opposed to any other kind of being. That view, which may be characterized as 'exclusive humanism', holds that it is some of the characteristics that set humans off from other beings which make respect for humans appropriate. Various characteristics can be and have been appealed to by various thinkers, but those which have a sufficiently direct connection with features of moral respect to be nonarbitrarily singled out can be grouped under the rough heading of 'rational autonomous moral agency'. I do not wish to challenge the view that these characteristics may be sufficient to warrant respect for humans who possess them, but I do want to challenge the view that they are necessary to warrant respect for a human; and if this challenge succeeds, the onus is then on the exclusive humanist to bring forward further reasons why respect for other beings should be ruled out.

My argument that respect is not peculiarly due to rational autonomous moral agents, proceeds in three stages, focusing on agency, rational freedom and moral accountability, respectively, as criteria of worthiness of respect.

Firstly, then, I show, there is no reason to restrict respect to moral agents as opposed to moral patients. In doing so, I also amplify the meaning of the term respect, for this is sometimes contrasted with care as a different type of moral consideration. The relevance of the distinction is manifest in the claim that while care may be possible in relation to nonrational beings, respect is not; and this is significant because only the latter, and not the former, has the form of obligation; and so only this is moral consideration in a full sense. However, I problematize this distinction, clarifying that a specific – and formal – sort of respect only is narrowly restricted to relations between persons, considered as moral agents, but that this formal respect is not wholehearted enough in relation to humans anyway. The reason why respect in a narrow sense is obligatory for agents in relation to one another is that *assent* to norms is required; but just because nonrational beings might not (all or always) be able to show assent as such, this does not mean that their responses (even just in somatic terms) can therefore be disregarded by agents. Other reasons would have to be given to explain why respect is not due to any being that has a good.

In the second section I go on to examine the view that there is a specific sort of respect that is only possible in relation to rational beings, questioning whether rational freedom is not relevantly different from other sorts of freedom which nonrational beings can also enjoy. Reasons for respecting *rational* capacities derive from *reverence* for rational nature. The question then becomes why one should have reverence for rational nature in view of the possibility that reverence could just as well or instead be appropriate for the natural order of things. When this question is posed, the restriction of reverence to rational agency looks like a rationalistic prejudice, since on many views of the natural order of things, rational agency is just one part of it. If one takes the latter sort of view, then one has reason to respect not just agents, but natural beings as such. I advocate such a view.

An implication of this, though, is that subjective human freedom may seem to be subsumed under an objective view of natural causation; a political implication of this is that with appropriate knowledge of the causality of others' actions, they may be treated as 'objects of policy' rather than as morally accountable agents. However, in the third section, I seek to show that the genuine worry here can be dealt with by admitting that one can never be assured of the adequacy of one's knowledge of others' motivations, and, accordingly, I argue that the attribution of moral accountability is not necessary for respect in the requisite sense.

I conclude, therefore, that humans have no good reason to withhold respect from nonhuman beings: and this issues in a prima facie obligation to work out what respecting them means in practice. If humans respect one another as rational moral agents, then fulfilling the demands of this mutual self-respect requires them to view rational moral agency as a source of responsibility in relation to their cohabitants on this earth, rather than as a mere privilege.

1 Respect is not due solely to moral agents

One clear difference between humans and nonhumans, and perhaps the only difference with real moral implications that need not be at all controversial, is that only humans are the addressees of the imperatives of human ethics.[1] Put in other terminology, only humans can be moral *agents*. In this respect, at least, there is reason to think that moral consideration for humans – or, more precisely, for one's fellow moral agents – will have a different character from that appropriate and possible in relation to nonagents. I shall attempt to specify what this does and does not imply with regard to ethical relations between humans and nonhumans.

In giving or showing moral consideration for another, one considers how one's action will affect them and takes one's estimate of the effects as reasons telling for or against the action. The other can be considered in two contrasting ways, though, as a 'patient' or as an 'agent'. As a patient, the other simply benefits or suffers from the effects of one's action; one's consideration of the patient is completed once one has assessed the likely benefits or suffering. (Of course, further questions may warrant consideration, such as whether the suffering/benefit is warranted or justifiable, but this is consideration of one's moral principles, their grounds, and so on, not of the patient.) Regarding the other as agent, though, consideration is more complex. As an embodied being, capable of suffering and benefiting, the agent is also a patient; as an agent, though, she acts, reacts, and in general may have relations of reciprocity with oneself, as well as with other agents. In most normal human interactions, the other is considered from both points of view, but the difference between the types of consideration can be important, especially when it comes to assessing the moral claims on us of nonagents.

The significance of the patient–agent distinction comes to the fore when we ask what it means to consider the other *'for their own sake'*. Considering the other purely as patient, this means no more or less than considering what, in one's own estimate, is likely to do them more good than harm. Considering the other as agent, however, on most versions of humanistic ethics, one must also – and sometimes perhaps instead – have regard to what *they* believe will do them good or harm;

and not only that, since one must also have regard to what they will; and, as agents, what they will may be independent of what does them personal good or harm.

A related distinction can be drawn between two types of consideration – between what I shall call subjectively motivated moral consideration and objectively motivated moral consideration. In the former case, one is motivated by a subjective disposition to 'care' about the good of the other; in the latter case, regardless of one's disposition, one recognizes an objective obligation to act in a way that manifests due regard for the other – the very notion of '*due*' regard making implicit reference to a notion of the right which one recognizes as objectively morally binding on one, whatever one's subjective disposition in regard to the being itself. Hence there is a well-established philosophical view which holds that relations between humans and nonhumans are a matter of compassion as distinct from morality in a strict sense,[2] while relations of respect hold only between agents; or, in the terminology I have chosen to adopt (as more directly related to recent debates in political theory), as a matter of care as opposed to justice (or obligation or rights).[3] I shall examine the implications of this contrast and go on to problematize it, on the grounds that both 'care' and 'due regard' capture something of what we normally mean by 'respect', and that therefore there are reasons to think that respect includes both care *and* justice.

Reasons for care for nonhumans

It would be uncontroversial to assert the possibility of some humans caring about some nonhumans, for it is just that: on the one hand, a possibility, and, on the other, one which does not necessarily imply generalizability to more than some nonhumans. Moreover, such care is not thought of as an obligation. Thus if we are to ask for reasons why one should care about nonhumans, then in a sense no answer can be given: that is, if care is understood as a disposition which one either has or does not have then one cannot be *obliged* to care. One can of course be obliged to show certain kinds of consideration in one's actions; and one can be obliged to engage in 'caring behaviour' (even when one lacks a subjective disposition to care): but precisely because they are obligations they are instances of the objective motivation that I am contrasting with the subjective motivation distinctive of care. Still, care can be inculcated – it can be favoured and it can be hampered. So the question 'Why should one care . . .?' could be understood as asking not after direct obligations, but after reasons why one might think it a good idea to inculcate, favour or develop that disposition rather than not. Certainly, if care is thought of simply in terms of feelings of compassion, it might not be wholly amenable to explanation in terms of reasons at all, but there are also aspects of care that can be explained in terms of interests.

Thus one reason why one should care about a nonhuman would be that so doing contributed somehow to the efficacy of the care one is already disposed to in relation to some other humans, or perhaps even just oneself. By developing this line of thought one comes to a view which many have found intuitively plausible – namely, that humans in general have an interest in developing kindly attitudes towards nonhuman creatures because if they are harsh or cruel in their dealings with them they are likely to be harsh or cruel in their dealings with humans too. The view was articulated by Kant: 'If [a man] is not to stifle his human feelings, he must practise kindness towards animals, for he who is cruel to animals becomes hard also in his treatment of men. . . . Tender feelings towards dumb animals develop humane feelings towards mankind' (Kant, 1963: 240–1). On this view, then, we owe it to ourselves and to other humans to show kindness towards nonhumans.

However, this line of argument can be criticized as too weak for establishing a general interest in the protection of goods of nonhumans, and in two respects: it is weakly motivated, and it is weak in what it obligates to. Firstly, regarding its motivational force, it rests on challengeable evidence: it would likely not be hard to find counterexamples to the claim that being cruel to animals makes people cruel to other people, or that being humane in relation to nonhumans makes someone more 'human' in their dealings with others. The argument appears to rest on a contingent psychological generalization that may simply not be true, or whose truth may at any rate be equivocal. Admitting even exceptions somewhat undermines the claim. For even if there were evidence that being *habitually* cruel to animals leads to treating humans badly, it would seem to leave insufficient reason for avoiding *occasional* ill-treatment of them (cf. Regan, 1988: 182–3). Thus the contingency regarding motivations parallels the optionality of moral principle, which is the second main criticism, concerning the kind of consideration for nonhumans that it is even *claimed* to provide: in supposing that caring concern for humans flows over to nonhumans, it nevertheless appears to offer no independent reasons for concern for nonhumans. Nonhumans may enjoy consideration, if humans happen to be so motivated, psychologically or morally, but this is more a question of humans' largesse than moral obligation in any firmer sense: thus while humans may have a good reason to care about nonhumans, where doing otherwise would somehow be humanly debasing, this stops short of being an obligation to give moral consideration to nonhumans regardless of effects on humans; it stops short, in other words, of requiring unconditional *respect* for them.

So while the claim that it is in humans' enlightened self-interest generally to avoid inflicting unnecessary harm on other beings is certainly not nothing, I wish to put forward the stronger argument that humans not only have contingent reasons to care about nonhumans, but also necessary reasons to respect them. Accordingly, in the next two subsections I shall discuss the two problems just outlined: I shall first explain why for practical purposes care is included in respect, and therefore can appear as part of an obligation, rather than as something supererogatory; I shall then seek to identify a motivating interest in recognizing such obligations.

Respect is for persons only?

The concept of respect is a complex one; but I take it that the general idea refers to a kind of attitude that one can adopt towards others when one views them as in relevant ways equal to, and independent like, oneself; similarly, as was earlier noted, self-respect is appropriate when one views oneself as equal to but independent of the others one respects.

The relevance of equality and independence in the attitude of respect can be highlighted by considering contrasting ways one might regard others: on the one hand, it can be contrasted with an attitude of awe or reverence, for this is an attitude one adopts towards another being to whom one does not presume to relate as an equal; on the other hand, it can be contrasted with an attitude of care or solicitude, in which, while not necessarily considering the other 'inferior', one nevertheless takes them to be less than fully independent, and therefore not equal in this particular regard.[4] Respect, then, is essentially an appropriate way of regarding other independent equals when relations among those equals are to be well-ordered.

If this is how respect is to be understood, then it is plain to see why some argue that while *care* for nonhumans may be appropriate, or even that *reverence* for the order of nature as a whole may be, *respect* is so peculiarly appropriate to relations between persons – since only of persons can independence and equality in the morally relevant sense be predicated – that it is simply not an attitude or relation that is genuinely possible between humans and nonhuman beings. This thought was articulated by Kant: 'Respect always applies to persons only, never to things. The latter can awaken inclinations, and even love if they are animals (horses, dogs, etc.), or fear, as do the sea, a volcano, or a beast of prey; but they never arouse respect.' (Kant, 1993: 80)[5]

Kant's verdict about the impossibility of respect for nonhumans depends on a rigid distinction between two mutually exclusive classes of beings – namely, persons and things. This distinction, borrowed from Roman law, is invoked in legal or ethical contexts to decide who or what counts as the kind of being that can have rights or be imputed obligations. An important application of it concerns the regulation of property relations: persons own; things are owned. Clearly, it is very important that humans not be considered as things, as entities that can be another's property or used simply as means to others' ends. Yet it is not so clear that prohibitions on certain kinds of treatment of human beings depend on their personhood. Indeed, it has to be noted that, on the one hand, not all humans have personhood in the requisite sense, since children and people with impaired faculties, for instance, do not; on the other hand, for legal purposes at least, entities other than human beings, like business corporations, for instance, can be accorded personhood. What is morally relevant in the distinction, for Kant, is that respect is due to persons only, because persons alone are defined as rational agents.

There is a perfectly cogent sense in which relations of respect are possible only between rational agents. What is necessary for respect, in this sense, is that there be a certain interchangeability of perspectives, a certain parity, symmetry or potential reciprocity, in the relation between one agent and another. In respecting the other, I, as an agent, consider how they would be affected by my action not only objectively (as a patient), but subjectively (as another agent); I consider not only how it affects their good, but also how they perceive it; and this involves considering what they would *will* that I should do. This thought is captured in Kant's idea of the universalizing of maxims which constitutes his categorical imperative. The right action is one that would in principle be decided upon by either of us. But the class of beings that can be considered in this way is limited to those with rational agency. The reason for this limitation can straightforwardly be illustrated by reference to the motto 'do as you would be done by': this injunction has purchase in relation to other beings who *could* do as I am considering doing; it does not have purchase in relation to beings who cannot; and since what I am doing, or at least part of what I am already doing is, *ex hypothesi,* deliberating as an autonomous rational moral agent, the whole consideration is only possible in relation to other agents.

By contrast, if I have to decide and act on the basis of an essentially objective view of the other's good, this may be to care for them, but it is not to respect them, in the above sense, because it cannot be. Thus, for instance, I may decide to act 'in their best interests' even though there is, in principle, no way of their assenting to my estimate of what *is* their best interest. In caring, the possibility of paternalism, misguidedness, and therefore also oppression, can never be entirely ruled out; and these are incompatible with respect in the narrow sense. In this view, then, care and respect are quite distinct, and, in some ways, mutually exclusive, attitudes. If I act out of care for the other, this is something other than respect.

But I shall argue for a more integrated view of care and respect, as well as of reverence, one which overcomes anthropocentrism in the (cosmological) sense I have argued it needs overcoming. I acknowledge that there is a sense in which respect is peculiarly relevant to persons, or rational agents; care to creatures (living nonrational beings); and reverence for the natural order of which we all (all beings) are part. But I shall argue that there is another, more appropriate, sense of respect which also includes care and reverence.

To show why respect for persons might not be due purely to their rational agency it is helpful to draw some distinctions. The first is between what one might call 'contemplative' and 'active' respect: if I hold a particular person in high regard, but actually never come to have any dealings with them, it seems appropriate to say I respect them, but only, so to speak, in contemplation, and this need not have any direct bearing on my actions;[6] active respect, by contrast, is something I show in my actions, and it is manifest when I show the other due regard. Now in contemplative respect my attitude may well tip over into something closer to reverence: it came quite naturally to me to describe contemplative respect for someone as holding them in *high* regard. There is something supererogatory here: it is as if, should I meet them, I would show not only active respect but something like deference. This is perhaps because something about them has singled them out for my attention, while respect is something I hold to be due, and in like measure, to anyone, regardless of their qualities or accomplishments, as something that 'goes without saying'. Conversely, of a person with whom I have direct contact, merely to contemplate respect for them, without acting on it, would not be to respect them. The distinctive features of respect I wish to focus on, therefore, are those of active respect only.

Now in the most relevant sense of active respect, what it means is that when considering how to act I take into account the likely effects on the other as reasons telling for or against the various proposals for action I am considering. An interesting feature of active respect, though, which is the converse of what was noted in relation to contemplative respect, is that the kind of consideration practically involved may often, and even typically, have characteristics of caring or solicitude: for if respecting an equal and independent other means allowing them space to develop their own projects, allowing them to speak, to disagree, and so on, then while this *might* be accomplished in a cool and indifferent manner, that manner is likely to be taken as *withholding* 'wholehearted' respect.

So while respect can in principle be distinguished from reverence on the one hand and care on the other, in practice it is an attitude that can be coloured by one or both of the others, and, when it is 'wholehearted', it is likely to be. I therefore think it is appropriate to draw this further distinction, between wholehearted and merely formal respect. This would enable us to accept Kant's verdict on the impossibility of respecting nonhumans, when this is understood as formal respect, but also to argue that for wholehearted respect, in practical contexts, that verdict may be questionable.

To draw this contrast is to focus on what is at issue between the position I am developing and an exclusivist humanist one. On a wholehearted interpretation of 'respect', as including the morality of care, it is effects on the other's good that require moral consideration; on the merely formal account it is the other's rational agency only. So, adopting the proposed view, respect for beings who simply have a good is possible.

However, while this argument undermines the radical distinction between care and moral obligation, it still only leaves care for nonhumans as a possible moral option. For this reason I now wish to argue, in addition, that there is a moral obligation to show wholehearted respect for beings just on the ground that they have a good: if humans have an interest in respecting one another in this way, they have no reason to withhold such respect from nonhumans.

Discourse ethics and consideration of nonhumans

I wish first briefly to consider what is the motivating interest for respect in relations between human agents. We have noted that the possibility of mutual respect arises with relations of reciprocity and the potential interchangeability of perspectives. This idea, captured in Kant's principle of universalization, is based on a kind of identification of one agent with another. Respect means, amongst other things, preserving the conditions that make reciprocity practically meaningful; and all agents have an interest in this. The idea of reciprocity which is captured in a somewhat formal and abstract manner in Kant's principle is linked more concretely to the conditions of ethical life by Habermas with his principle of discourse ethics. In what follows I shall indicate how the latter allows in a more wholehearted notion of respect, one that is motivated by an interest in integrity; once this is established, then there can be shown to be a stronger moral motivation than Habermas himself recognizes to respect the good of nonhuman creatures.

Discourse ethics requires respect for agents not as rational beings in the abstract but as articulators of what is good for them: therefore the normative principles arrived at in discourse are grounded in interests, as is required by the fundamental principle ('the D-Principle'): 'Only those norms can claim to be valid that meet (or could meet) with the approval of all affected in their capacity *as participants in a practical discourse*' (Habermas, 1990: 66). This leaves the question, however, of those beings who may be affected by human decisions but do not have the requisite capacity to participate in practical discourse. Although I have argued, in the previous chapter, that there is reason to expect discourse ethics to reveal enlightened interests in the protection of the environment, qua environment of humans, it is a different question whether there would be any equivalent interest in protecting nonhuman interests. Beings that are not communicatively competent cannot directly participate in this clarification of interests: they cannot directly influence participants' perceptions either of the participants' own interests or of the interests of non-participants; moreover, they cannot 'freely assent' to decisions reached. Beings who are not agents might figure in participants' deliberations, or they might not. So while the principles of discourse ethics may not rule out concern for nonhuman interests, they do not yield reasons for it to be obligatory.

However, there are suggestions Habermas makes that may yield the possibility of this further development. One particular suggestion I shall focus on is that compassion and solidarity – with nonhumans as well as humans – do 'appear in a discourse ethic that is consistently thought through to the end, at least as limit concepts' (Habermas, 1982: 246). This is on the grounds of 'anamnetic solidarity' with which we extend to nonhuman creatures 'compassion for the violation of moral or bodily integrity' (ibid.: 247).[7] To appreciate how this suggestion can be developed, though, it is worth quoting from Habermas's account of the function of morality as such, where he characterizes the moral intuitions which discourse ethics conceptualizes – something which is particularly significant for my argument since it is an account of the general interest in integrity. Accordingly, I reproduce the relevant passage:

> Social interactions mediated by the use of language oriented to mutual understanding are constitutive for sociocultural forms of life. This kind of communicative socialization through which persons are at the same time individuated generates a deep-seated vulnerability, because the identity of socialized individuals develops only through integration into ever more extensive relations of social dependency. . . . From this anthropological viewpoint, morality can be conceived as the protective institution that compensates for a constitutional precariousness in the sociocultural form of life itself. Moral institutions tell us how we should behave toward one another to counteract the extreme vulnerability of the individual through protection and considerateness. Nobody can preserve their own integrity alone. The integrity of individual persons requires the stabilization of a network of symmetrical relations of recognition in which nonreplaceable individuals can secure their fragile identities in a *reciprocal* fashion only as members of a community. Morality is aimed at a chronic susceptibility of personal integrity implicit in the structure of linguistically mediated interactions, which is more deep-seated than the tangible vulnerability of bodily integrity, though connected with it. (Habermas, 1993: 108–9)

From this, one can see why Habermas believes solidarity (including the 'caring' features of protection and considerateness) is built into ethics as such: without the committed reciprocity described here, ethics would not be possible. Humans have an interest in this commitment because of their own vulnerability. But this applies between agents – is there any reason for thinking it can or should be extended to nonhumans?

Habermas himself goes on to give some reasons why it might. In particular, he points out, there are ways in which we do communicate with animals that we involve in our social interactions. We have a responsibility toward them which 'is related to and grounded in the potential for harm inherent in all social interactions' (ibid.: 109). Between humans and animals there is a kind of intersubjective relation, and, accordingly, it is possible to adopt a 'performative attitude' toward them.[8] This means that in our interactions with them 'we should not confront animals in the objectifying attitude of a third person, nor just communicate about animals but *with* them. We must be able to ascribe characteristics of agents to animals, among others the ability to initiate utterances and to address them to us' (ibid.: 110). Then, he claims, we have duties which are rooted in the presuppositions of communicative action.

However, Habermas at the same time makes significant qualifications of these points. For one thing, the duties he speaks of here are only *analogous* to moral duties – they are not actual moral duties in the sense of having arisen through the assent of all concerned as participants in discourse, since nonhumans cannot strictly speaking participate in it. For another thing, they are only analogous to moral duties 'to the extent that the asymmetries in the interactions admit comparison with relations of recognition between persons' (ibid.: 110). In most cases the analogy will be partial at best, given how asymmetrical communications generally are. It is therefore evident that on Habermas's account it cannot be the purpose of morality as an institution to protect the interests of nonhumans in any very thoroughgoing way. In other words, it remains an optional matter of care, as opposed to obligatory respect.

The extent of our quasi-moral responsibilities in relation to nonhumans appears to depend on the degree to which communication with them resembles inter-human communications, rather than on the degree to which our actions have avoidably adverse effects on the beings concerned. The core of the problem is that the harms nonhumans are liable to, for Habermas, are not harms affecting their socio-personal integrity. Thus Angelika Krebs notes how, despite Habermas's 'halfhearted' efforts to accommodate them, this actually presents a pretty definitive obstacle to communicatively grounded ethical concern for nonhumans:

> if morality is the institution which protects socio-personal integrity it is obvious that nature does not fall under the objects which this institution protects. For no star, no ecosystem, no species, no stone, no plant, no animal can feel annoyance, grudge, humiliation on account of violated reciprocal expectations and demands. A species which becomes extinct, a plant which dies, a mouse which suffers in a mouse-trap do not resent that we did this to them. The mouse simply suffers, its bodily integrity is affected, there is no socio-personal integrity to be affected. (Krebs, 1997: 273)

So is there any way in which discourse ethics can be rendered compatible with intuitions of a more compelling moral status of nonhumans? Krebs suggests that this could be made possible by softening the distinction between bodily integrity and socio-personal in-

tegrity so that the range of beings subject to morally relevant vulnerability can be extended. This suggestion clearly squares with the 'integrated' view of integrity for which I argued in chapter 4. Indeed, it
would be worth questioning Habermas's view that the vulnerability of
personal integrity is more deep-seated than the vulnerability of bodily
integrity, especially as he grants that the two are connected. Thus a
solution might be to extend the understanding of the function of morality so that it not only protects socio-personal integrity – and bodily
integrity only if immersed in socio-personal integrity – but also protects
bodily integrity as such.

I would like to support this suggestion by adding that even among
humans the idea of socio-personal integrity is ultimately unintelligible
without incorporating considerations of bodily integrity. To this end, it
is worth considering the basis of solidarity between humans, the reasons for protecting socio-personal integrity, and whether those reasons
cannot apply to nonhuman beings, thereby expanding the idea of
'socio-personal integrity' to a broader sense of integrity. One thing to
note is that no human individual has *direct* experience even of other
human individuals' weal and woe: the experience is always mediated,
and always involves a degree of inductive consideration. Part of that
mediation is linguistic; but important parts of it are not. At the most
basic level, a child attains to communicative competence in the first
place by learning to superimpose linguistic skills on intersubjective
experiences otherwise mediated. Children who are not yet communicatively competent and are not yet moral agents are nevertheless beings
with whom mature, autonomous and communicatively competent
adults experience a powerful sense of solidarity. On the other hand,
many adults reach a point in their life when they cease to be communicatively competent: in relation to them, too, mature adults experience a
powerful sense of solidarity. So one is not born a mature autonomous
being, and may not die so. Is mature autonomy a condition which is
radically distinct from the conditions which precede and which may
follow it? We are what we have become, and are still becoming. Earlier,
pre-discursive, experience is not left behind (cf. Benhabib, 1992): aspects of one's earlier identity, like some of one's earlier beliefs, can get
trained out or transformed, but there is no radical break between child-
hood and adulthood. The vulnerability that ethics is intended to protect, therefore, is not generated by purely linguistically mediated
interdependencies. Once this point is granted, then the purpose of
morality can be redescribed in terms which are less indifferent to the
good of non-discursive beings. Moreover, it is important to recognize
how much of human ethics has to do with human *animality*: offences

against humanity are not offences just against their 'rationality'. Injustice can be predicated of crimes against humanity which cannot plausibly be interpreted as crimes against 'rational nature'. (A number of human rights obviously come here – beginning with the right to life and physical security.) Furthermore, it is also worth recalling that discourse ethics is not supposed to be a simple contractualist doctrine: the D-Principle is not just the principle of 'you scratch my back, I'll scratch yours': for assenting to norms is not just a question of self-interest; rather, it is assenting to their rightness. Hence it is the assent of people as participants in discourse, not as narrowly self-interested litigants. Participants who can experience solidarity with other humans can also experience it for other beings who are similar in relevant ways.

Nevertheless, the possibility of developing discourse ethics along these lines is blocked by Habermas's particular formulation of it because he believes the necessity and possibility of ethics derive from the vulnerability of socio-personal identity *in contradistinction* to bodily integrity.[9] Whereas the former is constitutive of ethical relations, the latter is extraneous to them. So if 'goods' like bodily integrity have to be accepted regardless of whether freely agreed, then the understanding of the function of morality would appear to be altered in such a way as to leave no distinctive role for discourse ethics at all. It will be recalled that one of the features of discourse ethics is the principled refusal to admit any substantive conceptions of the good, or 'teleological principles', in advance of seeing what norms participants actually assent to. The problem Krebs highlights is that to understand morality as protecting bodily integrity as such does precisely mean to introduce a teleological principle. For if there are goods associated with bodily integrity it must be possible to specify them quite independently of what participants in discourse may happen to agree on. So if the relevant teleological principles can be specified without recourse to discursive procedures, discourse ethics itself would be redundant. This is Krebs' own conclusion. Yet with this conclusion the link between human interests and nonhuman values that I've invoked discourse ethics to support would be broken.

So is there any way of avoiding that conclusion? Certainly, if the protection of bodily integrity were introduced as a normative ethical principle – if participants had, willy nilly, to discover and agree to this principle – there could indeed be no distinctive role for discourse at all. However, I shall argue that the protection of bodily integrity can appear as an obligation without introducing an extraneous teleological principle. The basis of this argument is that the principle of free agreement, the D-Principle, is itself not totally neutral with regard to teleological or material principles. As Krebs points out, one material principle *is* presupposed as a condition of possibility for discourse ethics (as, indeed, for Kantian ethics more generally), and that is *autonomy*. The reason why communication is ethically fundamental at all has to do with the axiomatic value of individuals giving their free assent to the norms that will bind them. In what follows I shall argue that autonomy can be understood in such a way as to provide reasons for protecting bodily integrity as well as for preserving discursive relations, and therefore that protecting bodily integrity does not require the introduction of a teleological principle 'from without'. If this suggestion succeeds, it will be seen that the socio-personal integrity of humans is by no means the privileged object of morality, even on the terms of discourse ethics, when these are consistently thought through to their limit – more consistently than in Habermas himself.

2   No more reason to respect rational freedom than any other kinds of freedom

The aim of this section is to show that there is no reason to withhold respect from nonhuman beings if the reason for according it to humans is that they are possessed of autonomy, understood as rational freedom. The first step of the argument is to analyse the meaning of 'rational freedom', in order to identify reasons for respecting beings possessed of rational freedom that do not also apply to beings possessed of any other sort of freedom. I shall claim that the only reason respect would be peculiarly due to rational beings derives from reverence for 'rational nature'. The question then is whether there is any more reason to revere rational nature than other kinds of nature. I shall suggest that there is not, and therefore that there is no moral reason why respect should be withheld from nonrational beings.

Analysing freedom

Rational freedom can be understood as the freedom to act in accordance with self-chosen or self-affirmed 'laws', laws which are chosen or affirmed on the basis of their accordance with the dictates of reason. The idea that reason effectively dictates laws is significant, since rational freedom is not presented as lawless or indeterminate. However, the determinacy of laws of reason differs from that of natural laws in a crucial respect: a person is governed by laws of nature which she has no choice whether to obey or not, but, we normally suppose, she can choose whether to act in accordance with laws of reason. Herein, in this power of choice, lies what is generally referred to by the idea of free will.

Predicating freedom of a rational being, though, is not necessarily the same as positing free will as this is understood by libertarians. It is possible to predicate freedom of a being which has rational capacities without invoking the idea of 'free will' at all. It would be quite useful to do this given that, despite strenuous efforts, philosophers have so far failed to provide a conclusive counterargument to scepticism about the existence of free will. In what follows, therefore, I offer what I think is a plausible description of the experience of subjective freedom, and which makes no reference to the idea of 'free will'. Since what is at issue is subjective experience of freedom, I've thought it appropriate to include a report on my own experience of the phenomenon.

Last evening, walking home along Middle Meadow Lane, I asked myself what it means to speak of freedom. At that time and place the question took quite specific forms. I was sure I was free, if I wanted to, to walk on the other side of the white line that divides the walk; I could simply skip across it – a free act. I did not do so, but I was confident of being *free* to do so, *if* I wanted. But I did not want to. Why not? To do so would have been a trivial act which in itself would prove nothing – I could be as unfree in skipping across as in not skipping across if a determinist chose so to describe me. My reason, as it appeared more decisively to me, was that this act would merely detract from what I was doing, in a meaningless way. I am walking home: this is my present project. I am on this side of the line, as it happens, because the other side is reserved for cyclists, and even if none are around at present, my practice is to avoid possible problems so that I am left free to pursue *my* projects, not the unchosen project of avoiding cyclists.

So I appear to have an idea of freedom as the pursuit of my projects. This idea is somewhat deepened when I think of less trivial and longer-term life choices I have made, and the courses of action they have committed me to. Thus freedom seems to mean sticking to my projects and commitments; unfreedom would mean being coerced or distracted away from them on to an unchosen path. It thus sounds like a kind of conformity, although it feels like a kind of consistency. Either way, it does not sound too much like what one usually means by 'freedom'. So I pose another question: do I remember making the initial choices that set me on these projects? Would they be nearer to 'real freedom'? The answer, it seems to me, is that the initial choices were just the same as this: I have always faced – when in a position of choice – a range of options some of which, in my judgement at the time, furthered my previously formed projects and some did not. In other words, I have always already been situated in a flow of short-, medium- and long-term projects. When I was younger, though, they seemed more open-ended. Dramatic changes of direction were (or seemed) more possible. This, I think, was because I had less invested in particular projects; I had made fewer specific path choices; I had a lack of commitment across a range of options. In this respect I feel less free now than then. But it is only one respect. My greater freedom then resided in the numerous unrealised possibilities that might in time have been realised; in one life, however, one can only realise a finite number of possibilities, so I could not in principle have realised all of them; hence that greater freedom was in other respects a kind of illusion (not the illusion of having the possibility of doing some things differently, but of having the possibility of doing anything and everything that I might have thought or dreamt of doing).

So, I concluded:

At any time I am free to do x, y or z – where these are feasible options – *not* to do just anything at all. I may feel that by planning a series of actions x_1, x_2, etc., I might get in a position, in principle, to do just anything at all. But all this says is that I choose a *project* – whose accomplishment will require *not* doing just anything at all at each stage, but precisely what is required. So the more decisively one seeks to assert freedom, the more decisively one binds oneself to future constraints.

The general conclusion yielded me by these reflections is that the experience of freedom is the *awareness* of making choices; it is not clear that it is also, or instead, something exercised in making them. That is to say, the exercise of choice itself appears to have been determined by previous choices and their outcomes. This account, then, is consistent with a strongly deterministic position like that of Spinoza, for instance.

On Spinoza's view, each action, considered under the attribute of thought, is conditioned fully by the array of other thoughts or mental processes with which it comes in contact. This leaves no place for a faculty of will in general of which freedom can be predicated. The unity experienced by – and *as* – the 'I' that makes specific choices at specific moments, is accounted for by Spinoza as he accounts for the identity of any particular thing in nature: every finite thing, including a human being, endeavours to preserve itself and to increase its power of self-maintenance, and this endeavour 'to persist in its own being' and realise its potentialities, its nature or essence, is what Spinoza calls its *conatus* (Spinoza, 1989: Part III). The sense of self experienced by the conscious human individual is just the self-experience of this *conatus* under the attribute of thought. Freedom and unfreedom, then, can be predicated not of some abstract unitary (nonnatural) 'will' but of the *conatus*. It is free when developing in accordance with its own essential determinations; it is unfree when prevented from doing so. Each facet of development requires its own type of freedom.

The existence of different types of freedom can be accounted for in terms of emergent powers. Indeed, the Spinozan view is consistent with what we know of the evolutionary development of the universe, which allows reality to be depicted in terms of more and less basic causal powers. Thus 'matter may be said to be more "basic" than life; life in turn may be said to be more basic than rationality (in the sense that we are rational animals), and hence human society and its history' (Collier, 1994: 46). 'The relations between the more and less basic domains are one-way relations of inclusion: all animals are composed of chemical substances but not all chemical substances are parts of animals, and so on' (ibid.: 107). It therefore also follows that anything belonging to a higher stratum of nature will be governed by more than one kind of law.

When freedom is accounted for in terms of emergent powers it can be characterized as what Andrew Collier calls 'Liberty of spontaneity' – that is, 'the power to act in accordance with our own natures (in this case, as rational beings), rather than being constrained by the nature of something alien.' Emergent powers exist at every stratum: 'There is a sense in which a tree is "free" from mechanical determination. It doesn't *break* mechanical laws (neither do we) but it grows according to its own nature in ways impossible for something subject *only* to mechanical laws . . . It has therefore got a degree of "liberty of spontaneity"' (ibid.: 119). This is all the more obvious in the case of animals. Possession of liberty of spontaneity is not, Collier points out, an all-or-nothing thing: 'It comes with the possibility of restraint, unfreedom, oppression. Hence it makes sense to talk of the freedom and oppression and liberation of animals, as it would not if they were Cartesian machines' (ibid.). As for humans, freedom is stratified and complex: our liberty of spontaneity does not exist at one level only.

What is distinctive about rational freedom is that it essentially consists in the capacity to be aware of one's motivations and to act on those which are coherent with previously formulated ideas. This is what Spinoza means, I take it, by distinguishing between mental events and states whose causes are 'internal' and those whose causes are 'external' to the individual. 'The former are classed as "actions" or affections in regard to which we are active and the latter as "passions" or occasions where we are passive in relation to our affections. . . . We are active or free when the causes of our actions are internal and unfree when these causes are external to us' (West, 1993: 292–3). Spinoza's view then is that, if the self is ruled by passive affections, it acts from reasons which are not its own and therefore acts less than rationally and less than freely. For Spinoza we are free to the extent that we act on the basis of adequate ideas. Passive emotions – such as rage, spite, cruelty, and so on – are really the confusion of ideas. Or, one could say, in the terms I have been using, that these negative emotions undermine one's integrity, understood as encompassing one's whole psycho-physical, social and spiritual being.

Rational freedom can then be seen to consist, above all, in an awareness of one's degree of integration and of the conditions for its promotion. Freedom from passive emotions is an important part of the meaning of autonomy for such beings; indeed, it might be said, self-control for humans is nothing other than full awareness of their own nature. If the human being is sufficiently in touch with its own nature – under the attribute both of extension and thought – it knows if it is doing well or not. Getting in touch with its own nature is not an 'act of will': it is certainly not an isolated act – it is a process; and it is not 'pure will', for it arises with practice. So the attainment of adequate ideas need involve nothing occult. Human beings can help themselves to this attainment in propitious circumstances: these circumstances always involve contributions of others; one does not develop the capacities referred to by libertarians under the heading of 'free will' on one's own, but in association, in a culture; one also helps others develop their circumstances. The whole way of thinking about free will as if on a model of a 'first' or 'uncaused' cause becomes redundant. All this is perfectly consistent with our experience of being free: we are free to reflect on what we have become, on what we might do, on what we ought to do.

A more general description of what is distinctive about a being with these capacities is that they are aware of *being*: that is, they are aware not just of being in determinate situations but aware of being as opposed to not being. It is perhaps this awareness which generates the sense of contingency that supports the notion of 'free will' – the idea that 'things could be otherwise'. For part of its grounding is the thought that not only could I have been otherwise, but also that 'I could have not been'. But the thought can also be grammatically misleading: 'I could have not been', or 'I could have been otherwise' makes the 'I' the subject of a verb. (It can even encourage a certain overconfidence about one's (individual and species) powers.) But being is not a kind of doing.

Rather, the affirmation that 'I am' is perhaps better understood to mean that 'being is here, manifest, in *this*, this *me*'. My mode of being as a natural being, and even as a spiritual being, does not necessitate any thought of 'free will', as contra-causal causality. Even spirituality, then, would not be something occult, but rather an 'in-touch-ness' with the order of being. This idea, while at root not entirely antithetical to a Western, Cartesian, perspective, is more directly elaborated in certain Eastern and mystical traditions, and these have been explicitly picked up by deep ecologists (cf. Fox, 1995: ch. 8) to demonstrate a basis in being – as opposed to morality – for respecting other species. This provides a prima facie reason for respect for all beings. It provides an inescapable well-disposedness towards all being – because *being* is ultimately undifferentiated. It inculcates an attitude of 'live and let live' in relation to other beings – which does not entail indifference to their fate when that comes under our control or influence, as so often it now does.

So, we can now address the initial question of this section: ought we to respect any being capable of freedom, or only those capable of rational freedom? Why should we restrict respect to beings capable of rational freedom rather than extend it to any beings with powers whose exercise can be enhanced or thwarted by the actions of we agents? The reason Kant restricts respect to beings possessed of rational nature is that it is only rational nature that conforms to the moral law: moral law is the source of all respect.[10] Yet the attitude to rationality as such, or to the moral law, on the definitions I earlier introduced, is one not of respect but of reverence. The question then is why one would revere rationality rather than nature as a whole. Unless rationality were to be seen as apart from nature (indeed, as somehow 'above' the rest of nature, and not just as a supervenient level within the totality of nature), then there could be no reason I can think of. Yet even if there were some special reason to revere rational nature, this would only seem to entail respect for persons to the extent that their acts and motives accord with it, and that would not be a sufficient basis for respect between humans anyway: it would be implausible to suggest we can or should respect persons only if and when they act purely according to the dictates of reason or for the sake of the moral law.

Yet perhaps it is not rational freedom which is the issue at all.[11] In playing off a Spinozan against a Kantian view of rational freedom, have I perhaps overlooked what it is that we feel we need to respect in our fellow human beings as free agents? Do we and should we not respect their capacity to choose, whatever choices they happen to make?

Surely, at least part of what it means to respect a free agent is to respect
their right to learn for themselves, and guide their lives according to
their own lights. To arrive at a moral view one has to learn, even from
one's moral mistakes, without necessarily deferring to others' authority. The idea here can be summed up as the suggestion that respecting
free human agents means regarding them as *morally accountable* for
their actions.

3 Moral accountability is not necessary for respect

There is thus a further objection to the Spinozan view which, at first
sight, appears to depend on objecting to the denial of free will, but
which is conceptually distinct from it. This is the argument that the
Spinozan view denies the possibility of moral accountability. After
sketching the basic objection in a form which appears to depend on a
belief in free will, I examine the argument of Peter Strawson who claims
that the objection holds good even if one suspends belief in the metaphysics of free will. However, I shall go on to show why I am sceptical
that Strawson's argument does not entail a tacit appeal to the metaphysics of free will, but also, more crucially, why I do not accept that
moral accountability in the sense he refers to it is either possible or
necessary for relations of respect.

The sense of accountability I accept is that according to which 'to
hold someone to account' is to ask of them an explanatory account of
their actions,[12] and expect from them an account which one can assess
according to cognitive criteria. In this sense, the idea of accountability
is compatible with a Spinozan position. On the view that opposes this,
for someone to be held morally accountable they must be considered
the authors of their own actions; and this means crediting them with
free will. Because positions like that of Spinoza deny free will and see
actions as essentially the products of determinations which operate
through the agent they are thus also taken to deny the possibility of
moral accountability and therefore to remove the possibility of mutual
respect in what is taken to be the relevant sense. Moreover, the view
that agents are not the authors of their own actions in as strong a sense
as they would be if acting with free will, also gives rise to political
worries: people appear to be viewed, in effect, as 'objects of social
policy' – and as such, potentially liable to whatever sort of 'therapy'
those with the power to administer it deem appropriate, from mild
inducements, through social engineering, to an out-and-out programme of totalitarianism. This view, bluntly, fails to recognize

people's rights of freedom, people's rights to be considered as subjects, or authors of their own actions.

Now the political worry is a serious one, I believe, but in order to address it properly, there is first a philosophical problem to deal with, namely, that, as stated, the articulation of the worry – and therefore its acceptance as a genuine concern – depends on subscribing to a belief in free will, in the strong libertarian sense of contra-causal causality. If one has no stronger reason for affirming this belief than for denying it, then one is apparently faced with the dilemma of either allowing that social relations can only be manipulatively regulated or of embracing a questionable metaphysics.

A way of avoiding the dilemma has been suggested by Peter Strawson, who claims that we can and do – indeed, cannot but – employ something like the conventional idea of moral accountability without necessarily having any commitment to the metaphysics of free will. At the heart of Strawson's argument is his insistence on the 'central commonplace' of everyday moral phenomena 'that we attach very great importance to the attitudes and intentions towards us of other human beings' (Strawson, 1974: 5). Our response to others' attitudes and intentions towards us he refers to as *reactive* attitudes: these are the 'non-detached attitudes and reactions of people directly involved in transactions with each other; of the attitudes and reactions of offended parties and beneficiaries; of such things as gratitude, resentment, forgiveness, love and hurt feelings' (ibid.: 4). Now these attitudes, on the Spinozan view, would seem for the most part to represent 'inadequate ideas': for the things that people do they do for reasons which come from a train of natural causes. Thus it would not be appropriate to praise or blame them for what they do; rather, one should seek to understand what makes them do what they do; and this would mean adopting what Strawson refers to as the *objective* attitude. Taking this objective view restricts the application of notions of accountability, since the idea that an agent is the sole sovereign author of their actions appears to be as untenable, indeed unintelligible, as the idea of free will; this means that the notion of accountability has no intrinsic moral meaning and can have only a pragmatic role: 'we treat someone as accountable for a given action if, and only if, we think that the chance of his doing it again may be raised or lowered by the sort of "therapy" which depends upon inducements or threats' (Bennett, 1984: 197).

Strawson's objection to the Spinozan position is that it is neither possible nor desirable completely to purge or repudiate the reactive attitudes and thereby adopt a purely objective attitude towards others. It is not possible to do away with them because, I take him to be

arguing, of the way we are constituted; and given that we are constituted in and through our social relations it is not *desirable* to do so
because to repudiate the attitudes would mean opting out of those
social relations. Now regarding the impossibility of entirely purging
reactive attitudes, I think one can simply concede Strawson's claim: for
it would be hard to deny the fact that humans are prone to reactive
attitudes, and one might well grant that for practical purposes these
may be impossible to eliminate entirely. While conceding this, though,
one need not thereby relinquish a Spinozan view of ethics, for the more
crucial question is whether it is desirable to try and do so, to the extent
it is possible, as Spinoza believes.

Regarding the undesirability of viewing others objectively, Strawson
raises two chief objections that I can discern: (1) to adopt the objective
attitude means seeing and treating the other as less than fully human or
rational, or less than a person; (2) in doing so one cuts oneself off from
normal human relationships.

1   To take the objective view is, on Strawson's account, to adopt
what is in effect a purely strategic attitude to the other: it means seeing
them as 'something to be taken account, perhaps precautionary account, of; to be managed or handled or cured or trained' (Strawson,
1974: 9). With an objective attitude, he claims, one views the other agent
as in important respects less than fully human or rational: 'If your
attitude towards someone is wholly objective, then though you may
fight him, you cannot quarrel with him, and though you may talk to
him, even negotiate with him, you cannot reason with him. You can at
most pretend to quarrel, or to reason, with him' (ibid.). It is thus an
attitude which may be appropriate when dealing with people whose
powers of reasoning are inhibited by abnormalities or immaturity, as
when we 'look with an objective eye on the compulsive behaviour of
the neurotic or the tiresome behaviour of a very young child' (ibid.),
but it is not normally appropriate when participating in ordinary adult
relationships.[13] To adopt this attitude habitually would be to see other
humans as lacking fully rational capacities, as in some respect incapaci-
tated; this would preclude proper moral consideration of their interests
(as autonomous beings); and so is morally undesirable. Indeed,
Strawson argues that it means one does not see others as morally
responsible for their actions.

2   It is also undesirable from the point of view of the one adopting
the attitude, since adopting this attitude exclusively would entail human isolation, says Strawson (ibid.: 11). The objective attitude 'cannot

include the range of reactive feelings and attitudes which belong to involvement or participation with others in inter-personal human relationships' (ibid.: 9). The reactive attitudes are an integral part of our relations with other people; take these away, Strawson seems to be saying, and one takes away any real involvement with them.

Now with this critique of the 'objective attitude', Strawson directly counters the Spinozan view according to which what is of ethical value is perceived and attained through overcoming reactive attitudes to arrive at more adequate – and in Strawson's terms, objective – knowledge. However, I do not think Strawson has done enough to show that view to be thoroughly mistaken. In fact, I shall argue, Strawson misrepresents what respect for agents means; correcting this enables us to see how respect for nonagents is also possible.

Defending the objective view on intersubjective grounds

I grant Strawson's claim that participant attitudes are a necessary condition for relations of respect between rational agents, since it does seem reasonable to suppose that only as participants in ethical life, confronting one another on equal terms, ready and able to do as they would be done by, can individuals properly respect one another; and this, of course, involves being able to reason with one another. However, I shall argue that participant attitudes and relations are not inconsistent with the adoption of an objective attitude; for while the objective attitude precludes (in the sense of suspending rather than abolishing) reactive attitudes, it does not preclude participant attitudes, and, in fact, is part and parcel of these when they are rational and reasonable.

It is interesting first of all to note, since we are speaking here of relations of respect between *agents*, that part of what is involved in taking a reactive attitude is that one casts oneself as a moral *patient*, the done-by rather than the doer. Thus one's blaming the other may simply be a manifestation of pique or subjective hurt. Yet to be consistent with respect, attributions of praise and blame have to be justifiable: emotional responses directed against individual persons in specific situations would be devoid of moral character unless connected with an *impersonal* kind of indignation over some breach of a generalized norm (cf. Habermas, 1990: 48). So if a (negative) reactive attitude is to have moral significance, it must include not simply the experience of subjective hurt, but also indignation at the breach of a generalized norm. One can then react as an agent, and not only as a patient.

With this clarification one can review the question of whether reactive attitudes might be necessary for respect: that is, whether, whenever a person has or manifests an attitude of respect for another person, it will always be possible to find a reactive attitude bound up with it. There is reason to doubt this to be the case. If in the relevant sense of respect it is due to persons who are capable of entering into reciprocal duties, and if a reactive attitude is appropriate when the other does either more or less than is expected of them as their moral duty, then reactive attitudes would seem by definition to arise as the exception rather than the rule of relations of respect. In fact, a failure of a person to do their duty might appropriately occasion as a reaction a loss of respect for that person. However, in everyday attributions of moral accountability, respect may be thought to be preserved by crediting the person with knowing that there is a reasonable expectation which she has failed to fulfil, or that she 'should have done otherwise'. Yet it is to be reiterated that the force of this 'should' comes from a generalizable norm, not from the personal reaction per se. One could make this judgement without experiencing any personal reaction at all.

The critical force of this point is brought out by noticing that one can make the judgement without holding the person morally accountable. One might say, for instance, 'you should have done otherwise, but I understand the motivational forces that made you act as you did, and I therefore realise that while morally you *should*, motivationally you *could not*'. This, of course, is precisely the sort of assertion that Strawson, like libertarians, wants to prevent (although he, unlike them, thinks this does not entail invoking free will). I too would want to prevent this way of talking between mature rational agents, but merely on the grounds that it is presumptuous: to assert that 'you could not have done otherwise' is to claim knowledge that is both uncertain and indeterminate. However, exactly the same point applies to the contrary assertion that 'you *could* have done otherwise'. If we cannot claim adequate knowledge of the action's etiology, then we cannot know one way or the other: so while it is presumptuous to 'explain away' the other's action, it is equally presumptuous to rule out the possibility of doing so – the presumption manifest, for instance, in saying a person's excuse is not valid. If we really are to remain neutral on the question of free will, as Strawson officially claims to be, then we do not form a view one way or the other. In short, neither an 'objective' view nor a 'reactive' view yields knowledge with guaranteed adequacy of the other's motivations.

Note that this is an empirical point about the possibility of attaining adequate objective knowledge, and does not bear on the question of the desirability of trying to do so.

Now when Spinoza talks about adequate knowledge of motivations, I take him not to be talking about the *other* person's motivations at all, but about one's own. What Spinoza commends is that one try to get an adequate understanding of one's own motivations. This involves taking what Strawson calls an 'objective view' of them. But if one does this in one's own case, it is not at all clear how presumption or lack of respect come into it. Indeed, when I earlier conducted my first-person subjective inquiry into freedom I entertained an 'objective view' of how my motivations are formed, finding no need to invoke the idea of 'free will', but did not thereby feel my dignity or self-respect were threatened; rather, I felt that I was developing as a self-understanding being – as would be expected by Spinoza, for whom, indeed, recognizing one's determinations is an integral part of the development of self-respect. I would find unintelligible the suggestion that my interest in understanding myself was an instrumental one – on the contrary, it seemed part of my interest in integrity, striving for cognitive coherence: so why would my interest in understanding another have to be understood instrumentally? I see no reason why it should: crediting others with the ability to review their own motivations *is* to show them respect; to deny their ability to do so would be to *deny* them respect.

Of course this does not license *me* to take an objective view of *their* motivations – especially since my knowledge is unlikely to be adequate to the task – but respect does require me to attend to the deliverances of their objective view (that is, listen to their explanations), and, correlative to this obligation, I am entitled to question the adequacy of their explanations. There would thus be a participatory relationship between us which could in principle be conducted wholly in the objective attitude.

The objective attitude is not inconsistent with participant attitudes, I would therefore argue. On the contrary, it is necessary to ethical participation. For part and parcel of a participant attitude is a preparedness to be corrected about one's imputation of intentions; and this does indeed entail a preparedness to accept an invitation to take a more objective attitude. This is no less a part of well-ordered relations between people, and arguably a more important contribution, than what might sometimes amount to little more than the knee-jerk reactive attitude. In sharing, discussing and developing with them an objective view of their own motivations the objective attitude may indeed, on the whole, be more appropriate than resenting their hurtful behaviour. To view the other objectively is potentially to question the 'story' they currently tell themselves about their own motivations and intentions. But, politically, if we subscribe to discursive democracy, that is precisely what we ought to do – being prepared, reciprocally, for it to be done tó us too. Respect is earned in the interplay, in the exchanges, that ensue. As the subjective and objective stories amend one another, one can envisage something approaching consensus emerging.

Strawson seems to take an unnecessarily restrictive view of the sorts of communication that are possible between persons. The agent's motivations may be inaccessible to the reagent, but the agent's reasons *can* be communicated to her, discussed by her, and even constructively criticized by her; conversely, the motivations may not be entirely accessible to the agent herself, and the reagent may also be able to contribute some illumination on this. Furthermore, if the reagent does not have access to the agent's motivations, neither does the agent have access to the motivations of the reagent's reactions, and hence will *not* know what to learn from them! As long as each remains locked within her own perspective, little ethical progress is likely to be made! So respecting people means communicating with them; not simply leaving them to be motivated as they happen to be. Developing this thought allows a reply to political worries about the Spinozan view and a better alternative conception of politics.

Reply to political worries

Central to libertarian worries about the Spinozan view is the paternalism (and worse) it can encourage. For while Spinoza's refusal to praise or blame could be viewed as radically tolerant, a problem critics see is the implied corollary that the normative regulation of society would be achieved by 'social engineering' and 'therapy' for inappropriate behaviour. In removing the notion of moral accountability, and seeing the individual as just a 'medium' or 'node' through which various determinations work, he removes what it is about the individual that is supposed to be owed respect. Thus the thought seems to be that if individuals are not credited with 'free will' they will be treated as mere objects of administrative social policy; the idea is conjured up of ideological brainwashing such as is associated with totalitarian regimes.

Yet what is at issue, politically, is the liberal presumption in favour of respect for an individual's right, at least in a loose sense of the term, to be accredited the best judge of her own interests, and not to be 'corrected' by others on the basis of an 'objective' diagnosis or inter-pretation. Accepting that individuals have a right not to have others' interpretations imposed upon them, however, does not entail accepting that they also have a 'right to be wrong' about their motivations; in fact, rather than allow the license this implies, there may be good reasons why they should, on the contrary, have duties to get clearer about their motivations. The liberal principle can be preserved, though, if, in the clarification of motivations and interests, individuals retain an overrid-ing right to give or withhold assent to any objective interpretation of them. Hence it seems to me that the political concern about taking an objective view of interests and motivations is sufficiently answered by recognizing that that view might always be wrong. Thus in the same circumstances, and for the same reasons, that a libertarian would feel impelled to posit free will, one can instead simply acknowledge inad-equate knowledge of motivations. The outcome would be the same restriction on paternalism or coercion.

An advantage of not refraining from the objective view altogether, though, is that the possibility is preserved of individuals becoming more enlightened about their interests, and, indeed, arriving at trans-formed views of them. In this regard, a refusal to take the objective attitude is vulnerable to familiar criticisms of positivistic and empiricist tendencies in liberalism (cf., for instance, Offe and Wiesenthal, 1985): that is, at any rate, as was argued in the previous chapter, there is no reason to accept people's deliverances about their preferences as incor-rigible statements of their legitimate interests. Adopting an 'objective attitude' in the context of a discursive clarification of interests does not violate individuals' rights, but nor does it allow simple acquiescence in the normative status quo.

In downplaying the moral significance of reactive attitudes, my ar-gument not only invokes a familiar political critique of liberalism; it also has bearing on the question of how concern for nonhumans can or should enter political theory. Strawson's account of reactive attitudes as part and parcel of 'normal relations' between persons can be criti-cized not merely for an unreflective acceptance of what is socially 'normal', but also for its unreflective assumption that the notion of 'persons' is relatively unproblematic. On Strawson's definition, per-sons are defined as beings with extension and consciousness, yet this, as others have noted (for instance, Frankfurt, 1982), leaves a puzzle about what other animals are. Strawson, of course, was not directly concerned about the ontological or moral status of other animals; but this perhaps partly accounts for why his argument holds no sway against the argument defended here that we *should* be.

My view is that we respect persons by attending to their accounts of their actions – and, of course, this means crediting them with knowledge of our shared moral norms and expectations, but at root this is just to credit them with what we take to be a species capacity for knowledge, communication and coherence between thought and action. While this may be a peculiarly appropriate way to respect persons, it is not incompatible with respect for other beings on the basis of *their* species capacities.

4   Justice for nonhumans

Having argued that there is no reason to withhold respect from nonhumans, I shall now argue that there is also some reason to grant it.

For the purposes of political theory, an important part of what it means to show respect – for nonhumans as for humans – is to provide justice for them. Hence I shall suggest that it is too limited an account of the normative core of basic social institutions which takes this to be provided by an account of justice that does not explicitly rule out speciesism as a form of injustice. Certainly, it is not obvious why humans' dealings with nonhumans could not in principle quite straightforwardly be deemed a matter of justice. There does not appear to be any *conceptual* obstacle in the way of a society deeming it wrong, and therefore unjust, for instance, to enclose animals in cruel conditions, to utilize their bodies as resources or objects of experimentation, to expropriate their habitats for human use, or to kill them for relatively trivial reasons of human convenience. Some societies have recognized such norms. The problem as it appears from the perspective of modern political theory, though, is that such conceptions of justice are *substantive* conceptions; they embody a commitment to a particular theory of what is good or of value (which not everyone subscribes to); and so, in being based on contestable but unfalsifiable premises, such conceptions are seen as dogmatic and unpersuasive by modern theorists of justice, who instead develop *procedural* accounts of justice.

The procedures are designed to discover what norms should have the binding force of obligation on those who are to be bound be them; nonhuman beings cannot be bound by any obligation and cannot participate in deciding what obligations there should be; therefore nonhuman beings can participate neither in the formulation nor the applying of just principles. Certainly, nonhumans cannot enjoy a range of specifically political rights, since they do not have the requisite capacities for citizenship; they clearly cannot participate in political processes. But a being does not have to be an agent to be considered a part of the polity, otherwise those human beings who do not meet the criteria of rational agency could not be either. Hence just as some humans are beneficiaries or recipients of norms of justice but not active participants in the formulation of them, so too nonhumans could be. So, for reasons elaborated more fully above, in section 1 of this chapter, this aspect of the problem would appear not to be decisive.

Nevertheless, even if there is no conceptual obstacle to considering nonagents as potential recipients of justice, there are difficulties in seeing why agents should accord them this status. Justice, as traditionally conceived, particularly on procedural conceptions, is confined to relations between beings with reciprocal obligations. There is an important principle underlying this conception: obligations are justified if and only if agents agree amongst themselves to be bound by them. On a contractualist view of this agreement there is an element of rationally self-interested reasoning: agents agree to be bound by principles of justice, even when it is not in their immediate self-interest, because they wish to preserve the institution of justice itself, since without it there would not be the peace and stability in their social relations which preserve the freedom they are assumed to desire. With regard to nonhumans, however, there are no social relations in the first place, and there is therefore nothing similar to preserve; there are no threats of civil disorder, and so no threats to ward off; there is no possibility of nonhumans undertaking any obligations on their part, and so no quid pro quo for agents attempting to introduce considerations of them. In other words, the idea of obligations to nonhumans appears to be thoroughly unmotivated.

Nevertheless, even if one accepts the contractualist interpretation of the basis of social obligations as described here (chosen because it is the least favourable to my case), there remains more to be said about what it is that the contractors may be thought to agree to. Justice is, in Rawls's telling phrase, 'the first virtue of social institutions'; and justice is a virtue of institutions not only because it is, as for Rawls, *fair*, but because it conduces to the good life. The form of justice is not, and cannot be, completely indifferent to its content. Indeed, contemporary proceduralists do not remove every conception of the good at all, but rather seek to minimize the commitment, to work with a 'thin' conception of the good (cf. Rawls, 1972) centred around the bases of self-respect.

In section 1 we saw reasons to think that self-respect entails a presumption in favour of care and humaneness in humans' dealings with nonhumans, and I think this can be reinforced by the following consideration. The good life for rational autonomous beings is not one of simple selfish pleasure; on the contrary, it would be realized in the exercise of those rational autonomous powers. Hence the key thought is that for a rational agent, no human action can be assumed, without inquiry, to be a matter of moral indifference. It would not be rational to start from the assumption that all is license, with any action allowed until proscribed by some obligation. On the contrary, for a rational agent, every proposed action should in principle be examined to see whether it does have any moral implications, and if so, whether it is morally required, permitted or prohibited. Actions that are assumed, without investigation, to be morally indifferent may be called wanton actions.[14] The significance of this is that one does not assume that one can do just as one likes until a reason for providing an obligation is produced. The burden of proof is thus quite different; and this can have quite striking consequences in relation to the treatment of nonhuman beings. The wanton treatment of nonhuman beings involves a deficit of justification exactly as *any* wanton action does. Such actions, moreover, are not only not justified, they are not *motivated* in the sense of being rationally compelling for an agent. Certainly, the features of agency which humans claim as the basis of their alleged prerogatives – to treat nonhumans just as they like – are absent when they do so. There is therefore quite literally no justification for wanton treatment of nonhumans.

Yet perhaps there can be detrimental treatment of nonhuman beings which is not wanton? This cannot be ruled out in a world where interests and moral principles can conflict. As was explained in chapter 3, it is possible to accept the requirement of consistency which commits one to avoiding injustices or arbitrary discrimination, in general, and thus also the particular form of injustice which can be called speciesism, and yet also believe that there are forms of discrimination against nonhumans which are not unjust because they are not arbitrary. Thus while the avoidance of speciesism depends on the consistent application of the basic formal principle of justice which requires that 'like cases be treated alike', the proscription of speciesism will gain no purchase when it is the likeness of cases which is itself at issue.

Clearly, such questions as when the suffering of humans and nonhumans is relevantly similar fall outside the scope of political theory. One principle that can be established for political theory, though, is that when likenesses can, prima facie, reasonably be claimed to exist, then the burden of proof should rest with those who wish to claim the contrary, to bring forward reasons to rule out the appropriateness of moral concern. This would not rule out the possibility of

people who sincerely hold beliefs about human distinctiveness in relation to nonhuman beings, perhaps on religious grounds, having their
beliefs respected; but it would be appropriate to apply quite stringent
tests of good faith with the aim of ruling out arguments for abuse of
nonhumans which are based on little more than what I referred to in
chapter 3 as human chauvinism. Reversing the burden of proof in this
way is consistent with, and in some ways analogous to, the reversal of
the burden of proof that occurs with the adoption of the 'precautionary
principle', thereby bringing interspecies and more narrowly environmental concern on a par with one another.

Certainly, as I also noted in chapter 3, people cannot directly be
forced to overcome human chauvinism: human chauvinism, as an absence of care about nonhumans, cannot be proscribed in the manner of
a duty for the same reason that an absence of care in general cannot –
since this requires that they *see* likenesses with other beings, and this
they will only do if they are *disposed* to do so. But dispositions can be
inculcated; the fundamental human interest in integrity and self-
respect means favouring institutions that favour rather than inhibit it.[15]

If legitimate consensus is moved by the force of the better argument,
then those who are partisan in favour of moral concern for nonhumans
can legitimately appeal to a non-formal feature of what counts as a
better argument within human ethics – namely, that considerations
tending to enhance virtuous conduct should take priority over considerations that would diminish it. Thus once reasons to care are articulated, the onus on any reasonable person, I think, is to produce not just
objections, but *better* reasons not to care.

Conclusion

In this chapter I have sought, in the first three sections, to show that the
differences with most obvious moral relevance between human moral
agents and nonhuman beings do not warrant any particular privileges
for the former: on the contrary, as I made explicit in section 4, when
they are consistently thought through they tend rather to imply greater
responsibilities.

Of course there remain many questions about what it means, in
practice, to respect nonhuman beings. Trying to find workable answers
to such immensely difficult and complex questions constitutes an
enormous problem in itself. What I have sought to show, though, is that
it is a problem that humans have good reason to address as such, and
that the difficulties in the attempt are that – difficulties – and not

impossibilities. Political theorists, I claim, cannot justifiably remain neutral or agnostic on the question of the moral considerability of nonhuman beings, and therefore they have the task of working out what this means in the context of devising social and political arrangements that affect them.

7

Political Theory for a Sustainable Polity

Introduction

Having now completed the argument in favour of dealing with ecological (both environmental and interspecies) concerns, along with other individual and social concerns, in terms of interests, this final chapter indicates some of the implications for political theory of doing so.

A general advantage, for the pursuit of ecological values, in assimilating these to human interests, is that they can then be brought under distributive principles, and in many cases lend themselves to protection as rights. Accordingly, in the first section I suggest how, on this basis, ecological values can be incorporated into a normative theory of the basic institutions of society. What this argument would amount to, in practice, would be a case for the constitutional recognition of ecological interests as on a par with generalizable interests in the securing and equitable distribution of other social goods. In the second section I highlight some of the questions such a proposal raises for political theory, both normative and explanatory. Among these are concerns about the legitimacy of entrenching a recognition of certain types of interest,[1] which are likely to be heightened when the protection of nonhuman goods is added in; there are also concerns about the effectualness of relying on constitutional measures in the context of a liberal state when global and regional developments tending already to undermine the state's privileged political position are compounded by the transboundary issues that characterize so many ecological problems. I do not claim to offer comprehensive answers to such questions, but I do want to claim that the questions merit being placed high on the agenda for further research by political theorists, since they go to issues at the core of their discipline, touching not only on the substantive meaning of social justice and the good life within a polity, but also on the nature of liberal democracy and the state.

1   Ecological values and basic institutions

What it means to incorporate ecological values into political theory at the level of basic normative principles, my argument suggests, is, firstly, to treat environmental services and resources as social goods whose distribution is a question of justice, on the grounds that they represent generalizable interests warranting recognition at the level of basic institutions. It also means entrenching a recognition that not all 'environmental goods' can or should be treated as resources or services, and that there should therefore be substantive restrictions on the utilization of certain environmental goods – especially, for instance, non-renewable resources and environmental features of special scientific or cultural interest: and this is on the ground that the enlightened interests in their protection are as legitimate as the enlightened interests in social justice as more conventionally understood. Furthermore, it means there should be the possibility of placing restrictions on the treatment *as* environmental goods of those nonhuman beings who 'have a good' of their own: this is on the ground, as set out in chapter 6, that it is unjustified to disregard their moral claims on us. Because they cannot directly press these claims themselves, a minimal requirement on the state would be to underwrite the provision of suitable fora and legal norms permitting a fair hearing for those groups who seek to represent them; it is also arguable, though, that at least some animals who are most seriously affected by planned human practices are entitled to constitutional guarantees of more direct protection.

Because these principles warrant incorporation into what Rawls calls the basic institutions of society, it is appropriate that they should receive articulation at the constitutional level. Accordingly, in this section I briefly flesh out the case for pursuing ecological ends by constitutional means, and indicate how the principles guiding the basic institutions of an ecologically sustainable society may look different from those of a more conventional liberal democracy.

Constitutional environmentalism and the case for rights

Why adopt a constitutional approach to environmentalism? One major reason is that environmental problems today are such that adequate

solutions to them will require large-scale cooperation within and between polities: to secure such cooperation it is necessary that there be
widely agreed general principles about its basis; for such principles to
be binding and legitimate within a polity they need to be set above the
vicissitudes of everyday political expediency. Principles established at
constitutional level appear to fit the bill. It is in fact noteworthy that
throughout the world, a growing number of states are writing environmental provisions into their constitutions; and some have also taken
the step of entrenching environmental rights.[2]

An advantage of pursuing environmental ends by means of constitutional rights is that in doing so one can draw normative and practical
support from an established discourse of fundamental human rights.
The human rights discourse, which does enjoy considerable consensus
in international law, embodies just the sort of non-negotiable values
which seems to be required for environmental legislation. Rights mark
the seriousness, the 'trumping' status, of environmental concern; they
articulate this concern in an established institutionalized discourse
(Aiken, 1992); and they link the concern to citizens' interests rather than
to supposedly 'objective' criteria (Wynne, 1994) of environmental
harm, thereby allowing what count as environmental goods or bads to
be seen as questions for political deliberation, and thus as related to
other aspects of social justice. Indeed, the view has been advanced, not
least influentially by the Brundtland Report (World Commission on
Environment and Development, 1987), that the goals of environmentalism can be presented as essentially an extension of the existing human
rights discourse. Certainly there is evidence that governments, as well
as social scientists and environmental campaigners, consider this a
natural extension of human rights.

Legal theorists have identified a potential for mobilizing existing
human rights, so that in campaigning for effective implementation
of existing international instruments, environmental protection will
follow automatically.[3] Thus, as Boyle (1996) argues, existing civil and
political rights can be mobilized to foster an environmentally friendly
political order and go a long way to enabling concerned groups to voice
their objections to environmental damage; moreover, serious environmental damage is frequently accompanied by civil and political oppression, and so there is reason to see common cause between struggles
against both.[4] Social and economic rights can also be mobilized to
contribute to environmental protection through substantive standards
of human well-being: rights to health, decent living conditions and
decent working conditions may all bear directly upon environmental
conditions. As well as this potential for mobilizing existing human

rights, there is also the possibility of reinterpreting them to enhance their environmental implications (Ksentini, 1994). The right to life, for example, could in principle 'be deemed to be infringed where the state fails to abate the emission of highly toxic products into supplies of drinking water' (Anderson, 1996: 7). The right to life might be deemed, more generally, to include the right to live in a healthy environment, a pollution-free environment, and even an environment in which ecological balance is protected by the state. In the European context, another human right which has been used to set precedents for environmental protection is the right to respect for one's private and family life and home.[5]

As well as mobilizing and adapting existing human rights, there is also the suggestion that new, more specifically environmental rights, may constitute part of a 'new generation' of human rights.[6] Since the Stockholm agreement of 1972, and the further impetus given by the Brundtland Report in 1987, the idea that humans have a fundamental right to an adequate environment has gained growing acceptance. If one accepts the immanent logic that has led from civil and political to social and economic rights, one can perhaps see how its further development can lead in the direction of environmental rights. For if certain social and economic rights are material preconditions for the effective enjoyment of civil and political rights, it seems no less evident that the effective enjoyment of an adequate environment is a precondition for the enjoyment of any of those rights.

Nevertheless, even setting aside worries about the human rights discourse itself,[7] with regard more specifically to environmental rights various issues raised by legal theorists command our attention.

To begin with, the idea of a human right to 'an adequate environment', understood as a substantive right, raises various problems. For instance, it is notoriously difficult to find legally serviceable definitions of 'adequate environment' or the kindred locutions to be encountered in contemporary constitutions. There are also associated problems of enforcement and adjudication – often establishing who the right is to be enforced against can be very difficult. Another problem is that of attaining a sufficiently strong and enduring consensus with regard to their inviolability in relation to competing – nonenvironmental – claims. So while some substantive rights could perhaps gradually be implemented – along with conceptually related rights to health, housing and education – it is realistic to expect greater prospects of success to depend on linking substantive claims to procedural claims.[8]

Procedural rights relevant to environmental protection include rights to know (i.e. a right to environmental information, including rights to government records and to independent ecological and health research which as a bearing on the ecological welfare, rights to be informed of development proposals); rights to participate in the determination of environmental standards; rights to object to ministerial and agency environmental decisions; and rights to bring action against departments, agencies, firms and individuals that fail to carry out their duties according to law. (Eckersley, 1996: 230)

As well as pragmatic considerations, there are also principled arguments favouring procedural rights – in particular, in relation to enhanced democratic participation in environmental decision-making. Environmental protection is never a purely technical affair:[9] it involves political decision-making about what is a problem and how to address it; and the outputs of decisions also have effects raising questions of distributive justice.

It also needs to be noted, though, that while democracy may be enhanced by procedural rights of participation in decision-making processes, effective opportunities to participate may be far from equal for all citizens; in fact, given that these rights are usually exercised most effectively by particular interest groups, there is actually a democratic case for placing constitutional constraints on their rights to influence decisions affecting the wider public. Participation rights are arguably most important for NGOs and other pressure groups. Certainly, NGOs fulfil an important civic function by holding governments and intergovernmental institutions accountable to the public (Bichsel, 1996: 252); advocacy groups give a voice to sectors of society not represented by other pressure groups and so these NGOs empower a greater number of citizens to participate in the political process (ibid.: 253). Nevertheless, while they help to broaden the political agenda, their own specific agendas can be more particularistic. NGOs are not democratic or even political institutions: their enhanced role needs to be subject to democratic constraints which constitutions can in principle provide (cf. Cameron and Mackenzie, 1996).

Another relevant development, which is potentially in tension with the rights approach, is that environmental security is now increasingly considered – by social scientists and governments alike – to be on a par with military and economic security as a concern touching the very stability of existing states (cf. Eckersley, 1995): hence the question of how states' security interests relate to citizens' and groups' interests in environmental protection is also one of constitutional significance. An advantage of rights, in relation to this issue, is that they set down certain markers for where citizens' interests, or citizens' interpretations of threats, should be recognized as legitimate by the state.

Certainly, one would not expect environmental rights themselves to be a panacea for all ecological and social challenges, but it is also worth noting that they are relevant even in relation to alternative environmentalist strategies. The principles these seek to apply – such as the 'polluter pays' principle, the precautionary principle, environmental impact assessment (EIA), and sustainable development – themselves raise rights issues. The operation of the precautionary principle and EIA, for instance, rely chiefly on procedural rights to know, and to influence proposed environmentally sensitive developments; and where the precautionary principle is accepted as a decision rule, as for instance in Europe, its implementation can be the basis of rights claims; also, there is no reason why claims to EIA procedures could not generate justiciable obligations (Anderson, 1996). As well as justiciable rights, there are also more fundamental rights issues that arise out of tensions within and between these principles. For instance, while the principle that the polluter should pay in practice typically issues in the right to buy tradeable permits to pollute, it could be interpreted to imply a right of others to be paid compensation by polluters.[10] Most generally, the principle of sustainability itself can be construed – as it is by Brundtland – as essentially a question of balancing competing rights – of equity, futurity and environment.

This question of balancing competing rights brings us back to the basic issue that environmental interests can conflict with interests protected by traditional human rights, particularly those of economic freedom and cultural development; and that environmental interests themselves are subject to conflicting interpretations. This leads to the question of whether and how different categories of interest – whether or not directly protected as justiciable rights – can be mapped onto other social goods, and subject to appropriate distributive principles.

Classifying environmental goods as social goods

On the face of it, while procedural rights could be viewed as a fairly straightforward extension of existing civil and political liberties, substantive rights might seem more akin to social and economic rights. It might therefore be tempting to see their respective objects as assimilable to two distinct types of social goods along the lines of the

Rawlsian distinction between liberties (subject to equal distribution) and income/wealth (subject to differential distribution). But this is problematic if the point of substantive environmental rights is to protect everyone equally. An alternative view would be that a substantive right to an adequate environment is a right of non-interference, albeit in the medium of environmental manipulation – and hence to be considered as an extension of liberty.

To preserve the Rawlsian distinction in an environmental context could mean differentiating between the right to an adequate environment, understood as freedom from environmental harms or bads, on the one hand, and a right to resource use, on the other. The significance of this would be that the former comes under the equality principle applied to liberties and the latter under the difference principle, as applied to economic goods (income and wealth). In practice, avoidance of ecological bads and enjoyment of ecological goods are not always easy to distinguish, since an unpolluted environment can be considered a resource, for instance, but conceptually the distinction is important – especially if one assumes that two different distributive principles are applicable to other basic social goods. So while I am not necessarily making a presumption in favour of Rawls's principles of justice, it is helpful to take these as an illustrative benchmark against which to introduce some general considerations about how ecological goods can be fitted into normative political theory.

(1)   *Liberties*. Rawls's first principle of distributive justice states that 'each person is to have an equal right to the most extensive total system of equal basic liberties compatible with a similar system of liberty for all' (Rawls, 1972: 250). Under this heading, in addition to standard personal, civil and political liberties, we might therefore also include a right to protection from some kinds of environmental harm. Thus as well as rights of free access to environmental information (civil), rights of fair access to environmental decision-making (political), and a right to fair hearing when representing interests of non-persons (legal) which this would yield, basic liberties could also include a right of freedom from (personal or collective) environmental harms. This could have far-reaching implications, since it focuses the issue of which environmental bads are to be seen as harms definitively to be avoided, as opposed to costs to be offset against benefits accruing from practices causing them. Part of the point here is to entrench a recognition that some environmental goods and services should not be considered as tradeable commodities at all (cf. chapter 5, section 2 above).

(2) *Income and wealth.* The principle for the distribution of this type of social good, the 'difference principle', states that 'social and economic inequalities are to be arranged so that they are . . . to the greatest benefit of the least advantaged' (Rawls, 1972: 302). If it is appropriate to consider freedom from environmental bads as a kind of liberty, then insofar as environmental goods are considered as resources, they would seem naturally to fall under this heading as part and parcel of an adequate definition of wealth.[11]

However, if one accepts Rawls's difference principle as appropriate to the distribution of income and wealth, one nevertheless needs to recognize that what this means, when ecological conditions are taken fully into account, is quite different from what it would be assumed to mean on typical liberal capitalist assumptions, and, indeed, on Rawls's own explicit assumption of *moderate* material scarcity (ibid.: 127–8). The difference principle specifies that inequalities are unjustified unless the (relatively) worse off members of society are (absolutely) better off with them than they would be without them: the standard implication of this, on the assumption of moderate scarcity, is that economic incentives to increase production are thereby allowed, since all can eventually benefit from it. This is because the more economic goods are generated, the more there are available for distribution; but if ecological costs are factored fully into costs of production the situation may look quite different. Thus if there are serious ecological constraints on economic growth, and therefore on what might 'trickle down', then relative improvements of the requisite sort may not be possible, and there may arise rather a need to provide an absolute baseline safety net.[12] The effect of this could be to provide for much greater socio-economic equity than would be expected on unecological liberal assumptions about the circumstances of justice (Benton, 1997).

(3) *Environmental goods that do not fall under either of Rawls's headings.* These are, chiefly, the goods which do not directly or tangibly accrue to an individual in such a way that asserting an interest or right in them could in principle be a clear-cut matter, and which therefore currently receive little recognition.[13] These are: (a) the kind of good represented as 'existence' or 'aesthetic' value; (b) goods of nonhuman beings.

Goods of type (a) could come in for indirect protection as afforded by discursive decision-making fora, and hence indirectly under the liberty principle; they could also be conceived under the heading of cultural values. In either case, however, the protection would not be direct or substantive. As was noted in chapter 5, participants in discourse may not agree to endorse the values in question. But this leaves the same situation as applies to cultural values more generally: these can be contested within and between cultures, and certainly the value attached to the physical environment has varied significantly over history and across societies. Appeals to cultural values, therefore, are unlikely to afford the guarantees of the strong (and non-relativistic) sort of protection envisaged by those theorists – such as O'Neill and Sagoff, discussed above in chapter 5 – who presuppose a strong connection between determinate environmental norms and cultural values in general. Nevertheless, it would arguably produce as strong protection as could be politically warranted. The key point, perhaps, is simply that mechanisms for democratic decisions be in place to ensure that decisions are taken at the appropriate level – that is, by those most clearly affected.

The situation regarding goods of type (b), however, is different. Here it is not simply a matter of conflicting human interests in relation to *their* environment, for it raises the issue of nonhuman interest-bearers, and thus the question of whether it is possible or desirable to expand the range of bearers of rights to include nonhumans. Whereas constitutional rights have hitherto been restricted to humans, claims that certain primates should also enjoy such rights are currently gaining support (Cavalieri and Singer, 1993); and claims for animal rights more generally are also being advanced; even rights for natural entities other than animals have been canvassed (cf. Stone, 1974). However, the more the range of bearers is expanded, the more problematic the rights discourse becomes both in principle and in practice: on the one hand, the less the new bearers resemble humans, the more tenuous appears – to many[14] – the connection with the reasons which give human rights their moral force in the first place; on the other, this expansion of rights may tend to dilute their force *as* rights, since there are likely to be so many competing claims that not all can adequately be redeemed, something which downgrades the discourse of rights as such. Certainly, there are many difficulties in drawing up and implementing legal rights for nonhumans, but this does not mean that other measures for the protection of nonhuman interests are not possible. The (probably insuperable) difficulties in the way of justiciable rights for (at least most) other creatures do not prevent some degree of constitutional level provision for their protection.[15]

It might nevertheless be objected that there appears to be no direct or immediately effective human interest in the pursuit of nonhuman goods, and so the claimed advantage of linking ecological values to human interests would not seem to apply here. My response to this problem is in part guided by the thought that the same point could be made in relation to many human goods too. Empirical individuals and groups often have no *immediate* interest in relation to other humans either, but this does not prevent them recognizing a more general or indirect interest in the provision of social and public goods. For theories accepting the assumption of such an interest, it does not need to be empirically proven whether individuals actually care about other humans in order for the equitable distribution of social goods to be justified. So on the basis of the argument of the last chapter – that there is no sustainable argument for pure human preference, and that self-respect entails respect for nonhumans – I would claim that it is not appropriate to demand a higher standard of proof in relation to nonhumans. So, without denying that there are considerably more difficulties dealing with nonhuman interests, I nevertheless maintain the claim defended in chapter 6 that political theorists have to recognize that relations with nonhumans can in principle, and should, be normatively regulated. In practice this is only likely to happen by being harnessed to and picked up by (human) interest groups. But what can be done is to allow such groups particular rights; to alter the burden of proof and rules of standing in relation to animal rights cases, for instance, and, more generally, to favour and promote institutions aimed at inculcating 'care' for nonhumans.

2 Ecological democracy

I am aware that such proposals, when considered for their political implications, raise many questions. I shall not attempt definitive answers to them, but I shall suggest how they might in principle be answered in a manner consistent with the broad normative principles I have proposed.

One question area concerns the potential conflict between constitutional and democratic principles. Well-known concerns about the 'democratic deficit' of constitutionally entrenched rights and norms[16] – in particular, their immunity to 'democratic' revision, and the 'undue' influence that can accrue to the judiciary – would seem to be accorded extra validity when even animals are seen as a virtual part of the polity! Against this it can be pointed out, though, that the standard line of reply – that there are certain principles and rights that merit immunity from the pure majority will of the populace at any given moment, and good democratic reasons for the judicial checking of legislative and executive power – would hold in relation to the protection of ecological interests if it holds for generalizable interests at all. This view is broadly consistent with what appears to be an emerging consensus about the relation between democracy and ecological values,[17] namely, that accepting the traditional value of democracy in allowing the reasoned articulation of competing views, it will favour the recognition of ecological values just to the extent that these are reasonably attended to; if these are insufficiently recognized at present, this is because actual democratic conditions fall short of what is required for the discursive practices they advocate. Certainly, constitutional provisions will not be sufficient to guarantee the development of an appropriate democratic culture, but they can nevertheless provide necessary conditions for it, such as rights of access to resources, education, information and political participation. Hence, in principle, there would appear to be complementarity between constitutional environmentalism and a commitment to discursive and – what for some it entails – ecological democracy. For the constitutional approach can be geared to underwriting the requisite conditions for enlightened will-formation whose purpose it is discursive democracy's to attain.

Nevertheless, the question of what ecological democratization can or should mean in practice is much more complicated. When constitutional proposals are advanced in the context of a liberal state they can always expect a mixed reception and in some ways unpredictable outcomes. What makes a liberal democracy potentially responsive to normative innovations also makes it responsive to the interests of those who would oppose them; so constitutional proposals aimed at shifting the effective balance of power are liable to meet resistance. The appropriate attitude to the institutions of liberal democracy, I would therefore suggest, is one of immanent criticism.[18] Hence we might appreciate that the normative ideal of a sustainable society is in some respects already implicit in modern constitutional democracies. Instituted and evolved to govern, by accommodation, plural and shifting constellations of interests that develop with the growth of a dynamic economy and the accelerating social changes brought with it, the political stability of a modern constitutional democracy is not premised on static social relations or productive forces. Liberal democracy is in many ways a flexible and resilient political form: its constitutional arrangements are typically such as to allow a range of freedoms to citizens and economic agents, with political regulation of them kept to that minimum necessary to favour an equilibrium of social and economic forces. This enhances its 'feedback' capacities – that is, its responsiveness to signals of ecological disruption emanating from various sectors of society.[19]

Nevertheless, the sustainability of liberal democracies with capitalist economies is premised on an assumption of the indefinite sustainability of economic growth – an assumption which appears seriously questionable from an ecological perspective. Moreover, the emphasis on growth, as opposed to what it is for,[20] combined with the domination of market values, means there can also be certain important interests people have whose effective expression is systematically blocked. Within liberal democracies, policy problems tend to be defined and disaggregated largely in response to the dominant pattern of interest representation (Dryzek, 1996: 113). Liberal democratic states have little disincentive to externalize ecological costs both spatially and temporally; they also provide very limited opportunities for vicarious representation of non-citizens' interests – or indeed, for the ecological interests of their own citizens (Eckersley 1996: 215). Longer-term and more generalizable interests tend to mobilize less effectively in the cut and thrust of normal politics than short-term partisan interests. Moreover, even those public interests taken up and advocated by non-state associations, such as environmental organizations, are vulnerable to liberal democratic 'framing devices' (ibid.: 215).[21]

The question of the extent to which reliance on institutions of the liberal state is appropriate involves not only normative, but also empirical considerations. Ecological imperatives are arising within, and in some respects bringing about, a changing political context, both nationally and globally, that calls into question previous assumptions about the nature and role of the nation-state. While the state remains the main source of constitutional and environmental law, and while international environmental politics is still strongly shaped by national interests, including those expressed in terms of 'environmental security', the pressures (governmental and non-) towards globalization on the one hand and the principle of subsidiarity on the other are bringing about noticeable changes. Indeed, it is arguable that the traditional conception of the nation-state as the bearer of a monopoly of legitimate force within a territory is gradually being undermined in each aspect of its definition: states no longer always have a *de facto* monopoly of force both because of the growing power and influence of transnational economic agencies and because of the increase in transnational legal agreements and legislation; states' legitimacy is increasingly called into question, among other reasons, because of their perceived inability adequately to respond to environmental crises (Beck, 1995); states are increasingly difficult to identify uniquely with a territory, not only because of competing claims of ethnic groups, within and across their borders, to collective rights of self-development, but also, and more especially, because when transboundary ecological processes are taken into view, the very notion of a bounded territory is undermined (Kuehls, 1996). With the emergence of new sources of legislative authority, of new political actors and rights-bearers, there is increasing conceptual, as well as normative, complexity involved in balancing the interests of individual citizens against both states and non-state collective agencies, and then again against environmental considerations. An adequate grasp of the import of empirically shifting power relations in this complex context therefore requires a sound theoretical basis.

Certainly, there are many political questions which obviously cannot and should not be dealt with at the constitutional level. Much debate about solutions to ecological problems concerns the area of social life that they come under: thus there is debate for instance about whether or when economic, fiscal, legal, legislative, or some other type of measure is appropriate. Within each area, there is then also room for debate about the normative basis of the measures to be taken: for instance, whether they are to be preventative, punitive, compensatory, redistributive, or incentive-providing. Given this range of uncertainties, combined with all the uncertainties regarding the nature, extent, impact and distribution of ecological problems, there is a strong case for enhancing the democratic capacities of state institutions to respond to new ecological imperatives formulated 'from below'. In particular, this could mean allowing more feedback and input from the associations of civil society.

Insofar as political theory is concerned with associations of civil society, a major concern is to understand not only the formal policy processes of the state, but also the opportunities that are or should be available for other political actors to influence policy-making. A rough definition of civil society, as this term is understood by NGOs (cf. Jacobs, 1996) and theorists of discursive democracy (Dryzek, 1996: 117), is that it is composed of all social life not encompassed by the state, on the one hand, or the economy, on the other. It is the site for the articulation and representation of those interests which are disadvantaged within the existing political system – including various new social movements and representatives of other environmental and animal rights constituencies. In its political aspects, civil society 'can be defined in functional terms as public action in response to failure of state and/ or economy' (ibid.); it 'can also be a source of pressure on state and

economic actors, through protests, boycotts, campaigns, and so forth'
(ibid.). Given the desirability, for both ecological and democratic
reasons, for greater discursive democracy (cf. Dryzek, 1987), there is
need to support and assess the ongoing research into appropriate design of deliberative institutions, on which many theoretical questions
bear (cf. Lafferty and Meadowcroft, 1996): examples here include public hearings (especially in association with impact assessment), right-to-
know laws, alternative dispute resolution techniques, public inquiries,
interest-group access, and so on (Dryzek, 1996: 111).

Nevertheless, while civil society is undoubtedly an important site
for the introduction into the political system of ecological values, there
is also need for a degree of caution, as I have already noted, about the
normative status of its actors and their claims. It is often assumed that
discourses emerging from deliberative fora or public spheres in 'civil
society' articulate interests that are necessarily more environmental
and more legitimate than those protected or promoted by the state. But
these interests are still particularistic, in relation not only to fundamental interests, but also to other legitimate interests and discourses. If
discursive democracy is to maintain its distinctiveness from political
horse-trading, it must aim to secure the conditions for conduct in
accordance with the Habermasian regulatory ideal of a discourse so
transparent as to articulate fundamental norms. Of course, in practice,
conditions approximating the ideal seldom if ever prevail. Hence there
is reason in practice to be cautious about what exactly to expect. It is to
be remembered that if participants are to ascertain what their interests
really are, this is not straightforwardly a case of discovering them, but
is always also likely to involve some degree of *transformation* of them.
So to embark on a process of interest-transformation can only be
legitimate if it does not undermine the protection of legitimate interests
as initially perceived (including the 'mere preferences' Sagoff excludes
from deliberation proper). This point cuts quite deeply into the argument for deliberative democracy: if it depends on a right of citizens to
participate in deliberative fora, then the terms and conditions of participation need to be established; the terms of participation must themselves make reference to interests – interests that need to be established
prior to any process of interest clarification.

Of course, the problem cuts both ways: interests not recognized as
legitimate can in practice get excluded merely because they do not fit
the dominant view (cf. Lukes, 1974). It seems clear, therefore, that there
is a need both for constitutional guarantees and limits regarding such
matters as the rights of participation and for maximum opportunities
for dissident views to have a hearing. In particular, while there are

strong arguments for strengthening the scope for action of associations of civil society, there must be safeguards against these undermining adequate recognition of other individual, including economic, interests. As was argued in chapter 5, it has also to be acknowledged that economic imperatives, while seriously qualified, are not entirely obviated by ecological considerations. For the time being, it has to be acknowledged that some of the most effective measures for environmental protection – such as ecological taxes – presuppose the continuance of property rights and economic freedoms; moreover, ethical concerns about the alleviation of poverty, as well as realism about the effective force of conventional economic interests, combine as reasons for caution about too swingeing or utopian a critique of economic development which neglects the co-requisite of global social justice.

But if critique has to take its cue from actually existing conditions, this does not mean it cannot draw its inspiration from a more utopian vision. A basic premise of any normative political theory, I believe, should be the desirability of finding institutions, processes and policies that favour the articulation of the most enlightened interests of the day – interests on the basis of which the very meaning of economic development would be transformed to take account of the quality of life of all – and this, on the grounds that the most basic political good is that of human self-respect and integrity.

Conclusion

For the most enlightened interests of the day to become the most effectual interests there is a long way to go – enlightenment, as a social process, does not come all at once. As should by now be clear, I do not wish to claim that it would be a straightforward matter to bring empirical interests to coincide with ecological goods. But I have assumed that it is only if they are linked to interests that ecological goods will be promoted at all.

Given the extensive discussion of interests, in my final remarks I return to what I take to be the normative implications of its first premise, that human beings are natural beings. Human beings enjoy, *de facto*, certain privileges – as I think it would be appropriate to call them – in virtue of their exceptional capacities for sociality, rationality and spirituality. My guiding thought, though, is that these *de facto* privileges do not entail *de jure* privileges in relation to their cohabitants of this world, or to this world itself, but responsibilities. Only through realizing their responsibilities can humans attain the dignity and integrity which is potentially theirs.

This thought is not extraneous to political theory – or to politics as such – but provides its ultimate *raison d'être*: for the purpose of organizing our lives politically is not merely to contain conflicts of interest that arise as if from a collision of material atoms in motion – which is a fundamentally reductive view not only of humans but of the nature of Nature – rather it is to find a way of living which brings human lives into harmony with the nature that they are. We have not made ourselves or the world; but we do make our way in it. Humanistic wisdom and ecological wisdom combine with spiritual insights in yielding the conclusion that we should aim to make our way – individually, collectively and politically – with humility and dignity, striving for adequate knowledge and for coherence of action with it, in an attitude of reverence for the greater whole of which we are just parts, but not without reverence too, for the nature which we ourselves are.

Notes

1 Introduction: Ecological Values and Human Interests

1 In this book I shall not be discussing the question of future generations. The interests of future humans cannot unproblematically be related to interests of living humans, but the problems they present are not of the same sort as the problems that ecological values do.

2 At the time of going to press, I am aware of only one sustained and systematic attempt to do so (which is also going to press): Dobson (Forthcoming).

3 I am going to argue that this argument has a qualitatively different significance, but for present I am just drawing attention to a range of views.

4 Leopold, for instance, formulated the suggestive and influential guideline that 'a thing is right when it tends to preserve the integrity, stability, and beauty of the biotic community. It is wrong when it tends otherwise' (Leopold, 1949: 224–5).

5 Making this move will certainly not remove all possible controversy: what 'ecological facts' are, and what assumptions any political theorist is 'really' committed to, will remain contested questions. But I think just afocusing on the point that this is what debate ought to be about is itself a significant step.

6 Cf. Soper (1995: 15–17) on nature as otherness.

7 I expand further on this in Hayward (1996b).

8 See, for instance, Andrew Dobson (1995) and Robert Goodin (1992). Luke Martell (1994) also gives this along with natural limits as a feature of green theory, although his actual development of the idea limits intrinsic value to sentient beings.

9 Of course, it remains open to radical greens to question whether shallow and reformist reasons are *likely* to have such thoroughgoing effects as actions based on 'deeper' reasons. This is certainly worth asking, but my point is that the question cannot be answered merely by inspecting alleged motivations.

10 An opposition between anthropocentrism and ecocentrism is the organizing principle of Eckersley (1992); cf Dobson (1995: 61): 'If there is one word
that underpins the whole range of Green objections to current forms of
human behaviour in the world it is probably "anthropocentrism".'

2 Intrinsic Value in Nature

1 See, generally, contributions to the journal *Environmental Ethics* over the
past 20 years (an index of past issues is accessible via the world wide web
at http://www.cep.unt.edu/enethics.html; and a search facility for this and
other topics in environmental ethics is located at http://www.cep.unt.edu/
search.html); see also the issue of *The Monist*, 1992, 72.2 devoted to 'The
intrinsic value of Nature'.

2 For I distinguish a human interest in considering them from the interests
that may be brought to bear – or indeed suspended – during the consideration. This differentiation of interests is explained more fully in chapters 4–
6.

3 For example, cf., e.g. Attfield (1987) on the need to establish moral
considerability first: this is necessary but not sufficient, he thinks, for the
predication of intrinsic value.

4 Given that states of affairs are complex, and that some substantially different states may have aggregate totals of component values that are equal,
decision-making problems will arise here too: but I shall treat this as a
problem of application rather than principle – see section 4.

5 I have put in the word 'arbitrarily' since euthanasia and just war provide
counterexamples which many find persuasive against an absolute prohibi-
tion. In fact, many think a penalty of death for certain offences against other
humans is not arbitrary either. I am not here entering any debate about the
circumstances, if any, in which killing might not be arbitrary.

6 See Attfield (1995) and Glover (1977): again, I am drawing attention to an
area of debate, not here entering it.

7 Attfield (1987; 1995) helps to clarify the issues here. Nevertheless, a number
of influential environmental philosophers do speak of the intrinsic value of
entities (see, for instance, Callicott, 1986; Elliott, 1994). In fact, Mathews
(1991: 119–20) argues that the refusal to do so is a peculiar anomaly of
utilitarian approaches to values; however, I disagree with this claim, and
think her own argument is vulnerable to the criticisms I make in the text.

Given, though, that the idea of entities having intrinsic value has been
taken up by theorists from other disciplines, including political theory, as
evidenced in the survey of Dobson (1995: 50), a further cautionary word is
in order. Whenever one speaks of value, there must be something of which
the value is predicated, and so it is not inappropriate to refer to that something, in a formal way, as an 'object', by way of contrast with the subject who
attributes the value: yet it is important to avoid eliding this formal idea with
that of a tangible object, as even O'Neill (1993) in an otherwise careful
analysis, tends at times to do.

8 Otherwise it would be problematic to say that happiness was intrinsically good, since its goodness could then depend on whose happiness it was. Judgements about the intrinsic value of something like happiness, therefore, rest on these two intuitions: happiness is *good*, and good *for any human*. Robin Attfield has pointed out to me that it also sometimes rests on related tenets such as that it is morally right to promote what is nonmorally good.

9 In seeking to specify the features which any intelligible notion of intrinsic value must have, my approach differs from that of John O'Neill, who distinguishes between different *varieties* of intrinsic value. I believe that the present approach enables – indeed, requires – us to press the analysis more deeply, but I am indebted to O'Neill for the initial set of distinctions that have made this possible.

10 Indeed, the idea of intrinsic value is more exactly contrasted with 'extrinsic value', a broader category of value of which instrumental value is just one variety: others include what Attfield (1995) has referred to as 'contributive' and 'inherent' values.

11 It will be noted that when Moore refers to value as a 'property', he stresses that it is a *nonnatural* property. Attempts to adapt his conception of intrinsic value to account for intrinsic values in nature as *natural* properties inevitably lead to confusion: such is the outcome, I would maintain, for the attempt of Elliot (1994), for instance.

12 O'Neill's own definitions are these:

> Weak: 'The evaluative properties of objects are properties that *exist* in the absence of evaluating agents.'
> Strong: 'The evaluative properties of objects *can be characterized* without reference to evaluating agents.' (O'Neill, 1993: 16 – my emphases)

I have modified his definitions, firstly, because I have a minor reservation about the idea of 'evaluative properties of objects', which introduces more terms in need of definition (and raises the problem noted in the previous note); and, secondly, because I have a reservation about the reference to 'evaluating agents'. The latter issue is one which will become central, and it arises with the possibility that not all evaluating subjects are moral agents. That is, we can distinguish between the evaluations of a moral agent who may or may not acknowledge the existence of values for others, and the evaluations of, say, nonrational or nonhuman beings for whom things can be of value but who can nevertheless not engage in the sort of evaluative activity characteristic of moral agents – these are beings, in other words, who can be 'moral patients'; that is, beings who can have a good, for whom things can have value, but who are not also moral agents.

13 The logic of deploying the notion of nonderivative value has been set out in a deliberately crude fashion to highlight problems that in practice would normally arise in less dramatic, and perhaps less intractable, ways. Cer-

tainly Attfield's particular intrinsic value theory is addressed to far more
subtly presented problems: for in the real world it is not normally a case of
choosing between one whole class of goods or another; moreover, his
theory is aimed not at guiding individual actions but at identifying principles to inform *practices*; he also believes it is possible to 'optimize' the
weighing of claims of individual instances of intrinsic value against aggreg-
ates of them.

14 For further explanation of what I mean by 'human chauvinist', see chapter
3, section 3, below.

15 I hope that what I have sought to establish here is clear, but in case it be
misunderstood, I reiterate the following: Attfield's own approach is to
argue for moral considerability first and then construct his intrinsic value
theory on its basis – so he does recognize the crucial step of establishing
moral considerability. Moreover, I am not denying that if the human chauvinist were persuaded to take this step, he could be brought to share
Attfield's substantive values. My only claim here is that there is no determinate sense in which these values are *intrinsic*.

16 I have made related criticisms of the proposal of Birch (1993) in Hayward
(1996a).

3 Anthropocentrism

1 In ethics, at least three interpretations of anthropocentrism are possible: (a)
it can refer to an exclusive concern with the good of human patients, such
that humans could be pictured as constituting a 'closed moral circle'; (b) it
can mean a greater, though not exclusive, concern with the good of human
patients such that they occupy the innermost of 'concentric moral circles';
(c) it can refer not to whom or what concern is *for*, but, rather, mean that the
concern as such is exclusively that *of* human agents (only humans can be
agents, but this is affirmed without prejudice to the potential range of
patients they can be concerned with). The third interpretation is consistent
with (a) or (b) or neither. (a) is objectionable, I shall agree with ecological ethicists; (b), though, is not necessarily objectionable; (c) cannot be
objectionable.

2 For further reflections on this question, see chapter 6.

3 The possibility that there might be more problems to overcome than
speciesism and human chauvinism is addressed in section 5.

4 See chapter 2 for reasons in support of this view against claims for strong
objectivity of values in nonhuman nature. My acceptance of the possibility
of 'weak objectivity' is conditional on interpreting 'objectivity' in terms
of intersubjective agreement about what it is reasonable to suppose is objectively valuable. Another point that is relevant in the present context is that
I am not claiming that valuers have to be humans, only that some of them
are.

5 There may well be critics of anthropocentrism who personally intend the
term to refer only to the *exclusion* of nonhumans rather than to imply any

particular commitment regarding the consideration due to humans. But given that this is just one plausible sense of the term (see note 1 above), I think it is ill-suited to convey their meaning.

6 Incidentally, some benefits can go to nonhumans, too – as in veterinary medicine, for instance. While this is not a decisive consideration – especially as vets can sometimes participate in objectionably speciesist practices – it does reinforce the point that human and nonhuman interests are not always straightforwardly opposed.

7 In the literature on biocentrism there does not appear to be a consensus on whether it is supposed to be an alternative to human-centred concerns, or an extension of them: as I show elsewhere (Hayward, 1995, chapter 2), some, like Paul Taylor (1981), tend to the former view while others, like Robin Attfield (1987), take the latter view. Relatedly, it makes a considerable difference whether biocentrism is understood to refer to life as such, or to living organisms more specifically: the latter is most usually intended, but on some usages the former is, and then it can almost be synonymous with 'ecocentrism', since the role of the abiotic constituents of ecosystems could be understood as indispensible for the maintenance of life as such.

8 Ecocentrism is contrasted with anthropocentrism and this contrast used as an organizing principle by Eckersley (1992).

9 I am not ruling out the possibility of there being such a reason, or, indeed, the possibility of eventually supplementing the idea of speciesism. The basic rationale for focusing on the latter is that living species have enough in common with humans for the 'anthropocentric benchmarks' I mentioned to apply. This does not preclude the development of ever more subtle benchmarks. For the time being, however, it seems to me that whatever intrinsic capacities rocks may have that are worthy of independent consideration, these unfold on such scales of space and time that human actions can have little effect on them.

4 The Enlightenment of Self-Interest

1 Even when the idea is subjected to critical scrutiny, as in the volume edited by Jane Mansbridge (1990b), one finds a noted analytical thinker like Jon Elster (1990) stating that the 'idea that self-interest makes the world go round is refuted by a few familiar facts' (p. 45) when these are merely facts that illustrate that not all human behaviour that is straightforwardly *selfish*. Mansbridge herself – in the context of a nuanced discussion of the relation of self-interest to altruism – expresses confidence that it is possible to demonstrate empirically when people are acting against their self-interest (1990a: 133). Yet such 'refutations' and 'demonstrations' beg the very sort of question that the book is intended to answer, namely, how you get *beyond* the view of which Mansbridge herself provides a nice illustration:

Hobbes himself, asked why he had just given sixpence to a beggar, answered, true to his belief in self-interest, 'I was in pain to consider the miserable condition of the old man; and now my alms, giving him some relief, doth also ease me'. Abraham Lincoln, having remarked to a companion that 'all men were prompted by selfishness in doing good or evil', and having subsequently run to rescue some trapped piglets for their mother, was asked, 'Now, Abe, where does selfishness come in on this little episode?' Lincoln answered, 'Why, bless your soul, Ed, that was the very essence of selfishness. I would have had no peace of mind all day had I gone on and left that suffering old sow worrying over those pigs. I did it to get peace of mind, don't you see?' (Mansbridge, 1990a: 140–1)

2 For a range of perspectives on this question area see, as well as Mansbridge (1990a), also Paul, Miller and Paul (1993).
3 The limits of this view are discussed in chapter 5.
4 This step is consonant with the further feminist insight into how the problem is to reconstruct relations within the family (as well as in the wider society), not simply to reverse the power hierarchy, nor simply to 'equalize' it either, since there are qualitative problems in the way of doing so.
5 It is also liable to be deeply unpleasant for the self involved if what is described corresponds, as I believe it does, to the condition known as autism.
6 There is further discussion of the ways in which interests can be enlightened in chapter 5.
7 The themes announced in this paragraph are recognizable as those which are central to the 'communitarianism' of, for example, Sandel (1982), Taylor (1990) and MacIntyre (1981); but this should not be taken as an unqualified endorsement of communitarianism, for reasons I shall return to in section 5.
8 In fact, it has been put to me that no political theorist seriously proposes altruism as a basic assumption anyway. Nevertheless, as I hope becomes clear, there are various issues that can best be brought to light by analysing the proposal. I would also observe that some of the arguments for ecological values – such as were critically examined in chapters 2 and 3 – could be said to amount to the advocacy of what might be called 'eco-altruism': for there are evident structural similarities between the critiques of human- and individual self-interest.
9 I have not been able to locate a systematic analysis of this definition; but the fact that it is often intended is evidenced by the index entry for 'self-sacrifice' in Mansbridge (1990b): 'see *Altruism*'. In the text I have taken a correspondingly 'commonsensical' view of the meaning of the meaning of self-sacrifice. Nevertheless, this hardly does justice to the rich connotations of the concept of 'sacrifice', and I think that unpacking these would yield further insights into how problematic this whole area is.
10 The qualification is necessary because in section 6 I shall mention a more strenuous sort of supererogation which exceeds this.
11 This is the kind of 'altruism' that Bernard Williams characterizes as 'a general disposition to regard the interests of others, merely as such, as

making some claim on one, and, in particular, as implying the possibility of limiting one's own projects' (Williams, 1973: 250). I accept that this disposition is a necessary feature of morality, but all it requires is that one acknowledge moral obligations with regard to others: it is not a disposition which is altruistic in any of the senses I have distinguished. In fact, it is consistent with universalism, which can be characterized in contradistinction to both egoism *and* altruism (cf. Hospers, 1982: 134–5).

12 If it is the case that one cannot be a 'self' on one's own (see Taylor, 1990: 36), it is also the case that one cannot be an 'altruist' on one's own – and I mean this in a nontrivial sense – since it is as possible to position an other as an egoist as it is to impose altruism on them (cf. Mellor, 1992), and this is not to capture what is virtuous in one's regard for others.

13 See Hayward (1997b). Some writers, including Habermas (1990: 200), use the term 'solidarity' to denote something more akin to empathy, in contradistinction to justice, so given that I later draw on Habermas's work, it is important to signal this terminological discrepancy. My usage is, I think, closer to that of Ernst Bloch (1961), for whom solidarity is part and parcel of that impetus for justice that comes 'from below', and is inspired no less by a sense of general human dignity than compassion with the concrete sufferings of one's fellows. (It is this Blochian idea that is implied by the next sentence in the text, where reference is made to 'taking sides': this is done on the basis of universalizable principles – for instance, standing with oppressed against oppressor.)

14 Suppose a friend is suffering from a serious illness, it may not seem inappropriate to say one wants to show 'solidarity' with them, in the sense of standing by them, giving what help and comfort one can, but this sense seems appropriate because the illness itself is effectively seen as an enemy to be struggled against, and to that extent it is personified: although we know the illness 'could not do otherwise', as an actual person could, we will sometimes be in a frame of mind to think we can influence and overcome the illness in the way we could a personal opponent.

15 The idea of an interest in integrity was first introduced in conjunction with an interest in self-respect. I am focussing on integrity since this is more fundamental than, and a precondition of, genuine self-respect.

16 This idea here is rather like the Spinozan idea of *conatus*, a striving to preserve in one's being (for more on this, see chapter 6).

17 MacIntyre, however, speaks of the integrity of a human life as a whole, and tends to equate narrative integrity with moral integrity: on tensions between the two, which are particularly relevant in the context of the more fragmented ethical life characteristic of modernity, see Susan Stephenson (1998).

18 If, as Kitwood says, integrity can be regarded as 'something more profound than virtue' (Kitwood, 1990: 183), its 'psychological substratum', then integrity 'is not a content-full virtue, like courage or generosity . . .' (ibid.: 210). Indeed, it has been pointed out by writers from a variety of disciplinary and theoretical backgrounds that if integrity is a virtue, it is a peculiar sort of

virtue: McFall refers to integrity, within morality, as a *higher-order* virtue; David Owen, commenting on Nietzsche, refers to integrity as a *ruling* virtue, in the sense that it represents a formal standard of excellence (Owen, 1995: 118). However, it is precisely the idea of integrity as a *formal* virtue – if a virtue at all – that gives rise to worries about what substantive moral commitments it might entail.

19 For a fuller discussion of the difference between preferences and commitments, see chapter 5, section 5.

20 This can obviously also happen in more subtle – ideological – ways, and I have only taken the illustration of overt brutality to make the point.

21 This is discussed further in chapter 6.

5 *Human Interests and Environmental Values*

1 For a classic discussion of this problem, see Olson, 1965.

2 Although note that the strong libertarian tendency in FME is somewhat counterbalanced by the public choice strand (see Eckersley, 1993).

3 These are characterized by not being excludable (that is, it is impossible to target particular consumers and exclude others) and by being able to withstand non-rival competition – for example, environmental goods like clean air and environmental bads like air pollution (Eckersley, 1993: 7). This has not stopped some free market enthusiasts trying to advocate privatization even here, but they have generally had to settle for 'the next best thing' – tradeable pollution rights.

4 See, for example Habermas (1990). I am not claiming that Habermas has the last word on this, or that his approach is immune to criticism, only that it allows us to move beyond what is problematic in Sagoff. One particular limitation of Habermas's approach is discussed in chapter 6, in relation to the question of moral consideration for nonhuman beings.

5 So while I would accept Keat's point that appropriate dealings with the environment need not necessarily be theorized with reference to its contribution to the satisfaction of *immediate* human interests, this nevertheless seems to me merely a question of degree of immediateness: for if these terms have meaning at all it is because they have meaning as social goods.

6 Barry (1965: chapter 10) provides a more detailed discussion of the relation between interests and wants (and wants can be considered, for my purposes, as having the same status I am attributing to preferences).

7 Reeve and Ware (1983) question whether meaningful talk of interests is limited to matters amenable to human or social control; I am with Barry (1965) in accepting the quite conventional view that it is.

8 The notion here is akin to the idea of having an interest as can be recognized in civil law as a basis for legal standing in relation to a particular matter: it refers to the capacity to be affected for better or worse by an action or proposed action of another. It meets the criteria for *admissibility* regardless of the *merits* of special claims that might eventually be pressed. Every action is liable to affect some third parties in some way: practically no action at all

would be possible if it had to respect every conceivable 'interest'. Hence, in law, rules of standing specify circumstances, qualifications and nature of harm that are relevant: likewise in political theory, some account is needed of which interests are such as to require socially sanctioned respect.

9 This is the locution always used by Barry, because his focus is on the meaning of interests only in what I call the special sense.

10 On my reasons for focusing on interests rather than needs, and the distinction between them, see the considerations that were offered at the end of section 6 in chapter 4. Another relevant consideration is also provided by Doyal and Gough (1991: 315n3), where they quote Thompson:

> The notion of an interest defines the range and type of activities and experiences that partly constitute a meaningful and worthwhile life, and it defines the nature of their worth. These types of activities are primary goods and because they are good something which deprives us of them is bad and harmful.

11 If I say I need something, I am making an assertion in which there is an implicit claim that its truth or otherwise is objectively verifiable. This does not mean that all needs are objective in a sense that would prevent the purely subjective apprehension of one's needs being the apprehension of a real need; it just means that statements referring to the existence of a need admit of truth-testing, whatever the test might involve. Statements about needs, in short, are, in principle, corrigible. Preferences, by contrast, cannot be true or false (even if reports of them can), for sincere statements about them are in principle incorrigible.

12 Cf. Sen (1990). Commitments, as opposed to mere preferences, are also at issue for O'Neill (1997) – cf. Keat (1997: 132) – although, as I observe in the text, they are not discussed in relation to interests.

13 For a critique of chrematistic economics, see Martinez-Alier (1990); Daly and Cobb (1990); and for a concise summary, Hayward (1995: 89–94). The Greeks used the term *chrematistics*, in contrast to *oikonomia*, to refer merely to 'the manipulation of property and wealth so as to maximise the short-term monetary exchange value to the owner' (Daly and Cobb, 1990: 138).

6 Human Self-Respect and Respect for Nonhumans

1 In saying this I am not taking any view on whether any nonhumans have ethical relations (cf L. Johnson, 1985); nor am I suggesting that all humans in fact have full moral capacities.

2 Below I discuss this view as it appears in Kant and Habermas in particular.

3 The care *vs* justice debate was initiated by Gilligan (1982); for a range of comment, see Larabbee (1993), and also Benhabib (1992), chapter 5; and on its relevance to interspecies concern, see Hayward (1997b).

4 Of course, one can care about a loved one while also considering them one's equal; in fact, as I go on to suggest, respect and care are seldom

found in isolation from one another: this fact, however, does not of itself undermine the validity of the analytical distinction between care and respect.

5 As Caygill (1995) notes, the term '*Achtung*' is used by Kant in ways that correspond to both 'respect' and 'reverence'; in the passage from which I've quoted, he contrasts the attitude of respect with 'wonder', which would indicate that he means by it something different from what I've characterized as reverence.

6 I say direct bearing, since of course I may seek to emulate them in my actions, but this is indirect relative to the sense I am discussing. In contemplative respect one does not 'make contact' with the other; active respect is an aspect of a real relationship.

7 See also Habermas (1993: 105–11). Dews (1995) usefully analyses this as a distinct argument from the earlier one of Habermas (1982).

8 He maintains this in Habermas (1982; 1993). On the 'performative attitude' itself, see also Habermas (1990: 23–9; 47–8).

9 Closer to my position in this regard is Apel (1992); cf. also Krebs (1997) on how Apel's development of discourse ethics is compatible with intuitions of a more compelling moral status of nonhumans.

10 'The *object* of reverence is the law alone . . . All reverence for a person is properly only reverence for the law . . . of which the person gives us an example' (Kant, 1948: 67). On the translation of '*Achtung*' as reverence, see note 5.

11 I would argue that whatever view of autonomy one takes, its possession by rational agents does not supply a reason for restricting respect to them. On the one hand, if autonomy is understood and valued purely as freedom of spontaneity, then liberty of spontaneity has to be valued *wherever* it occurs. It is worth noting that advocates of strictly negative freedom, as a kind of liberty of indifference – if they are consistent in maintaining, as for instance Berlin (1991) does, that criteria of rationality should not be built into its definition – are committed to the recognition of 'liberty of spontaneity' wherever it occurs, and, in particular, at whatever *level* it occurs. This includes kinds of freedom to be understood by reference to persons' bodily vulnerability to human interference; creatures other than humans can suffer this sort of harm. Indeed, Bentham was consistent enough, as animal liberationists have since highlighted (for example, Singer, 1991), in contrasting pleasure to pain, to see that this applied to any sentient creature. If, on the other hand, autonomy is understood in more specifically *rational* terms, it provides no direct reason for valuing any other form of liberty of spontaneity, but it does provide a reason for seeking to get adequate ideas about the good of any being capable of having a good, and, out of consistency, acting with respect for it.

12 Cf., for instance, MacIntyre (1981: 209).

13 I say normally, because Strawson does admit that sometimes it can be; what he argues though, is that it cannot be complete or long lasting – it is either temporary or a prelude to breaking from the strains of involvement.

14 I say every action should *in principle* be examined: I am naturally not
suggesting that in practice anyone could do this with literally every action;
but I assume that actions do fall under established headings embedded in
practices, and when novel moral issues are raised, then an agent would
think through the implications of acting one way rather than another.

15 It is worth recalling that in Gilligan's original formulation of it the care ethic
was set out as a description of a moral style actually encountered in empirical research, one to which the dominant view of ethics appeared to be
structurally blind. It involves *critical* knowledge of how ethical dispositions
are determined, or interests perceived. A way of proceeding therefore,
analogous to Gilligan's research, is to investigate whether there is already
'another voice' in moral conversations which dominant accounts of ethics
tend to be deaf to. One could thus seek to test the hypothesis that we already
do care in some ways, but do not adequately realize this cognitively (because of cultural and ideological repressions), and do not adequately act on
it (because channels for doing so are blocked off). The hypothesis that our
care for other species is actively repressed could be tested by examining, for
instance: how children's attitudes towards animals and meat are formed;
why food packaging attempts to remove all trace of its animal origins; how
attitudes to nature in general as radically other are formed; and so on. There
does seem to be a good deal of evidence of our cognitive alienation from the
rest of the natural world, and, indeed, from our own animal nature (cf.
Dickens, 1996). For clues on how to counter this alienation, one might
investigate the discourses of the growing number of vegans, vegetarians
and campaigners for animal welfare with an ear to a 'voice' that others
might recognize as their own under more propitious circumstances; one
might also inquire of those respondents of environmental cost–benefit ques-
tionnaires why they are prepared to recognize 'existence value' of certain
'environmental goods', including living entities; comparative studies with
societies that evince a more direct relationship with nonhuman parts of
nature could also be illuminating.

This way of proceeding has several advantages over ethical approaches
which seek to establish a more abstract calculus of the 'intrinsic value' of
nonhuman entities: in identifying what people already do care about one
avoids the need for the sort of moral exhortation that is hard to justify and
hard to make effective; it also usefully shifts attention onto the social factors
that inhibit its full expression, since if care does not translate into action this
is not necessarily due to lack of motivation to act, but to lack of channels for
action. If society were organized differently, the care could manifest itself.
In focusing on the social and cultural dimensions of the problem one avoids
playing – usually ineffectively – on individual conscience and instead
focuses on collectively agreed norms. With such norms in place, their form-
alization into something akin to constitutional principles becomes a real
possibility.

The proposition that consensus may move towards a greater concern for
nonhuman interests is only a hypothesis, not a foregone conclusion. I have

suggested, though, that the hypothesis is not self-evidently counterfactual, and have very roughly indicated some sorts of ways in which it might be tested.

7 Political Theory for a Sustainable Polity

1 Albeit general interests as opposed to special interests, as differentiated in chapter 5.
2 Practically all national constitutions drafted or revised in the past decade have included some environmental provision: the total number is something in excess of 70. Those which specifically provide environmental *rights* include: Angola (1991) Art. 24; Argentina (1994) Art. 41; Belarus (1994) Art. 46; Belgium (1994) Art. 23.4 (an environmental right is included as part of the right to a life of human dignity); Brazil (1996) Art. 225; Bulgaria (1991) Art. 55; Chechnya (1992) Art. 34; Chile (1980; 1997 reforms) Art. 19.8; Columbia (1991) Art. 79; Congo (1992) Art. 46; Costa Rica (1994) Art. 50; Ecuador (1996) Arts 44–8; Ethiopia (unofficial draft, 1994) Art. 44; Honduras (1982) Art. 145; Macedonia (1993) Art. 43; Mongolia (1992) Art. 16.2; Nicaragua (1987) Art. 60; Norway (1995) Art. 110b; Paraguay (1992) Art. 7; Philippines Sec. 16, Art. II (Douglas-Scott, 1996: 110n10); Portugal (1992) Art. 66; Russia (1993) Art. 42; Slovakia (1992) Art. 44; Slovenia (1991) Art. 72; South Africa (1996) Art. 24; South Korea (1987) Art. 35; Spain (1992) Art. 45; Turkey (1980) Art. 56. The Czech Constitution provides that the Czech and Slovak Charter of Fundamental Rights and Freedoms of 1991, which includes an environmental right, is 'a part of the constitutional order of the Czech Republic' (see Lippott, 1995). Countries without declared environmental rights in their constitutions, but whose Supreme Courts have ruled them to be inferred by existing rights include India (see Anderson, 1996) and Pakistan (see Lau, 1996). State constitutions in the USA which provide environmental rights include: Hawaii, Illinois, Pennsylvania, and Massachusetts. In Canada, Ontario has an Environmental Bill of Rights.

Although the wording varies somewhat between constitutions, the commonest formulation makes reference to a right to a clean and/or healthy environment. Up-to-date information on constitutions is readily obtainable via the Internet. Useful collections can be found at the following sites: http://www.psr.keele.ac.uk/const.htm (Keele University); http://www.uni-wuerzburg.de/law/index.html (Bayerische Julius-Maximilians-Universität, Würzburg); http://www.law.utexas.edu/foreign/(Tarlton Law Library).
3 On the general advantages of using existing human rights rather than introducing new ones, see Merrills (1996).
4 While in a European context, for instance, there have been very few cases of applying existing civil and political rights directly to environmental complaints, and even these have met with mixed success (Churchill, 1996; Douglas-Scott, 1996), elsewhere, especially where civil rights are less well-protected, this linkage is much more important: for example, see the

chapters by Anderson, Fabra, Lau and Harding in Boyle and Anderson (1996).

5 Article 8 of The European Convention provides that 'everyone has the right to respect for his private and family life [and] his home'. This provision has been used to set precedents for environmental protection, most significantly in the case of *Lopez-Ostra* v. *Spain*.

> Here, for the first time, the organs of the European Convention found a breach of the Convention as a consequence of environmental harm. The applicant suffered serious health problems from the fumes from a tannery waste treatment plant . . . Her attempt to obtain compensation from the Spanish courts was completely unsuccessful. The European Court of Human Rights held that there had been a breach of Article 8. (Churchill, 1996: 94)

Desgagné sees this as a development in the case law of the European Commission which reflects a growing awareness of the links between protection of human rights and protection of the environment (Desgagné, 1995: 263).

6 'Third generation or solidarity rights – usually [including] peace, development and a good environment – generally inhere in groups rather than individuals . . .' (Boyle, 1996: 46). Boyle notes that not all human rights lawyers favour the recognition of these as human rights; see also Sunstein (1993).

7 Scepticism about fundamental rights has been renewed at each stage of their development, but the common theme of objections – from the misgivings voiced by Burke and Bentham concerning the French Declaration, and Marx's critique of their class base, through various mutations of legal positivism to contemporary postmodernist objections to imperialism – is that the rights discourse (at each stage of its development) presents as universal a set of norms that are in fact particular. Today, this scepticism most often attaches to claims about their cultural relativity. But given the existence of an African Charter, European and American Conventions as well as International Covenants binding on all member states of the United Nations, such generalized scepticism would seem to be moot (although for a more principled response, see Vincent, 1986). A similar point would apply to criticisms of the rights discourse as an ethical discourse, to be contrasted with other ethical vocabularies, although I have tried to accommodate some of the concerns about its limitations both in chapter 6 of this book, and, more explicitly, in chapter 4 of Hayward (1995). Where serious and legitimate disagreement remains, in my view, is over issues within the discourse, concerning the content and weight of certain specific rights (especially in areas such as property and family life), and related questions (as signalled in note 6) of whether rights attach to individuals only, or also to collectivities. Such issues would obviously need to be addressed within the overall resesarch programme here proposed.

8 Robyn Eckersley suggests that 'the effectiveness of any substantive environmental rights presupposes the establishment of a wide range of environmental procedural rights' (Eckersley, 1996: 230). She also illustrates how they can blend together: 'Instead of an abstract, ambiguous "right to clean air and water", an environmental bill of rights . . . might declare, say, that citizens have a right to ensure that environmental quality is maintained in accordance with the standards set by current environmental laws (standards which would undergo regular public review)' (p. 230).

9 Cf. Benton and Redclift (1994); to suppose it is is to subscribe to one particular – managerial and positivistic – ideology: for an analysis of ideologies underpinning different environmental discourses, see Williams and Matheny (1995).

10 A different, but conceptually related, issue, which has attained particular significance in the USA, is whether environmental protection is a public good, so that individual property-owners obliged to contribute to it have a right to compensation, or a matter for competing rights of affected individuals (entailing no compensation) has involved constitutional interpretation. This issue – turning on the distinction between 'takings', which require compensation, and 'regulation', which does not – has provoked dispute at the constitutional level. It has been argued that despite enshrinement of individual property rights in the Constitution, their constitutional inviolability has already been all but eroded in practice: 'the Supreme Court has virtually abandoned all of the means it had established for preventing legislative interference with property rights' (Nedelsky, 1990: 247). Nedelsky argues that 'Either some other concept or value will have to replace it as a symbol of limited government, as the core of constitutionalism, or we may be facing a change in constitutionalism itself.' (p. 253)

11 Russ Manning (1981) notes that health, which ought to be considered a primary social good, is conspicuously missing from Rawls's list – rather, he lists it as a *natural* primary good (along with vigour, intelligence and imagination: (Rawls, 1972: 62). He assumes health is not so directly under social control. Environmental issues (and not only) lead us to challenge this assumption (Manning 1981: 159).

12 Note, though, that the *general* conception of justice would support this; see Rawls (1972: 303).

13 It will be noted that I am not including the question of concern for future generations under this heading, my reason being that theirs would not be a different type of good; and while, because not yet existent, they are a different type of 'bearer', the issues are of a different kind; indeed, it is arguable that distribution in relation to future generations can be dealt with *within* a Rawlsian paradigm, as, to some extent, they already are, via his 'just savings' principle. There remains, of course, much to be said on this topic.

14 Although see chapter 6 for critical discussion of their reasons. It is a different matter, though, to grant that in the nature of the case there are some

sorts of rights that simply cannot apply to animals – such as rights to political participation: see Benton (1993) for a fuller discussion.

15 Hence in Europe, for instance, Directorate General XI (DGXI), which is responsible for implementing the European Union's Environmental Policy, has so far issued the 'Birds Directive' and 'Habitats Directive'. For up-to-date information, see the DGXI website: http://europa.eu.int/en/comm/dg11/dg11home.html.

16 For recent statements of these concerns, see Bellamy (1995) and Waldron (1993); the view I would wish to support, by contrast, is set out by MacCormick (1993).

17 This, at any rate, is my estimate of how the argument has gone; but there are of course a variety of other views: for a sense of the terms of the debate see the three collections edited, respectively, by Doherty and de Geus (1996), Mathews (1996) and Lafferty and Meadowcroft (1996).

18 Cf. Hayward (1995) *passim*. It is noteworthy that even (eco-)Marxists now advocate 'democratizing' the state, not overthrowing it (cf. O'Connor, 1988). For a dissenting view, from an anarchist perspective, see Carter (1993).

19 For more on the general pros and cons of liberal democracy in relation to environmental decision-making, see Dryzek (1987; 1992).

20 For more on the significance of this, see Hayward (1995, chapter 3).

21 There is also the question of how far deliberative democracy can be generalized for society as a whole: in particular, there is the problem of coordination between 'deliberative communities'; and also the issue of how abstract norms of free and impartial public discussion can provide a check against the power and interests of elites. Hence it is pertinent to ask, with Eckersley: 'should not green institutional design start from the premise of power disparities rather than from a regulative idea that is unlikely ever to obtain in practice?' (p. 218).

Bibliography

Aiken, William 1992: 'Human rights in an ecological era'. *Environmental Values*, 1.3: 191–203.

Anderson, Michael R. 1996: 'Human rights approaches to environmental protection: an overview', in Alan E. Boyle and Michael R. Anderson (eds), *Human Rights Approaches to Environmental Protection*. Oxford: Clarendon Press.

Apel, Karl-Otto 1992: 'The ecological crisis as a problem for discourse ethics', in A. Ofsti (ed.), *Ecology and Ethics*. Trondheim: n.p.

Attfield, Robin 1987: *A Theory of Value and Obligation*. London, New York and Sydney: Croom Helm.

Attfield, Robin 1995: *Value, Obligation, and Meta-Ethics*. Amsterdam and Atlanta, GA: Editions Rodopi BV.

Badhwar, Neera Kapur 1993: 'Altruism versus self-interest: sometimes a false dichotomy' in Ellen Frankel Paul, Fred Dycus Miller and Jeffrey Paul (eds), *Altruism*. Cambridge University Press.

Barry, Brian 1965: *Political Argument*. London: Routledge and Kegan Paul.

Beck, Ulrich 1995: *Ecological Enlightenment*, trans. Mark A. Ritter. New Jersey: Humanities Press.

Bellamy, Richard 1995: 'The constitution of Europe: rights or democracy?' in R. Bellamy, V. Bufacchi and D. Castiglione (eds), *Democracy and Constitutional Culture*. London: Lothian Foundation.

Benhabib, Seyla 1992: *Situating the Self*. Cambridge: Polity Press.

Bennett, Jonathan 1984: *A Study of Spinoza's Ethics*. Cambridge University Press.

Benton, Ted 1993: *Natural Relations: ecology, animal rights and social justice*. London: Verso.

Benton, Ted 1997: 'Ecology, community and justice', in Tim Hayward and John O'Neill (eds), *Justice, Property and the Environment: social and legal perspectives*. Aldershot and Brookfield, Vermont: Ashgate Publishing.

Benton, Ted and Redclift, Michael 1994: *Social Theory and the Global Environment*. London: Routledge.

Berlin, Isaiah 1991: 'Two concepts of liberty', in D. Miller (ed.), *Liberty*. Oxford University Press.

Bhaskar, Roy 1989: *Reclaiming Reality*. London: Verso.

Bichsel, Anne 1996: 'NGOs as agents of public accountability and democratization in intergovernmental forums', in William M. Lafferty and James Meadowcroft (eds), *Democracy and the Environment: problems and perspectives*. Cheltenham and Brookfield, Vermont: Edward Elgar.

Birch, Thomas H. 1993: 'Moral considerability and universal consideration'. *Environmental Ethics*, 15: 313–32.

Birnie, Patricia and Boyle, Alan 1992: *International Law and the Environment*. Oxford: Clarendon Press.

Bloch, Ernst 1961: *Naturrecht und menschliche Würde*. Frankfurt: Suhrkamp.

Boyle, Alan E. 1996: 'The role of international human rights law in the protection of the environment', in Alan E. Boyle and Michael R. Anderson (eds), *Human Rights Approaches to Environmental Protection*. Oxford: Clarendon Press.

Brealey, Mark 1993: *Environmental Liabilities and Regulation in Europe*. The Hague: International Business Publishing.

Callicott, J. Baird 1980: 'Animal Liberation: a triangular affair'. *Environmental Ethics*, 4: 311–38.

Callicott, J. Baird 1986: 'On the intrinsic value of nonhuman species', in B.G. Norton (ed.), *The Preservation of Species: the value of biodiversity*. Princeton University Press.

Cameron, James and Mackenzie, Ruth 1996: 'Access to environmental justice and procedural rights in international institutions', in A.E. Boyle and M.R. Anderson (eds), *Human Rights Approaches to Environmental Protection*. Oxford: Clarendon Press.

Caranta, Roberto 1993: 'Governmental liability after Francovich'. *Cambridge Law Journal*, 52: 272–97.

Carter, Alan 1993: 'Towards a green political theory', in A. Dobson and P. Lucardie (eds), *The Politics of Nature*. London: Routledge.

Cassano, Franco 1989: *Approssimazione: esercizi di esperienza dell'altro*. Bologna: Il Mulino.

Cavalieri, Paula and Singer, Peter 1993: *The Great Ape Project: equality beyond humanity*. London: Fourth Estate.

Caygill, Howard 1995: *A Kant Dictionary*. Oxford: Blackwell.

Churchill, R.R. 1996: 'Environmental rights in existing human rights treaties', in Alan E. Boyle and Michael R. Anderson (eds), *Human Rights Approaches to Environmental Protection*. Oxford: Clarendon Press.

Collier, Andrew 1994: *Critical Realism: an introduction to Roy Bhaskar's philosophy*. London: Verso.

Daly, Herman E. and Cobb, John B. 1990: *For the Common Good: redirecting the economy toward community, the environment, and a sustainable future*. London: Green Print.

Desgagné, Richard 1995: 'Integrating environmental values into the European Convention on Human Rights'. *American Journal of International Law*, 89: 263–94.

Dews, Peter 1995: *The Limits of Disenchantment: essays on contemporary European philosophy*. London: Verso.

Dickens, Peter 1996: *Reconstructing Nature: alienation, emancipation and the division of labour*. London and New York: Routledge.

Dobson, Andrew 1995: *Green Political Thought*, 2nd edn. London: Routledge.

Dobson, Andrew (forthcoming): *Justice and the Environment: concepts of environmental sustainability and theories of distributive justice*. Oxford University Press.

Doherty, Brian and de Geus, Marius 1996: *Democracy and Green Political Thought*. London: Routledge.

Douglas-Scott, S 1996: 'Environmental rights in the European Union – participatory democracy or democratic deficit?', in Alan E. Boyle and Michael R. Anderson (eds), *Human Rights Approaches to Environmental Protection*. Oxford: Clarendon Press.

Doyal, Len and Gough, Ian 1991: *A Theory of Human Need*. London: Macmillan.

Dryzek, John 1987: *Rational Ecology: environment and political economy*. Oxford and New York: Basil Blackwell.

Dryzek, John 1992: 'Ecology and discursive democracy: beyond liberal capitalism and the administrative state'. *Capitalism, Nature, Socialism*, 10: 18–42

Dryzek, John 1996: 'Strategies of ecological democratization', in William M. Lafferty and James Meadowcroft (eds), *Democracy and the Environment: problems and perspectives*. Cheltenham and Brookfield, USA: Edward Elgar.

Eckersley, Robyn 1992: *Environmentalism and Political Theory*. London: UCL Press.

Eckersley, Robyn 1993: 'Free market environmentalism: friend or foe?'. *Environmental Politics*, 2.1: 1–19.

Eckersley, Robyn 1996: 'Greening liberal democracy: the rights discourse revisited', in Brian Doherty and Marius de Geus (eds), *Democracy and Green Political Thought*. London and New York: Routledge.

Eckersley, Robyn (ed.) 1995: *Markets, the State and the Environment*. London: Macmillan.

Elliot, Robert 1994: 'Ecology and the ethics of environmental restoration', in Robin Attfield and Andrew Belsey (eds), *Philosophy and the Natural Environment*. Cambridge University Press.

Elster, Jon 1990: 'Selfishness and altruism', in J. Mansbridge (ed.), *Beyond Self-Interest*. Chicago and London: Chicago University Press.

Ferré, Frederick 1994: 'Personalistic organicism: paradox or paradigm?', in Robin Attfield and Andrew Belsey (eds), *Philosophy and the Natural Environment*. Cambridge University Press.

Fox, Warwick 1995: *Toward a Transpersonal Ecology*. Dartington: Green Books.

Frankfurt, Harry G. 1982: 'Freedom of the will and the concept of a person', in G. Watson (ed.), *Free Will*. Oxford University Press.

Gilligan, Carol 1982: *In a Different Voice: psychological theory and women's development*. Cambridge, Mass. and London: Harvard University Press.

Glover, Jonathan 1977: *Causing Death and Saving Lives*. Harmondsworth: Penguin.

Goodin, Robert 1992: *Green Political Theory*. Cambridge: Polity Press.

Goodpaster, Kenneth 1979: 'From egoism to environmentalism', in K.E. Goodpaster and K.M. Sayre (eds), *Ethics and Problems of the 21st Century*. Notre Dame and London: Notre Dame University Press.

Habermas, Jürgen 1982: 'A reply to my critics', in John B. Thompson and David Held (eds), *Habermas: critical debates*. London: Macmillan.

Habermas, Jürgen 1990: *Moral Consciousness and Communicative Action*, trans. C. Lenhardt and S.W. Nicholsen. Cambridge: Polity Press.

Habermas, Jürgen 1993: *Justification and Application*, trans. Ciaran Cronin. Cambridge: Polity Press.

Hardin, Garrett 1968: 'The tragedy of the commons'. *Science*, 162: 1243–8.

Hayward, Tim 1994: 'Kant and the moral considerability of non-rational beings', *Philosophy* Supplement 36: 129–42; and in R. Attfield and A. Belsey (eds), *Philosophy and the Natural Environment*. Cambridge: Cambridge University Press.

Hayward, Tim 1995: *Ecological Thought: an introduction*. Cambridge: Polity Press.

Hayward, Tim 1996a: 'Universal consideration as a universal principle: a critique of Birch'. *Environmental Ethics*, 18.1: 55–63.

Hayward, Tim 1996b: 'What is green political theory?', in I. Hampsher-Monk and J. Stanyer (eds), *Contemporary Political Studies 1996*, Vol. I, PSA Conference Proceedings: 79–91; also published as University of Edinburgh Waverley Paper 96–3.

Hayward, Tim 1997a: 'The double role of organisms in general: the key to distinguishing between environmental and animal ethics'. *Ethik und Sozialwissenschaften*, 8: 41–3.

Hayward, Tim 1997b: 'Interspecies solidarity: care operated upon by justice', in T. Hayward and J. O'Neill (eds), *Justice, Property and the Environment*. Aldershot and Brookfield, Vermont: Ashgate Publishing.

Held, David 1995: *Democracy and the Global Order: from the modern state to cosmopolitan governance*. Cambridge: Polity Press.

Hirschman, Albert O. 1977: *The Passions and the Interests: political arguments for capitalism before its triumph*. Princeton, NJ: Princeton University Press.

Holmes, Stephen 1990: 'The secret history of self-interest', in J. Mansbridge (ed.), *Beyond Self-Interest*. Chicago and London: Chicago University Press.

Hospers, John 1982: *Human Conduct: problems of ethics*, 2nd edn. New York, Sydney, Toronto and London: Harcourt Brace Jovanovich, Inc.

Jacobs, Michael 1995: 'Sustainability and "the market": a typology of environmental economics', in R. Eckersley (ed.), *Markets, the State and the Environment: towards integration*. London: Macmillan.

Jacobs, Michael 1996: *The Politics of the Real World*, written and edited for the Real World Coalition. London: Earthscan.

Johnson, Lawrence E. 1985: *A Morally Deep World: an essay on moral significance and environmental ethics*. Cambridge University Press.

Kant, Immanuel 1948: *The Moral Law: Kant's Groundwork of the Metaphysics of Morals*. London, Hutchinson.

Kant, Immanuel 1963: *Lectures on Ethics*, trans. Louis Infield. New York: Harper and Row.

Kant, Immanuel 1993: *Critique of Practical Reason*, 3rd edn, trans. Lewis White Beck. New York and Oxford: Macmillan.

Keat, Russell 1994: 'Citizens, consumers and the environment: reflections on the economy of the Earth'. *Environmental Values*, 3: 333–49.

Keat, Russell 1997: 'Environmental goods and market boundaries: a response to O'Neill', in Tim Hayward and John O'Neill (eds), *Justice, Property and the Environment: social and legal perspectives*. Aldershot and Brookfield, Vermont: Ashgate Publishing.

Kitwood, Tom 1990: *Concern for Others: a new psychology of conscience and morality*. London: Routledge.

Krebs, Angelika 1997: 'Discourse ethics and nature'. *Environmental Values*, 6.3: 269–79.

Ksentini 1994: *Final Report of the UN Sub-Commission on Human Rights and the Environment* (UN Doc.E/CN.4/Sub.2/1994/9).

Kuehls, Thom 1996: *Beyond Sovereign Territory*. Minneapolis and London: University of Minnesota Press.

Lafferty, William M. and Meadowcroft, James 1996: 'Democracy and the environment: congruence and conflict – preliminary reflections', in William M. Lafferty and James Meadowcroft (eds), *Democracy and the Environment: problems and perspectives*. Cheltenham and Brookfield, Vermont: Edward Elgar.

Larrabee, Mary Jeanne (ed.) 1993: *An Ethic of Care: feminist and interdisciplinary perspectives*. London: Routledge.

Lau, Martin 1996: 'Islam and judicial activism: public interest litigation and environmental protection in the Islamic Republic of Pakistan', in A.E. Boyle and M.R. Anderson (eds), *Human Rights Approaches to Environmental Protection*. Oxford: Clarendon Press.

Leopold, Aldo 1949: 'The land ethic', in Aldo Leopold, *A Sand County Almanac*. Oxford University Press.

Light, Andrew and Katz, Eric (eds) 1996: *Environmental Pragmatism*. London and New York: Routledge.

Lippott, Joachim 1995: 'Response to Cass Sunstein's "A Constitutional Anomaly in the Czech Republic?"'. *East European Constitutional Review*, 4: 92–3.

Lukes, Steven 1974: *Power: a radical view*. London: Macmillan.

MacCormick, Neil 1993: 'Constitutionalism and democracy', in R. Bellamy (ed.), *Theories and Concepts of Politics*. Manchester University Press.

Macpherson, C.B. 1962: *The Political Theory of Possessive Individualism*. Oxford University Press.

MacIntyre, Alasdair 1981: *After Virtue: a study in moral theory*. London: Duckworth.

Manning, Russ 1981: 'Environmental ethics and John Rawls' Theory of Justice'. *Environmental Ethics*, 3: 155–65.

Mansbridge, Jane 1990a: 'On the relation of altruism and self-interest', in J. Mansbridge (ed.), *Beyond Self-Interest*. Chicago and London: Chicago University Press.

Mansbridge, Jane (ed.) 1990b: *Beyond Self-Interest*. Chicago and London: Chicago University Press.

Martell, Luke 1994: *Ecology and Society: an introduction*. Cambridge: Polity Press.

Martinez-Alier, Juan 1990: *Ecological Economics: energy, environment and society*, with Klaus Schlüpmann, paperback edn with new introduction. Oxford: Blackwell.

Marx, Karl 1954: *Capital*, vol. 1, trans. S. Moore and E. Aveling. London: Lawrence & Wishart.

Mathews, Freya 1991: *The Ecological Self*. London: Routledge.

Mathews, Freya (ed.) 1996: *Ecology and Democracy*. London: Frank Cass.

McCarthy, Thomas 1990: 'Introduction' to Jürgen Habermas, *Moral Consciousness and Communicative Action*. Cambridge: Polity Press.

McFall, Lynne 1987: 'Integrity'. *Ethics*, 98: 5–20.

Meadows, Dennis L., Randers, Jorgen, and Behrens, William H. III 1972: *The Limits to Growth*. New York: Universe Books.

Mellor, Mary 1992: *Breaking the Boundaries: towards a feminist, green socialism*. London: Virago.

Merrills, J.G. 1996: 'Environmental protection and human rights: conceptual aspects', in Alan E. Boyle and Michael R. Anderson (eds), *Human Rights Approaches to Environmental Protection*. Oxford: Clarendon Press.

Midgley, Mary 1994: 'The end of anthropocentrism?', in Robin Attfield and Andrew Belsey (eds), *Philosophy and the Natural Environment*. Cambridge University Press.

Moore, G.E. 1903: *Principia Ethica*. Cambridge University Press.

Naess, Arne 1989: *Ecology, Community and Lifestyle*, trans and ed. David Rothenberg. Cambridge University Press.

Nedelsky, Jennifer 1990: *Private Property and the Limits of American Constitutionalism: the Madisonian framework and its legacy*. Chicago and London: University of Chicago Press.

O'Connor, James 1988: 'Capitalism, nature, socialism: a theoretical introduction'. *Capitalism, Nature, Socialism*, 1: 11–38.

Offe, Claus and Wiesenthal, Helmut 1985: 'Two logics of collective action', in Claus Offe *Disorganized Capitalism*, ed. John Keane. Cambridge: Polity Press.

Okin, Susan Moller 1990: 'Reason and feeling in thinking about justice', in C. Sunstein (ed.), *Feminism and Political Theory*. Chicago and London: Chicago University Press.

Olson, Mancur Jr 1965: *The Logic of Collective Action*. Cambridge, MA: Harvard University Press.

O'Neill, John 1993: *Ecology, Policy and Politics: human well-being and the natural world*. London and New York: Routledge.

O'Neill, John 1997: 'King Darius and the environmental economist', in Tim Hayward and John O'Neill (eds), *Justice, Property and the Environment: social and legal perspectives.* Aldershot and Brookfield, Vermont: Ashgate Publishing.

O'Riordan, T. and Cameron J. (eds) 1994: *Interpreting the Precautionary Principle.* London: Earthscan.

Owen, David 1995: *Nietzsche, Politics and Modernity.* London, Thousand Oaks (California) and New Delhi: Sage.

Paul, Ellen Frankel, Miller, Fred Dycus and Paul, Jeffrey (eds) 1993: *Altruism.* Cambridge University Press.

Pearce, David, Markandya, Anil and Barbier, Edward B. 1989: *Blueprint for a Green Economy.* London: Earthscan.

Plant, Raymond 1974: *Community and Ideology: an essay in applied social philosophy.* London: Routledge and Kegan Paul.

Pollis, Adamantia and Schwab, Peter (eds) 1980: *Human Rights: cultural and ideological perspectives.* New York: Praeger.

Rawls, John 1972: *A Theory of Justice.* Oxford University Press.

Reeve, Andrew and Ware, Alan 1983: 'Interests in political theory'. *British Journal of Political Science,* 13: 379–400.

Regan, Tom 1988: *The Case for Animal Rights.* London and New York: Routledge.

Routley, Richard and Routley, Val 1979: 'Against the inevitability of human chauvinism', in K.E. Goodpaster and K.M. Sayre (eds), *Ethics and Problems of the 21st Century.* Notre Dame and London: Notre Dame University Press.

Ryder, Richard D. 1992: 'Painism: the ethics of animal rights and the environment', in Richard D. Ryder (ed.), *Animal Welfare and the Environment.* London: Duckworth in association with the RSPCA.

Sagoff, Mark 1988: *The Economy of the Earth.* Cambridge University Press.

Sandel, Michael J. 1982: *Liberalism and the Limits of Justice.* Cambridge University Press.

Saward, Michael 1993: 'Green democracy?' in A. Dobson and P. Lucardie (eds), *The Politics of Nature: explorations in green political theory.* London and New York: Routledge.

Sen, Amartya K. 1990: 'Rational fools: a critique of the behavioural foundations of economic theory', in J. Mansbridge (ed.), *Beyond Self-Interest.* Chicago and London: Chicago University Press.

Singer, Peter 1991: *Animal Liberation,* 2nd edn. London: Thorsons.

Smith, Adam 1986: *The Wealth of Nations.* Harmondsworth: Penguin.

Soper, Kate 1995: *What is Nature?* Oxford: Blackwell.

Spinoza, Benedictus de 1989: *Ethics,* ed. G.H.R. Parkinson. London: Dent.

Stephenson, Susan 1998: 'Graham Swift and the politics of integrity', in A. Dobson and J. Stanyer (eds), *Contemporary Political Studies 1998* Vol. 1, PSA Conference Proceedings: 32–44.

Stone, Christopher 1974: *Should Trees Have Standing?* Los Altos, CA: William Kaufmann Inc.

Strawson, Peter F. 1974: 'Freedom and resentment', in P.F. Strawson, *Freedom and Resentment and Other Essays*. London: Methuen.

Sunstein, Cass R. 1993: 'Against positive rights'. *East European Constitutional Review*, 2: 35–8.

Taylor, Charles 1990: *Sources of the Self*. Cambridge University Press.

Taylor, Paul 1981: 'The ethics of respect for nature'. *Environmental Ethics*, 3: 197–218.

Thomas, Caroline (ed.) 1994: *Rio: unravelling the consequences*. Ilford: Frank Cass, 1994.

Vincent, R.J. 1986: *Human Rights and International Relations*. Cambridge University Press.

Waldron, Jeremy 1993: 'A rights-based critique of constitutional rights'. *Oxford Journal of Legal Studies*, 13: 18–51.

Weale, Albert 1993: *The New Politics of Pollution*. Manchester University Press.

West, David 1993: 'Spinoza on positive freedom'. *Political Studies*, XLI: 284–96.

Weston, Anthony 1996: 'Beyond intrinsic value: pragmatism in environmental ethics', in Andrew Light and Eric Katz (eds), *Environmental Pragmatism*. London and New York: Routledge.

Williams, Bernard 1973: *Problems of the Self*. Cambridge University Press.

Williams, Bernard (with J.J.C. Smart) 1987: *Utilitarianism: for and against*. Cambridge University Press.

Williams, Bruce A. and Matheny, Albert R. 1995: *Democracy, Dialogue and Environmental Disputes: the contested languages of social regulation*. New Haven and London: Yale University Press.

World Commission on Environment and Development (WCED, Chair Gro Harlem Brundtland) 1987: *Our Common Future*. Oxford University Press.

Wynne, Brian 1994: 'Scientific knowledge and the global environment', in Ted Benton and Michael Redclift (eds), *Social Theory and the Global Environment*. London and New York: Routledge.

Index